Re-designing Learning Contexts

What do we mean by the word 'context' in education and how does our context influence the way that we learn?

What role can technology play in enhancing learning and what is the future of technology within learning?

Re-designing Learning Contexts seeks to redress the lack of attention that has traditionally been paid to a learner's wider context and proposes a model to help educators and technologists develop more productive learning contexts. It defines context as the interactions between the learner and a set of interrelated resource elements that are not tied to a physical or virtual location. Context is something that belongs to an individual and that is created through their interactions in the world.

Based on original, empirical research, the book considers the intersection between learning, context and technology, and explores:

- the meaning of the concept of context and its relationship to learning
- the ways in which different types of technology can scaffold learning in context
- the learner-centric 'Ecology of Resources' model of context as a framework for designing technology-rich learning environments
- the importance of matching available resources to each learner's particular needs
- the ways in which the learner's environment and the technologies available might change over the coming years
- the potential impact of recent technological developments within computer science and artificial intelligence.

This interdisciplinary study draws on a range of disciplines, including geography, anthropology, psychology, education and computing, to investigate the dynamics and potential of teacher–learner interaction within a learning continuum, and across a variety of locations. It will be of interest to those teaching, researching and thinking about the use of technology in learning and pedagogy, as well as those involved in developing technology for education and those who use it in their own teaching.

Rosemary Luckin is Professor of Learner-Centred Design at the London Knowledge Lab, Institute of Education, University of London. She has graduate and postgraduate qualifications in Artificial Intelligence and Cognitive Science and has taught learners in schools, colleges and universities.

Foundations and Futures of Education

Series Editors:

Peter Aggleton *School of Education and Social Work, University of Sussex, UK*
Sally Power *Cardiff University, UK*
Michael Reiss *Institute of Education, University of London, UK*

Foundations and Futures of Education focuses on key emerging issues in education as well as continuing debates within the field. The series is interdisciplinary, and includes historical, philosophical, sociological, psychological and comparative perspectives on three major themes: the purposes and nature of education; increasing interdisciplinarity within the subject; and the theory–practice divide.

Language, Learning, Context
Talking the Talk
Wolff-Michael Roth

Education and the Family
Passing success across the generations
Leon Feinstein, Kathryn Duckworth & Ricardo Sabates

Education, Philosophy and the Ethical Environment
Graham Haydon

Educational Activity and the Psychology of Learning
Judith Ireson

Schooling, Society and Curriculum
Alex Moore

Gender, Schooling and Global Social Justice
Elaine Unterhalter

Re-designing Learning Contexts

Technology-rich, learner-centred ecologies

Rosemary Luckin

Routledge
Taylor & Francis Group

LONDON AND NEW YORK

For James and Catherine

First published 2010
by Routledge
2 Park Square, Milton Park, Abingdon, Oxon, OX14 4RN

Simultaneously published in the USA and Canada
by Routledge
270 Madison Avenue, New York, NY 10016

Routledge is an imprint of the Taylor & Francis Group, an informa business

© 2010 Rosemary Luckin

Typeset in Galliard by
Pindar NZ, Auckland, New Zealand
Printed and bound in Great Britain by
CPI Anthony Rowe, Chippenham, Wiltshire

British Library Cataloguing in Publication Data
A catalogue record for this book is available from the British Library

Library of Congress Cataloging-in-Publication Data
Luckin, Rosemary.
Re-designing learning contexts: technology-rich, learner-centred ecologies / Rosemary Luckin.
    p. cm.
Includes bibliographical references and index.
1. Active learning. 2. Intelligent tutoring systems. 3. Interactive computer systems. I. Title.
LB1027.23.L82 2010
371.33—dc22   2009039989

ISBN13: 978–0-415–55441–1 (hbk)
ISBN13: 978–0-415–55442–8 (pbk)
ISBN13: 978–0-203–85475–4 (ebk)

Contents

Figures and Tables

Figures

Tables

Acknowledgements

In this book I discuss the concept of context and develop a design framework for technology-rich learning that is based upon a model that recognizes the key part played in any learner's progress by the other people with whom he or she interacts. The process of writing this book has been a learning experience for me and it has certainly relied upon a great deal of support from a range of people, without whom there would be no book. The flaws in the end product of this book-writing activity are of course my own responsibility.

I would like to thank my colleagues at the London Knowledge Lab and at the Ideas Lab, for providing such fertile and stimulating research environments; the teams who worked on the projects that I report in Part 2 of the book and the students, teachers and parents who made the empirical studies possible: Katerina Avramides, Ben du Boulay, Wilma Clark, Daniel Connolly, Amanda Harris, Joe Holmberg, Lucinda Kerawalla, Erika Martinez-Miron, Robin Mudge, Darren Pearce, Lydia Plowman, Genaro Rebolledo-Mendez, Richard Siddons-Corby, Hilary Smith, Hilary Tunley, Roland Tongue, Joshua Underwood and Nicola Yuill; colleagues who have read various book chapters and offered invaluable feedback, in particular: Madeline Balaam, Michael Reiss and Michael Young. Wilma Clark, Fred Garnett and Joshua Underwood also deserve a special thank you for their insightful and intelligent comments in the formation of the design framework as well as a great deal of chapter reading. The members of the Learner Generated Context research group and the Becta Research Advisory Group have been a great source of refreshing ideas and enthusiasm that has roused my sometimes flagging energy to complete the book-writing task; and my friends have been brilliant at putting up with me during the writing process and asking at just the right moment how it's all going: Barbara Bush, Ann Fletcher, Kim Issroff, Lynne Murphey and Carol Shergold. I also thank Catherine and James not only for their careful and conscientious data analysis, but for being them, for being there, and for adding meaning to my life.

Abbreviations

AI   Artificial Intelligence
CSCL   Computer Supported Collaborative Learning
CSCW   Computer Supported Collaborative Work
HCI   Human Computer Interaction
ITS   Intelligent Tutoring System
MAP   More Able Partner
SDLC   South Downs Learning Centre
ZAA   Zone of Available Assistance
ZPA   Zone of Proximal Adjustment
ZPD   Zone of Proximal Development

Part 1
Background

1 Contexts for learning

My first job after completing my doctoral thesis was as a research fellow on the Multimedia, Education and Narrative Organization (MENO) project, which explored the relationship between narrative and teenage learners' use of multimedia resources to support their learning in school. I worked alongside Lydia Plowman who drew my attention to the concept of 'Lines of Desire', a term borrowed from architecture and planning that refers to the routes that people take through open or semi-open spaces, in preference to those marked out as paths by planners. These can be seen, for example, on housing estates and in parks, where people are allowed some freedom to wander. I found this concept offered an appealing metaphor as I considered how learners might be able to look around them and find out enough information about the people, buildings, books, pens, technologies and other artefacts within their landscape, to chart a learning trajectory that would meet their needs. I still find this concept to be a useful one when I consider the design of technology-rich learning activities. I also find it offers a useful analogy for my own attempts to understand more about the concept of 'context', as I explore the different ways in which various communities of researchers talk about context.

I quote Michael Cole (1996) at the outset of my account of my personal line of desire through work that talks about context: 'I will not aspire to a definitive treatment of context in this book.' Rather I will look at the different ways of talking about context and, like Cole in his pursuit of a cultural psychology, I will attempt to extract some useful conceptual tools to guide my development of a context-based framework for the development of technology-rich learning activities. Nardi (1996) highlights the wide range of work that has illustrated that it is impossible to understand how people work or learn without also taking into account the people and artefacts that are part of the completion of their work or learning: 'Thus we are motivated to study context to understand relations among individuals, artefacts, and social groups' (Nardi, 1996: 69). I note, however, that pinning down what we mean by context is not an easy task. Nardi (1996: 69) states the problem clearly: 'How can we confront the blooming, buzzing confusion that is "context" and still produce generalizable research results?'

I confront this problem by looking across a range of ways in which context is talked about, and within this chapter discuss work that has been drawn from different disciplines, including geography, architecture, planning, anthropology, psychology, education, cognitive science and computer science. I acknowledge that each of these disciplines works within its own frame of reference with its associated and differing language, philosophy, concepts and methodologies. I also acknowledge that I run the risk of using these tools inappropriately as I blend them together in order to try and understand more about how best we might talk about, and use, the concept of context. I consider this a risk worth taking in order to avoid the narrow perspective that I believe has not served research into educational technology well.

One thing that became very clear to me as I explored the research landscape was that there were common themes of concern that transcended disciplinary boundaries and many excellent examples of interdisciplinary research. I do not, therefore, divide the text that follows exactly according to the disciplinary home from which it emanates. There is, however, a narrative that begins with work drawn from geography and architecture, that moves into discussions about research from anthropology and psychology and onto work drawn from education and computer science. There are many points of overlap along the way, in particular where digital technology is a feature of the research.

Discussions about context can be found in texts from the multiple sub-fields within geography research. This includes political, social, education, cultural and human geography. The importance of context is clear within this literature, as are the vastly different ways in which the term is used. In their evaluation of the impact of Information and Communication Technologies (ICTs) on everyday activity, Schwanen *et al.* (2008, 520) argue that:

> while geographers have made many contributions to the understanding of how ICTs mediate everyday life, perhaps the most significant of those is their emphasis on the spatial and historical contingency in the effects of the Internet, mobile phone and related technologies: context always matters . . .

They also note that researchers define context in diverse ways: for example, in relation to institutional arrangements, or with respect to the configuration of physical infrastructure. However, there is general agreement that the effects of the ways in which ICTs mediate everyday life 'cannot be separated from the contexts in which they are situated' (Schwanen *et al.*, 2008: 520).

This work by Schwanen and colleagues is explicitly about ICT use. Their views, however, resonate with similar sentiments expressed in work that is not about the use of technology. There is a variety of different ways of, and purposes for, using the term 'context'. In the social sciences we talk about the 'cultural turn' as a point of cross-disciplinary shift. Across geography and many related disciplines there has also been a move towards a greater attention to culture and meaning in preference to large-scale scientific approaches. This is referred to as the 'spatial turn' (see Soja, 1989), and is reflected in seminal work completed by Doreen Massey, who argued that space does not simply reflect the social relations of society but that the spatial and the social are mutually constitutive (Lambert and Morgan, 2009). From this spatial turn geography 'has emerged as a key point of reference within this disciplinary convergence' (Cosgrove, 2004: 57). As a consequence 'space' has become a major focus of attention and the subject of a diverse range of conceptual perspectives and a variety of analytical methods. Clearly, I can only scratch the surface of this huge debate here and I focus in particular upon work that discusses space alongside context, in order to try and extract some useful themes.

Casey (2001: 683), for example, describes space as 'the encompassing volumetric void in which things (including human beings) are positioned'. He distinguishes this from place, which is described as 'the immediate environment of my lived body – an arena of action that is at once physical, historical, social and cultural' (Casey, 2001: 683). In this sense, 'place' is presented as dominantly subjective and experienced: 'there is no place without self and no self without place', whilst space is presented as an abstraction. He argues that place and space can be further distinguished from one another by considering landscape, which acts as both the context for, and as an attribute of, place. He draws attention to the fact that landscapes have horizons, whereas places are enclosed and as individual entities have no such horizon. It is when places are connected that they gain horizons, which draw attention to new possibilities as well as closing off what the eye can see.

The complexity of context is evident in the work of Williams (2002) in a review of the changing geographies of care between hospital and home settings. She portrays 'context' as complex, social, interactional and institutional. She links the notion of context to a notion of 'place identity' and suggests that a synthesis of the subjective and objective dimensions of place is framed by the 'context of action through which individuals trace paths and institutional structures are sedimented' (Williams, 2002: 145). Koskela (2000) discusses the social shaping of 'space' in a study of urban video surveillance. Human interactions and processes frame particular spaces, as does the physical reality of the architecture of a space. This means that the notion of 'space as container' is important for understanding how space frames social interaction. She argues that power and emotion are negotiated differently in terms of how surveillance affects people. The conceptualization of space as 'container' is useful in her view, because it shows how this framing and negotiation occurs by positioning the actors in relation to each other, to artefacts or objects within their environs and to general conceptualizations of social space. Cummins *et al.* (2007: 1830) also consider the complexity of context and suggest that in order to make progress, future research should consider 'individual exposure to multiple "contexts" in time and space'. Here, they tie the notion of context to action spaces, and culture and temporal units in a concept they describe as 'time-space biographies', that map out 'an individual's movement around a more or less regularly frequented "action space", over meaningful units of time (such as a day, week or month)' (Cummins *et al.*, 2007: 1830). Discussions about time in relation to context are frequent. Kapler and Wright (2005), for example, track military activity across time and space and identify connections between activity spaces to produce a geographic and temporally situated narrative. Their visualization, called 'GeoTime', is relational and allows connections to be made between entities (people or things), locations (geospatial or conceptual) and events (occurrences, facts or action times).

Knowledge is also discussed alongside context, in particular with respect to tacit knowledge. Gertler (2003) focuses on the relationships between tacit knowledge and institutions, arguing that existing work has limited tacit knowledge to experiential and cognitive considerations and given insufficient attention to the 'role and origins of social context' and the foundations of context and culture. This emphasis upon the social can be found again in Gertler and Wolfe (2005), where context is equated with local, proximate interaction and dialogue. Pain (2004), too, is concerned with knowledge, but from the slightly different perspective of the methods that can be used to encourage local participation in research. She describes social geographers as having a 'particular sensitivity to context' and emphasizes that participatory research is 'designed to be context-specific, forefronting local conditions and local knowledge, and producing situated, rich and layered accounts' (Pain, 2004: 2).

I am struck by the extent to which much of the discussion so far, whilst not about education, deals with issues, such as institutions and social interactions that are relevant to education. There are also, of course, consistencies with work that talks specifically about notions of context, space and place, specifically with respect to education and from a geographer's perspective. Gulson & Symes (2007), for example, suggest that the treatment of space and place in educational studies is underexamined, undertheorized and underdeveloped. They describe context as something that needs to be integrated with space and argue that through its scientific, geo-mathematical abstracted conceptualization 'space' has been 'uprooted from its contexts'. Descriptions of space as 'an empty vessel within which action took place, or as an effect of social, political and economic relations' (Gulson & Symes, 2007: 100), have been unhelpful for the social sciences and have impeded the appreciation of space as a social entity 'where it is what individuals and societies do with space that 'counts'.

Catling (2005) appears to distinguish between 'environment' as physical and 'context' as social in his descriptions of the role and impact of the school environment. He suggests that the school environment emphasizes the provision of 'an orderly environment and context to engender good and "right" behaviour' (Catling, 2005: 341) with respect to what the school considers to be the child's learning, and on what external authorities deem as necessary requirements and controls, rather than with the child's lived experience. He distinguishes between the fixed, cartographic entity of the school environment and buildings, and the dynamics of the school setting as a 'social, cultural and political space for enacting, deepening and developing the meaning and interplay of people in place' (Catling, 2005: 341). Such descriptions of the school environment introduce the power and politics of the way that space is managed, an issue that is also noted by other researchers looking outside of education. P. Rogers (2006), for example, discusses the way in which spatial management of new urban spaces can generate 'tactical legislation' and prescriptive categories of acceptable behaviour and activity, thus introducing a layer of governance that puts property-holders and developers at odds with the provision of spaces aimed at youth. From an urban informatics perspective, Klaebe *et al.* (2009) offer a way in which this tension can be tackled in their review of the impact of urban renewal strategies. They suggest that narrative networks between real and virtual spaces have the capacity to influence urban design and participation over time, by contributing ongoing data that frames ways in which physical spaces are conceived, perceived and lived in.

Literature drawn from researchers with an interest in urban settings and the built environment reflects plenty of discussions about space and place and introduces an emphasis upon affect. Stenglin (2008), for example, describes space in its broadest sense as that which encompasses 'the organization of indoor and outdoor spaces as well as built spaces and spaces in the natural environment' (Stenglin, 2008: 426). Stenglin is also concerned with issues of affect and argues that affect in three-dimensional spaces 'can delight, calm, awaken and overwhelm us'. She argues that understanding affect is important for understanding interpersonal relationships within the built environment, and that it provides 'emotional entry points for interacting with the different spaces we encounter in our daily lives' (Stenglin, 2008: 441). There is an emphasis upon affect, subjective experience and social behaviour within work that explores the built environment. This resonates with the earlier discussions of work by people such as Williams (2002), and Gulson & Symes (2007). It is also linked to discussions of embodiment that crop up later in this chapter through work by Dourish (2001) written from a Human Computer Interaction stance. Jones (2005), in a study of a cyclist's interactions with the urban environment, proposes an intense relationship between people and their environments. He uses notions of embodied negotiation of space and makes a clear distinction between the notion of affect as emotion, and affect as embodied experience, arguing that the latter provides for a much deeper understanding of the self in its interactions. Jones links embodied action to a tool, in his example a bicycle, the environment, which for him is the urban landscape, and the physical and emotional experience of action. He presents a somewhat unusual framing of context as performance. Kraftl & Adey (2008) argue that affect is a ubiquitous and a vital part of the urban landscape of cities, which allows emphasis to be placed on 'encounters with spaces of practice' in a more reflective, reflexive manner.

The physical and the digital environment

I opened my discussion of the geography literature with work that was concerned with ICT. I return to that theme now to consider the crossover between concerns with the built environment and with the digital environment, or the blended physical and digital environment, before standing back to consider what can be learnt from the discussion so far. Kerckhove & Tursi (2009: 53) observe that: 'The proliferation of the microchip renders the everyday spaces of our existence alive, capable of interacting and reacting to our passage'. Manovich (2006) discusses augmented space from the point of view of both urban space (built environment) and human constructed space, or what Manovich terms 'cellspace'. Cellspace is defined as 'physical space that is "filled" with data, which can be retrieved by a user via a personal communication device' (Manovich, 2006: 221). The data that fills this cellspace comes from networks and embedded objects. He questions whether spatial form in its physical manifestation becomes a minor irrelevancy that purely acts as a support for information spaces that are manifested digitally or whether, in fact, the two combine to produce an entirely new experience which lends primacy to neither one nor the other; a 'phenomenological gestalt'. This is a question that becomes pertinent once again when I discuss embodied interaction.

Benyon (2006) draws on cognitive psychology to contribute to the debate on the distinction between 'space' and 'place' in his comparison of navigation in physical and digital space. He argues for the personal nature of an individual's interaction that 'seeks to subjectively centre themselves in a space attempting to reach a focus'. This activity, he argues, leads to the creation of places that 'contain actions, activities and social interactions'. He emphasizes the importance in the design of permeability, which he argues is about support for the movements of individuals. 'The availability and use of paths depends both on their physical existence and their visual appearance. Permeability is also dependent on public and private space, the connectivity of routes and the nature of the environment' (Benyon, 2006: 12).

In my appeal to the 'lines of desire' metaphor at the start of this chapter I drew on an artefact from architecture and wanted to use it to consider how individuals might build something coherent around their learning needs through the possibilities within their environment. Benyon's work seems particularly relevant to this analogy. He defines navigation as a way of finding out about, and moving through, an environment. He links navigation to notions of location and meaning and suggests that objects in an environment may have different meanings for different people. He also highlights the possibilities of social navigation and suggests that we 'use a wide range of cues from the behaviour of other people and the traces of their behaviours, to manage our activities' (Benyon, 2006: 14). In this manner, we find our own way by talking to or by following others. In order to attach our own meaning to a space and in so doing to create our own place, we need information or feedback about the environment or 'signposting'.

At this point I want to take a moment to consider what I can learn about context from the discussion so far. Clearly context matters and its significance needs recognition. It is complex and for some it is not a singular entity, but rather a multiplicity to which we are serially exposed. The language that surrounds the use of the term 'context' makes reference to local issues, local conditions, local knowledge, acknowledgement of social, interactional and institutional elements and a sense of history through 'sedimented structures' (Williams, 2002). Context is associated with action and time, emphasizing that it is a dynamic entity and is associated with connections among people, things, locations and events in a geographic and temporally situated narrative. It is distinguished from the physical environment and described as social. It is discussed in the language of emotions and affect, as performance, and as linked to culture and to tacit knowledge.

Discussions that link context to space and place are frequent and we see space portrayed as an abstraction, an encompassing void that contains people and things, as a container within which people and artefacts can be usefully related to one another; and as something that needs to be integrated with context in order to ensure that it is seen as a social entity that is shaped by what people do. Place, however, is more immediate and more connected to people and their subjective lived experience. Place is something that is framed by form, function, human interactions, design and legislation; and defined by power, policy and politics. We also see the introduction of the term 'landscape', as a context and attribute of place, which brings with it the notion of a horizon and boundaries. Discussions that link the physical and the digital recognize the significance of the changes that technology can make to the potential of everyday spaces and what can be learnt from linking our interactions across the physical and the digital.

Context and culture

I have already introduced the subject of culture and return to it again here, because it has an important role to play in my understanding of context. I take time to consider Michael Cole's (1996) illuminating text on cultural psychology. His aim is to reconstruct the cultural-historical approach to development and in so doing to create a conception of culture that can constitute a cultural psychology. As part of this process he discusses context at some length. Cole discusses two approaches to culture: the internal approach, which looks to the interpretation of the internal psychological structures for the sources of coordinated cultural activity; and the external approach, which looks to the visible manifestations of human action for coordinating artefacts, such as routines and rituals. Cole uses the dual nature of mediated artefacts to formulate an explanation that takes him beyond this division. He links artefacts to schemas and scripts as a way of conceptualizing the 'context-specificity of thinking' and of grounding cultural theory in people's everyday activities. He suggests that the combination of people, roles, objects, sequences and relations in scripts can serve as 'guides to action'. Cole notes the simplified nature of schemas, which require considerable user interpretation, and proposes that in order to formulate an account of culturally mediated thinking, both the mediational artefacts and the circumstances in which they mediate thinking need to be specified. The identification of the role of circumstances grounds the introduction of the term 'context' as a potential descriptor for these circumstances.

Cole acknowledges the difficulties and complexities associated with context: a term that is 'perhaps the most prevalent term used to index the circumstances of behaviour' (Cole, 1996: 132). He states the limitations of his aim as being to 'distinguish between two principal conceptions of context that divide social scientists' (Cole, 1996: 131) and to identify some useful guiding concepts. The first conceptualization of context is as 'that which surrounds'. This is often represented in diagrams as a series of concentric circles with a particular activity of interest at its centre. For example, two children playing a computer game in their bedroom, with layers of concentric circles that surround this activity that represent the game-playing episode, the organization of the bedroom, the organization of the family, the organization of the home, and so on. The aim with this conceptualization is to understand how the activity at the centre is influenced by what is depicted in the surrounding concentric circles. This way of talking about context separates the activity being studied from the influences surrounding it and is open to the criticism that context is portrayed as a container for an activity or event, rather than context being part of the same situation.

The second conceptualization of context discussed by Cole is that which builds on the metaphor of weaving. This allows the boundaries between a task and its circumstances to be seen as 'ambiguous and dynamic'. This weaving together description of context requires that we interpret mind in a relational way:

> In short, because what we call mind works through artifacts, it cannot be unconditionally bounded by the head or even by the body, but must be seen as distributed in the artifacts which *are woven together* and which weave together individual human actions in concert with and as part of the permeable, changing, events of life.
>
> (Cole, 1996: 136)

Cole notes the move towards using 'activity' and 'practice' in place of the words 'context' and 'situation'. He suggests that the use of the word 'practice' is motivated by a desire to combine the two conceptualizations of context, and that the use of the word 'activity' is well explained by Engestrom's description of an activity system (Engeström, 1987). An activity system integrates the object and its social orientations without privileging either. Cole notes that the artefact-mediated actions depicted by the traditional activity triangle can only exist in relation to the bottom components of the activity system triangle as illustrated by Engeström: the social rules, the other people in the community and the division of labour between the subject and the community. In this conceptualization, a context is an activity system and cognition is distributed across all the components. Cole considers the unit of analysis of an event and an activity and cites Wentworth (1980) who stated that 'context may be thought of as a situation and time bounded arena for human activity. It is the unit of culture' (Cole, 1996: 142).

There are some important issues within Cole's treatment of culture and context that I want to highlight. First, he focuses on mediation and upon artefacts as mediators of human activity. Second, he focuses on the special structure of artefact-mediated action and the basic activity triangle. He draws our attention to the existence of both the mediated and unmediated link between subject and object and stresses that 'the emergence of mediated action does not mean that the mediated path replaces the natural one, just as the appearance of culture in phylogeny does not mean that culture replaces phylogeny' (Cole, 1996: 119). The two routes, the cultural and the natural 'operate synergistically'. Cole notes that this notion of artefact-mediated human action is only the starting point for a cultural-historical psychology and that it needs elaboration in order to enable discussions about 'aggregations of artefacts'.

In Cole's discussion of scripts as artefacts he cites the work of Hutchins (1995), and argues that cognition and culture need to be considered as parts of a larger system. I too find myself reminded of Hutchins' view of culture – as 'an adaptive process that accumulates partial solutions to frequently encountered problems' (Hutchins, 1995: 354) – when I read Cole's descriptions of the way in which scripts leave much unspecified. Hutchins challenges what he sees as the marginalization of culture by cognitive scientists and anthropologists, along with history, context and emotion. He criticizes the 'special place' that was awarded to the 'powers and limitations of the mind, as if these can be established without reference to culture'. This, he claims, has led to cognition being 'unhooked from interactions with the world'. Hutchins also discusses systems of socially distributed cognition, in which the social interactions of a group produce group properties which are not the same as the properties of the individual members of that group, and which are not predictable from these individuals' properties. He presents a framework for 'Distributed Cognition' that uses the metaphor of an 'ecology of thinking' to describe human cognition as interactions within an environment 'rich in organizing resources'. He studies cognition and learning in everyday situations and describes the ways in which novice navigators become expert in terms of a system of interactions in a dynamic system that includes the learner and the other people who are helping them learn, plus all the other elements with which they interact.

Hutchins draws our attention to the importance of both the interpersonal interaction and our interaction with artefacts in the world. This attention to the physical environment as well as the social can also be found in the work of others, such as Goodwin (2003, 2007) an applied linguist, who argues, for example, that we need to take the structure of the environment into account through 'environmentally coupled gestures'. In Goodwin (2007) he describes the interactions between 11-year-old Sandra and her father as they complete Sandra's maths homework in the parental bedroom. Sandra is working on fractions in her workbook and Goodwin demonstrates how Sandra's father helps Sandra complete an answer through combining language, gestures and the structure of the environment so that the different media 'mutually elaborate each other to create a whole that is different from, and greater than, any of its constituent parts' (Goodwin, 2007: 55).

The symbolic representations of the fractions in Sandra's homework are linked to their instantiations in the written forms of the homework book. The father attends to the position of his body with respect to Sandra and shifts his gaze between the homework book and Sandra to ensure that she is looking at what he has just pointed her towards. These environmentally coupled gestures are 'systematically positioned within a larger arrangement of the participants' bodies' (Goodwin, 2007: 57). This type of arrangement is particularly important for education and apprenticeship. The importance of other bodies and their history is emphasized in what Goodwin (2009) refers to as cooperative semiosis; a continuous transformation process through which signs that are secreted into the environment by people are built upon by others to produce sign operations that create a new environment. Thus action and meaning are built through a social process.

Over the past two decades, there has been a great deal of attention given to approaches in which cognition and learning are 'fundamentally situated' (for example, Brown, Collins & Duguid, 1989; Brown, 1990; Lave, 1988; Lave & Wenger, 1991). I talk about learning in greater depth in Chapter 2 and restrict discussion here to the notion of situatedness. Situatedness brings with it a need to clarify what we mean by a situation. Cole (1996) suggests that a situation offers a way to give context an appropriate relational role. Suchman (1987) talks about situations with respect to social behaviour, which is understood between participants through their reference to the 'situation particulars'. A second term 'setting' is also important to notions of situatedness. This is defined by Lave (1988) as 'a relation between acting persons and the arenas in relation with which they act'; it is something over which a person has some control. From these approaches knowledge is no longer an abstract entity, it is an activity in and with the environment.

As is apparent in these discussions of situated learning and made explicit by Cole, the concept of activity and activity theory is important. In activity theory the meaning of context is quite specific: 'the activity itself is the context' (Nardi, 1996). There is no notion of context as a container: 'People consciously and deliberately generate contexts (activities)' (Nardi, 1996: 73). Activity theory is complex (Nardi, 1996), and its basic features are explained by Wertsch (1979), Nardi (1996) and Kaptelinin *et al*. (1999). Human activity is the unit of analysis for activity theory and this consists of a flexible hierarchy of three levels of analysis: activities, actions and operations. The distinction between these levels is made on the basis of: the motive of the activity and the object to which it is directed, the goal of an action and the conditions under which an operation is carried out. The object gives the activity durable direction and a moving target with a horizon of possible actions (Engeström, 2009). Motives are not necessarily conscious, whereas goals are necessarily conscious and can be broken down into sub-goals. Human activity is mediated by tools and sign systems that have structure and that have been shaped by others over history. A key difference between activity theory and the situated cognition process can be seen in the transformation processes of internalization and externalization through which the external and the internal are unified (Nardi, 1996). Internalization is the process by which the interpsychological process becomes intrapsychological. Externalization is the process by which an internal activity is transformed into an external one, for example when it needs to be adjusted or repaired, or when it needs to be done in collaboration with others.

Many of the features of activity theory can be found in the work of Vygotsky (1978, 1986), whose sociocultural approach influenced, amongst others, the work of Cole that I discussed earlier. I talk further about Vygotsky in Chapter 2 when I look at learning theories, but I also want to highlight the key aspects of this work here, in order to integrate them with my discussion of context. The basic ideas of Vygotsky's approach are presented in the 'general law of cultural development', which states that:

> Every function in the child's cultural development appears twice: first, on the social level, and later, on the individual level; first, *between* people (*interpsychological*), and then *inside* the child (*intrapsychological*). This applies equally to voluntary

attention, to logical memory, and to the formation of concepts. All the higher functions originate as actual relations between human individuals.

(Vygotsky, 1978: 57).

The strength of this statement should not be overlooked (Wertsch, 1985a). It implies that processes such as that of concept formation are social activities attributable to groups as well as individuals: 'consciousness is a product of society, it is produced' (Leont'ev, 1979). Human development, therefore, requires that society provides opportunities for shared consciousness or understanding and the symbolic tools to mediate the communication of ideas (Bruner, 1984). Vygotsky extends the concept of tools within labour activity by applying them to psychological signs as well as to tools of production. There is, however, an important distinction that must be recognized: tools like the plough are externally directed and cause some change to occur in the object to which they are applied. A psychological tool or sign such as language is internally directed and does not necessarily change the object of the psychological operation (Wertsch, 1985b).

The link between the external activity of the 'interpsychological' activity of the individual's culture, and the 'intrapsychological' processes within the mind allows the internalization of the higher mental processes from their social origins. This process of internalization is central to Vygotsky's work. It is not a simple 'transfer' or 'copying' process; the structure and functions of the process change during its internalization and lead to the formation of an 'internal plane of consciousness' (Leont'ev, 1979). The individual gains control over, or masters, the external sign forms of their social activity (Wertsch & Stone, 1985). In this way the learner is able to use these sign forms to mediate and organize their own activity. The individual's psychological functioning that emerges from this process reflects the nature of the culture from which it was derived (Wertsch, 1984).

The importance of mediated behaviour to the development of higher psychological processes has already been mentioned. Language is a sign system that provides a means of organizing human activity and of passing the results of human activity from generation to generation. However, Vygotsky stresses that sign systems used within a culture are more than a means of storing past activity; they are also a means of forming future activity. Children interact with adults in a society within which a sign system is available; through this mediated social interaction internalization takes place. The mastery of the mediational means that exist within the social interactions of the individual lead to their mastery of the mediational means of that individual's own cognition (Wertsch, 1979).

My investigation of work from psychology and anthropology has produced both similarities to, and differences from, the descriptions of context already identified. The description of context as that which surrounds was seen in the earlier discussions of space and place, was identified by Cole and can be associated with a loss of the sense that context is part of a task. The description of context using the weaving metaphor gets us over this problem by reinstating the connection between a task and its circumstances. We could now conceptualize context as the circumstances in which artefacts mediate thinking, a frame of reference that is time-bounded. This, however, fails to portray any intentionality on the part of people and any sense of activity. The discussions of activity theory help here and offer us a view of context as an activity system in which cognition is distributed across all the components: something that can be created through human activity. The emphasis placed by Cole on the importance of both the mediated and the natural path within artefact-mediated action highlights the importance of the physical reality of the world as well as our mediated interactions. This echoes Hutchins' claim that cognitive science has 'unhooked cognition from interactions with the world'; a point emphasized in Goodwin's notion of 'environmentally coupled gestures', which also recognizes that artefacts are only artefacts when they are being used, which is consistent with the activity theory idea that using a tool and knowing how to use a tool are a fundamental part of that tool (Kaptelinin *et al.*, 1999). Both Hutchins and Goodwin promote the way in which action and meaning are built through social interaction that is not predictable from, and is greater than, the individual elements of those interactions. Social interaction in relation to an arena is, of course, a key component of situated cognition.

When it comes to the mind, learning and knowledge, there are a variety of views, but all have a strong emphasis upon interactions and connections. From Cole we have the view that the mind is 'distributed in the artefacts which *are woven together*' (Cole, 1996). For Vygotsky all higher-order psychological processes have their origins in relationships between people. Hutchins provides us with the idea of an 'ecology of thinking' (Hutchins, 1995) to describe human cognition and learning as a system of interactions that includes the learner, other people who are helping them learn and all the other elements with which they interact. Nardi (1996) likens this to an activity system. From a situated cognition perspective, knowledge is no longer an abstract entity; it is an activity in and with the environment. The main location of difficulty in extracting a consensual view about context from this work can be found in their different views about human agency and direction. As Nardi points out the situated approach is too contingent and lacks 'more durable, stable phenomena that persist across situations'. There is a lack of intentionality, goal-directed activity and future horizons of possibilities. The processes of internalization and externalization are the basis of cognition in activity theory, whereas from the situated perspective, learning remains a social interaction that is increased by participation in a community of practice.

Technology and context

Earlier in this chapter, I discussed Kerckhove & Tursi (2009) and noted their suggestion that the proliferation of the microchip has brought our everyday spaces alive and able to interact and react in different ways. I now look to computer science to see in what ways context is discussed and used. The work I discuss has arisen largely from within the ubiquitous computing community, that has paid particular attention to defining context in a manner that will enable the development of 'context aware' applications. It is, therefore, motivated by a technical device design aim. Context has been defined by Dey (2001), for example, as 'any information that can be used to characterize the situation of an entity. An entity is a person, place, or object that is considered relevant to the interaction between a user and an application, including the user and applications themselves' (Dey, 2001: 7). Others have critiqued this notion of context. Chalmers (2004), for example, has examined a number of the approaches, origins and ideals of context-aware systems design and, in particular, the way that history influences ongoing activity. He suggests that an individual's experience and history is part of their current context. There is an interesting and useful parallel here with the cultural approach of Cole and activity theory. All the resources within a context will be culturally defined and, therefore, bring with them a historical definition that will influence a learner's ongoing interactions. Dourish (2001) identifies the challenges that ubiquitous computing technology has brought to human-computer interaction design and the confusion that surrounds what it means for a device to be context-aware. He proposes greater attention be paid to the nature of human activity.

Working from a Human Computer Interaction (HCI) point of view Fitzpatrick (2003) highlights the popularity of spatial metaphors for the design of Computer Supported Collaborative Work systems. She notes that such metaphors exploit our human familiarity with interacting in physical spaces and take advantage of new technological advances. The ways in which spatial metaphors have been used have been extremely varied. Fitzpatrick provides an excellent review that encompasses 2-D and 3-D virtual spaces, media spaces and virtual and mixed reality environments and draws our attention to the design challenges; for example, the need to explicitly detail every aspect about a space and how people can interact with it, and the issue of embodiment, which she defines as: 'how people are identified and represented in the space'. Dourish (2006) notes the different behavioural constraints provided by the concepts of space, in terms of its geometrical organization, and place in terms of social interaction rules. Place, like space, has also been studied as a design metaphor, from the point of view of power (Dourish & Bell, 2007), for example, which resonates with early discussions arising from the geography literature and with issues of privacy (Benford, 2005).

It is worth pausing for a moment to consider the work of Dourish in more depth, in particular his 2001 text on embodied interaction. Written from an HCI perspective, this is motivated by the observation that increased computational power, plus an expansion in the ways in which computers are used, has resulted in a need to explore new forms of human computer interaction. His goal in elucidating the concept of embodied interaction is to 'provide resources to designers and system developers, by giving them tools they can use to understand and analyse their designs' (Dourish, 2001: 3). His intention is not to try to turn the threads he has extracted about tangible and social computing into a uniform theory. Embodied interaction is defined as: 'interaction with computer systems that occupy our world, a world of physical and social reality, and that exploit this fact in how they interact with us' (ibid.). It specifies how computers and the world 'fit together'. Dourish (2001) is also keen to emphasize that embodiment is not a feature of particular technologies, but a feature of interaction; 'embodiment is a question of how the technology is used'.

There is a similarity to be drawn between Hutchins' (1995) concerns with the narrowness of cognitive science and Dourish's (2001) concerns about the procedural foundations of HCI. His central focus is upon interaction as the 'means by which work is accomplished, dynamically and in context'. The central argument proposed by Dourish (2001) is that tangible computing and social computing are parts of the same research programme that can be brought together within embodied interaction. He describes tangible computing as computation distributed 'across a variety of devices, which are spread throughout the physical environment and are sensitive to their location and their proximity to other devices' (Dourish, 2001: 15). Social computing involves the incorporation of 'social understanding into the design of interaction itself'. The reasons Dourish (2001) cites for bringing these two approaches to computing together are fourfold. First, because they have the same underlying principles concerned with the way in which people interact directly with the world, both physically and socially. He is at pains to stress that embodiment is about more than physical reality and that it applies to conversations as well as objects. Second, because both approaches focus upon the concrete nature of activities and artefacts rather than their abstractions, embodiment is a core common element between them. In a similar manner to Hutchins' comment about cognitive science 'unhooking' cognition from the world, Dourish suggests that:

> In the real world, where the artefacts through which interaction is conducted are directly embodied in the everyday environment, these are all manifested alongside each other, inseparably. Tangible and social computing are trying to stitch them back together after traditional interactive system design approaches ripped them apart.
>
> (Dourish, 2001: 19–20)

Third, the idea of embodiment is grounded in older research, in particular the work done within phenomenology and the view that the world is full of meaning, and fourth that this older existing research can provide a foundation for embodied interaction. There is an explicit acknowledgement of intentionality in Dourish's notion of embodied interaction, he sees 'embodiment as the source for intentionality, rather than as the object of it'. This is reminiscent of Nardi's (1996) comments about activity theory. Tangible and social computing encourage people to incorporate technology into their world and everyday practice to communicate the meaning of their actions and interactions rather than meanings 'encoded in the technology itself'. Dourish (2001) highlights three aspects of meaning: ontology, intersubjectivity, and intentionality. The first he sees as being about form and meaning, the second about how people come to share meaning even though they cannot access each others' mental states, the third he describes as the relationship between a thought and its meaning.

This focus upon meaning is interesting, particularly in the light of the differences highlighted earlier between the situated and activity theorists. Dourish (2001) offers the concept of coupling as a useful way to understand the relationship between embodied action and meaning. Coupling is presented as a means of turning the world into a set of tools: 'first, users can select, from out of the variety of effective entities offered to them, the ones that are relevant to their immediate activity and, second, can put those together in order to effect action' (Dourish, 2001: 142). Coupling provides for 'how meaning is made manifest from moment to moment and turned to use'. The technologies that Dourish cites as those which support embodied interaction 'make manifest how they are coupled to the world, and so afford us the opportunity to orient to them in a variety of ways' (Dourish, 2001: 154).

Dourish (2001) has offered a more human-focused perspective to ubiquitous computing, a theme that is found also in Y. Rogers (2006). Rogers suggests that ubiquitous computing research has not managed to achieve the 'dream of comfortable, informed and effortless living', largely because the variability in why, what, when and how people act 'makes it difficult, if not impossible, to try to implement context in any practical sense'. She suggests a change of course towards 'designing for engaging user experiences' (Rogers, 2006: 405), which requires 'a shift from *proactive computing* to *proactive people*'. She calls for the creation of technologies that can be 'ecologies of resources' that meet people's needs, with people as the drivers in control. Dourish (2001) also uses an ecological metaphor when he likens interactional approaches to computation to ecosystems, as the 'interplay between different components', as do Crabtree & Rodden (2008) in their consideration of the hybrid ecologies that occur between physical and digital space. But what might these ecologies of resources be like? In particular, what might they be like for learners?

The ways of talking about context that can be found in this computer science literature include entities and interactions. They recognize the importance of history and human activity and the widespread use of spatial metaphors for interaction design. Distinctions are drawn between space and place that are not far removed from those encountered in geography and architecture. The work on embodied interaction pulls together the physical reality and the social interactions of our experiences of the world that offers a computer science perspective to some of the ideas from Cole, Hutchins and Goodwin that were discussed earlier, and a means for us to reconnect our thoughts with the real world. Discussions of meaning highlight its ubiquity in the world, the role of social interaction and of human agency, and the images presented are of people selecting proactively from a variety of tools, those that can be used to make something they desire happen in the world, as opposed to technologies acting smartly to interpret and meet a person's need.

The complexity of context is evident from the outset of this chapter's review of a varied literature. My particular interest is in learning; it is not surprising, therefore, that I am particularly struck by Gulson & Symes' (2007) observation that the treatment of space and place in educational studies is underexamined, undertheorized and underdeveloped. I suggest the same is true about context with respect to the use of technology to support learning: *we need to reconnect technology, learning and context in the way in which we design and use technology to support learning.* Discussions that link context to space and place are frequent and traverse texts from geography to computer science. Space is portrayed as abstract and encompassing; a container for people and objects through which their interrelationships can be specified; something that needs to be integrated with context to highlight its social aspect. Place is connected to people and their subjective lived experience. It is something that is framed by human interactions and interventions, both positive and negative.

Context matters to learning; it is complex and local to a learner. It defines a person's subjective and objective experience of the world in a spatially and historically contingent manner. Context is dynamic and associated with connections between people, things, locations and events in a narrative that is driven by people's intentionality and motivations. Technology can help to make these connections in an operational sense. People can help to make these connections have meaning for a learner.

A learner is not exposed to multiple contexts, but rather has a single context that is their lived experience of the world; a 'phenomenological gestalt' (Manovich, 2006) that reflects their interactions with multiple people, artefacts and environments. The partial descriptions of the world that are offered to a learner through these resources act as the hooks for interactions in which action and meaning are built. In this sense, meaning is distributed amongst these resources. However, it is the manner in which the learner at the centre of their context internalizes their interactions that is the core activity of importance. These interactions are not predictable but are created by the people who interact, each of whom will have intentions about how these interactions should be. If we accept that context is centred around an individual, then its timescale is that individual's life and its boundaries are those of that individual's interactions. This is where I find the concept of landscape particularly useful in the way that it focuses on the fact that landscapes have horizons that draw attention to new possibilities, as well as closing off what the eye can see.

In the next chapter, I will focus on the ways in which learning can be conceptualized in order to refine this description of context through the integration of a compatible definition of learning. At the end of this current chapter, I borrow and adapt a phrase from Dourish (2001: 3) who states that he is 'more concerned with interaction than I am with interfaces, and more concerned with computation than I am with computers'. In this book my concern is more with learning than with the particularities of any education system, and I am more interested in interaction than in technology.

2 Learners and learning

The aim of this book is to explore the concept of context, to develop a context-based model of learning and to use this model to develop a design framework for the development of technology-rich learning activities. The purpose of this design framework is to guide and support the development of technology-rich learning activities that can enable learners and teachers to make best use of the learning resources that are available to them. In particular, the framework aims to engender the development of activities that use technology to overcome the traditional physical and temporal constraints that are part of many learning environments. There is nothing new about the suggestion that one should explore the educational context in which learning takes place in order to understand more about learning. Work such as that completed by Mercer (1992) suggests that the organization of learning resources, including the computer, influences the manner in which these resources are used. Similarly Wood *et al.* (1999), when evaluating Integrated Learning Systems, concluded that the impact of technology upon learning was heavily dependent on the specifics of the educational environment into which the technology was introduced. This type of work is useful in confirming the importance of looking at the wider environment, but is limited by a focus that is mainly on specific environmental locations, such as school classrooms.

In Chapter 1 I discussed what the word 'context' means more broadly and to a wide community of researchers. I proposed that we might talk usefully about context, in relation to learning and learners, as a dynamic process associated with connections among people, things, locations and events, in a narrative that is driven by people's affective motivations. Technology can help to make these connections in an operational sense. People can help to make these connections have meaning for a learner. I suggested that learners are not exposed to multiple contexts, but rather that each learner has a single context that is their lived experience of the world and which reflects their interactions with multiple people, artefacts and environments. In this chapter, I focus on learning so that I can refine my description of context through the integration of a compatible definition of learning. My aim is to identify a theory of learning that is consistent with the previous discussions of context and which can be interpreted and integrated with these discussions. This interpretation will then be used to develop a context-based model of learning that can be made operational and can form the foundation for the design framework. In my presentation of this interpretation I include consideration of the roles to be played by different participants in the learning process: for example, learners, teachers, trainers, peers and parents.

In the discussions in Chapter 1, I introduced several viewpoints that specifically relate to learning; for instance, work from the sociocultural tradition, such as that of Vygotsky, activity theory, Michael Cole's cultural psychology, Hutchins' distributed cognition approach and the situated and communities of practice approaches. The description of context upon which I settled favoured an intentional role for people, a learner-centredness that defines context as an interactional concept, combining a learner's active experience of their physical reality with their mediated experiences through human-made artefacts. I acknowledge the importance of the process of internalization through which an individual's distributed meaning-making interactions lead that individual's development. This narrows down the compatibility of the theories introduced in Chapter 1 to those from a sociocultural stance. The relational attributes of activity systems certainly make them appealing for my purposes, but my desire to focus upon a learner at the centre of their context's interactions, paired with my desire to get to grips with formal as well as informal learning, means that I need to probe a little deeper for an appropriate definition and theory of learning. I therefore begin with a focus on the sociocultural approach of Vygotsky (1978, 1979, 1986, 1987) as introduced in Chapter 1. This work reflects concerns about school learning and, therefore, offers a route into the consideration of formal learning.

The sociocultural approach of Vygotsky is developmental and describes an individual's mental development as an interaction between that individual and their sociocultural environment. The nature of these interactions influences the nature of their resultant mental processes; the interpsychological becomes intrapsychological via the process of internalization. The Zone of Proximal Development (ZPD) represents the crystallization of this internalization process, and was introduced with particular reference to the school-aged child. Vygotsky (1986) proposed his own theory concerning the nature of the relationship between instruction and mental development – a subject of considerable debate at the time of his writing – and suggested that the measurement of a child's mental development had been given too little attention. He proposed that a child's ability to solve standardized problems unassisted merely reflected the completed part of their development and that this was not the whole story. The ZPD was introduced within this context and was defined as:

> The discrepancy between a child's actual mental age and the level he reaches in solving problems with assistance indicates the zone of his proximal development; ... Experience has shown that the child with the larger zone of proximal development will do much better in school.
>
> (Vygotsky, 1986: 187)

Vygotsky (1986) distinguished between spontaneous concepts, of which the child has direct sensory experience in their everyday life, and scientific concepts, which are triggered by an 'initial verbal definition' that is then systematically applied until the concept becomes a 'concrete phenomenon'; a process that involves 'strenuous mental activity' (Vygotsky, 1986) on the part of the child. The emergence of higher psychological processes is the central issue in the development of the child at school age. The relationship between instruction and development is presented as one in which instruction or learning pulls along development; the conscious awareness of the scientific concepts preceding that of the spontaneous concepts. The child may, therefore, become conscious of the spontaneous concepts rather late. This is not saying that the concepts do not exist, merely that the child is unaware of their existence. The experience of the spontaneous concepts within the learner clears a path for the development of the scientific concepts, which then reach a higher level of development and in so doing create a structure that will allow the further development of the spontaneous concepts. The nature of the two development systems is revealed by the relationship between the child's actual development and their ZPD. When instruction is aimed at what the child cannot quite achieve, rather than at what they can do unaided, then it can play a major role in the development of the child's higher mental processes. Through the cooperation of adults, consciousness and volitional control can be provided, that was originally lacking in the spontaneous concepts. The purpose of constructing a ZPD is to focus the dialogue between the instructor and the child. The learner can then reflect upon this dialogue and reformulate it into their own thought (Bruner, 1984).

The *process* of the ZPD becomes clearer in Vygotsky (1978), in which it is described as something that must be created through instructional interactions; something that 'awakens' the internal developmental processes and can only operate when the child is interacting with other people in the environment. This once again highlights the idea that the process of internalization, crystallized within the ZPD, is social. Consideration of broadly sociocultural approaches to the process of educational practice highlights the key role played by the construction of interactions, because it is these that create opportunities for the participants' intellectual development. The learner and the more able 'other' must both be active participants. The nature of these 'developmental interactions' is complex (Bruner & Bornstein, 1989) and the provision of the correct environment, in terms of social space and cultural continuity, is important. The nature of the world experienced by the child is influential and the interactions with and within this world, which are mediated by tools such as language, are of great importance for intellectual development. Opportunities by which both a learner's verbal and non-verbal participation in an activity can be provided and accounted for (Freedman, 1995), as well as the presentation of the intended activity to the learner, must use the available resources to enhance the activity so that the learner can recognize aspects that they understand, and which are within their 'range of competence' (Bruner & Bornstein, 1989). The ZPD is not exclusive to asymmetrical interactions between a teacher and a learner within the classroom. Mutually cooperating peers are also encompassed by the ZPD and the process of peer collaboration has been considered by many, for example Tudge (1992), Saxe *et al.* (1993), and Wood *et al.* (1995).

The participants' past experience also influences the interactions that create the ZPD. Each participant brings with them a continuum of interactive experiences to which the current episode will form an extension; the nature of the current episode will, therefore, be derivative of the individual learner's history as well as that of their teacher or learning partner (Smagorinsky & Fly, 1993). This attention to the previous experiences of the learner, including the learning strategies they have developed, highlights the need for those working with the learner to gain a good knowledge of the learner.

A further factor to bear in mind, when considering the nature of the interactions between learner and more able other intended by Vygotsky and colleagues, is that of terminology. As we highlight in Luckin (2008) and Luckin *et al.* (in press) there are ambiguities associated with the Russian term '*obuchenie*' used by Vygotsky to describe the learning and teaching process. There is no single English equivalent and the term itself is often translated as 'instruction', or sometimes 'learning' and 'teaching' are merged to form 'teaching/learning' (Clarke, 2003), or 'teaching-learning' (Davydov & Kerr, 1995). The problems of translation have been debated by a variety of scholars (Davydov & Kerr, 1995; Daniels, 2001; Clarke, 2003; LeBlanc & Bearison, 2004). The important point here is that there is a sense of mutual cognitive growth within both the learner and their more able other or teacher (LeBlanc & Bearison, 2004).

Contemporary educational practice has been influenced by a sociocultural approach and the emphasis within education has switched from the individual towards a drive to recognize the social and communicative nature of cognitive development (Mercer, 1992). The classroom life of a child is made up of many varied social transactions. Children and adults are interdependent and a 'collective' ZPD exists (Moll & Whitmore, 1993), with each individual class having its own unique culture and brand of learning environment (Smagorinsky & Fly, 1993). Examples of the sociocultural approach in action can be found in the 'developmental learning' of Tharp & Gallimore (1988). A child's educational activities can be viewed as social contexts in which dynamic teaching and assessment take place and provision is made for the 'shared construction of knowledge and understanding' in responsive teaching (Stremmel & Fu, 1993).

Theories of learning

The discussion of context in Chapter 1 highlighted the integral role played by people's environments, including the artefacts and people that constitute this environment. With respect to education, and as pointed out by Bransford and his colleagues in their seminal book about how people learn, the influence that learning theories have upon our environment is not to provide 'a simple recipe for designing effective learning environments; similarly, physics constrains but does not dictate how to build a bridge' (Bransford *et al.*, 2000: 131). Rather, the various phases of learning theory development have each influenced aspects of the contemporary education environment. My exploration therefore considers the manner in which each theory has influenced some of our current educational environments, and the nature of the relationship that can be drawn between each theoretical position and the sociocultural approach. This is not an exhaustive survey of the many theories about human learning, but rather a discussion of the theories in relation to the work of Vygotsky and to the setting in which the learners operate in our design activities.

Behaviourism

The first theory of learning to be used systematically in the design of education systems is behaviourism. Behaviourist researchers were interested in observable phenomena and objective relationships that would enable them to produce a science of behaviour that did not need to call on mental states (Wood, 1988). Ivan Pavlov (1849–1936) conducted the early work of behaviourism with animals and introduced classical conditioning, which others, such as Watson & Rayner (1920), applied to the study of children. The definition of learning was limited to a learner's acquisition of a new association with a behaviour, for example being afraid, and a stimulus, such as seeing a rat. At a similar point in time Edward Thorndike (1898) introduced the concepts of trial and error, and reinforcement. His approach, referred to as operant conditioning, proposed that a learner's response to a particular situation could be strengthened when the learner was offered a subsequent reward. Thorndike conducted an extensive analysis of particular tasks in spelling and arithmetic and suggested that desirable relationships, or bonds, needed to be identified and strengthened through practice. One of Thorndike's followers, Skinner, was particularly interested in the concept of reinforcement and punishment (Skinner, 1938). Skinner was also interested in machines for teaching; an interest that can be linked to his concerns with classroom management (Skinner, 1968). He argued that teachers were not able to intervene in students' learning as often or at the optimal time after each student's actions.

The definition of learning within this paradigm was still based upon learners acquiring new associations between a behaviour and a response, but there was a new emphasis upon what could be done to strengthen or weaken these stimulus-response pairs. Other behaviourist researchers were less radical and argued that the consideration of an organism's mental representation of the world was also important. Edward Tolman, for example, argued that reinforcement was required for performance, but not for learning (Tolman & Honzik, 1930). Tolman identified the role of expectancy, and suggested that the best predictor of learning was what the learner perceived, or expected, to be the consequences of their actions. This notion of expectancy can also be related to the phenomenon of learned helplessness (Seligman, 1975); that is, a phenomenon that has important implications for the design of educational tasks and environments, where learners' early experience of problems that they find too difficult can result in them withdrawing their efforts.

Behaviourism has come a long way from its conception with Pavlov's dogs; it is still however focused on observable outcomes, and lacks any clear statement about the learner's agency, or the specification of a role for elements outside the stimulus response pairs. Despite this, it has had an important influence on the nature of the elements within each learner's context. It grounds some aspects of the ways in which institutions and education systems operate and its researchers identified many issues that are still the subject of contemporary research and discussion: such as motivation, how teachers should be supported, and the negative effects of punishment.

A further development of the work started by the behaviourists and in support of Skinner's notion of programmed instruction can be seen in the work of Bloom *et al.* (1956), who published *Taxonomy of Educational Objectives*. This offered a classification of learning levels, or goals, organized hierarchically across three types of domain: Cognitive (Knowledge); Affective (Attitude); and Psychomotor (Skills). In the Cognitive domain, for example, six categories of behaviour are identified. These range from the simplest to the most complex: Recall; Comprehension; Application; Analysis; Synthesis; Evaluation. The idea is that a learner must master the simplest before moving on to the next level of complexity. Bloom *et al.*'s *Taxonomy* offered the behavioural objectives needed for the type of programmed instruction envisioned by Skinner. A further relevant development can be seen in work that explored the analysis of learning tasks (Miller, 1953). Gagne (1965) subsequently used this task-analysis approach and developed a model of instruction for human learning. He identified different types of human learning, each of which required a different instructional approach. This provided an extension of the drill and practice approach of the behaviourists and suggested that different types of learning required different conditions for learning. He identified the need to assist learners in more complex problem-solving activities and to take other cognitive processes, such as memory, into account when designing instruction (Gagne 1965, 1987).

An approach that offers a stark contrast to that of the behaviourists and a complement to the work of Gagne is the view that man is an information processor. This was popular in the 1950s and '60s and offered a focus on what was happening inside the heads of people as opposed to what was merely manifested in their observable behaviour. The approach is not a 'theory' in the strict sense, but rather a set of related terms and concepts that offer a language with which models of human activity and theories can be constructed (Wood, 1988). The emphasis was upon understanding the processes that went on inside the heads of people and the language that was used included terms such as skills, actions, goals and control. The juxtaposition of these developments with the development of computers resulted in a propensity for talking about minds in similar ways to computers, for example with discussions on symbol manipulation, rule-based systems, sequential representations and memory load.

This approach to psychology as cognitive science was further influenced and developed by the interdisciplinary enterprise of Artificial Intelligence (AI). AI has progressed from an initial belief that symbol manipulation and the reproduction of particular skills and abilities, such as being able to play chess, would lead us to the creation of intelligent machines. Connectionist models and parallel distributed processing became important themes in the 1980s, and the 1990s saw the emergence of a group of people who were interested in what was being called 'Artificial Life'. This involved the study and modelling of simple organisms and a recognition that the environments within which these organisms lived were important. Simple robots that could react appropriately in their environment were developed *(see* Steels & Brooks, 1995) in clear contrast to the early work building artificial systems in toy domains (Winograd & Flores, 1985).

Constructivism

Constructivism offers yet another contrast to the behaviourist and information processing approaches for several reasons. Constructivism as formalized by Jean Piaget is an articulation of the manner in which knowledge can be constructed by learners, also referred to as 'genetic epistemology', because of its focus on the process through which learners construct knowledge as they develop cognitively. Piaget's constructivism encompasses a much richer set of factors than the behaviourist approaches discussed above (Piaget, 1970). The importance awarded to development recognizes that there are changes over time: changes that are influenced by the learner themselves through their actions, their physical and their representational maturity; and changes that are influenced by things 'outside' the learner, that is, the physical world and the people with whom the learner interacts. The recognition of a role for things both within the head and things outside of the head of the learner requires assimilation and accommodation processes that specify internalization. A constructivist approach awards little influence to the child's environment; this is limited to the assimilation of environmental affordances. The emphasis upon action rather than language is another limiting factor, particularly upon the potential of other people to influence the learner. The role of others is also limited by the emphasis upon conflict and the need for learners to come into contact with things that do not fit into their existing representational system, in order for development to occur. It should be noted, however, that cultural influences were not totally ruled out by Piaget, who acknowledged that the formal operations performed by learners may reflect the subset of formal operations prevalent in the adults in their community (Cole, 1996).

There are other approaches where the learner's environment is given a greater role. Maria Montessori developed a method of education *(see* Montessori 1959, 1969) that promoted the importance of the child's environment. She proposed that the stages in the child's development were closely linked to the content and environment of the curriculum. However, the important environment for Montessori was not that which occurred naturally as part of the child's social culture, but one that needed to be manufactured specially for the child. The method by which the child's development was influenced by their environment was also distinct. Montessori (1969) saw children as accumulating material by means of their 'absorbent mind'; a clear contrast to the strenuous mental activity leading to the creation of mental processes envisaged by Vygotsky. The role of the teacher in a Montessorian paradigm was to prepare the didactic material and environment appropriately. If the child's attention was not aroused by the environment alone, the teacher should be 'seductive' to gain the learner's attention (Montessori, 1959). Once the child's interest had been roused, the teacher was to withdraw into the background. Their job was the presentation of fresh material when the child had exhausted that already available; it was not to help the child to solve problems.

Constructivism, like behaviourism has had a great influence upon the way in which many educational systems operate. Piaget's constructivism has also been the basis for developments in educational technology, most notably through the Logo work of Seymour Papert (1980). Montessori, too, has continued to influence the education environment and the Montessori method is still practised, for example, in independent Montessori schools worldwide.

My desire to elucidate a context-based model of learning based upon a learner's interactions in the world makes the emphasis within situated and legitimate peripheral participation on evolving, continuously renewed sets of relations particularly interesting. However, as I pointed out in the discussions in Chapter 1, there is a lack of intentionality and direction of action in these situated approaches. There is also a lack of recognition of the role of internalization. Hedegaard (1998) also criticizes the situated cognition approach for its overreliance upon social practices in everyday life. Within a Vygotskian approach, the differences between everyday learning and school learning are recognized. Children's school learning must be anchored in everyday life situations, subject matter areas and the learner's development. The situated and apprenticeship models pay due attention to the first of these anchors but insufficient to the second and third (Hedegaard, 1998).

Scaffolding

My focus in this book is upon interactions, in particular interactions between learners and their teachers, or more able others. The ZPD requires assistance for the learner from a more able other. The nature of this assistance is, however, left underspecified in Vygotsky's writing. Seminal work done by David Wood (Wood *et al.*, 1976), in which he coined the term 'scaffolding' to describe tutorial assistance, is particularly relevant. Effective scaffolding is presented as something more than the provision of hints and graded help. It involves simplification of the learner's role and interactions in which learners and their More Able Partners (MAPs) work together to achieve success, but the contributions from each vary according to the child's level of ability (Wood, 1980). The model of effective teaching proposed by Wood involves the use of the contingent teaching strategy, which requires the MAP to adopt the following approach:

> Where the learner fails to understand or comply with a preceding instruction n, then more help or control should be given on instruction n +1. Where the learner succeeds, any help offered should exert less control than on instruction n.
>
> (Wood *et al.*, 1992: 14)

Three different aspects of contingency have been identified: instructional contingency, which is concerned with the level of the next intervention; domain contingency, which is concerned with issuing instructions which are appropriate to the materials selected by the learner; and temporal contingency, which is concerned with how long the learner should be left struggling (Wood *et al.*, 1992).

The scaffolding approach represents one way of pinning down the nature of the assistance that teachers can provide for children as they learn and has been used in much subsequent research (for example, Palincsar *et al.*, 1993; Rosson & Carroll, 1996). Mercer (1995) suggests a process of 'guided construction of knowledge' in which a variety of teaching strategies are provided to suit 'different kinds of learning and different kinds of understanding', complemented by constant guiding strategies to support whichever teaching strategy is adopted. Bliss *et al.*, (1996) highlight the difficulty they observed in the implementation of scaffolding. They examined scaffolding in school and suggest that before scaffolds can be constructed, or even planned, a careful analysis of the domain is essential, indicating potential links to the child's existing, intuitive knowledge.

The role of these MAPs in the interactions that create a learner's context is fundamental and requires that these MAPs assist learners towards cognitive growth. The scaffolding metaphor is particularly useful in specifying how this assistance can be provided. Its origins are certainly in the social interactions between learner and MAP; it is, however, difficult to implement.

The Zone of Collaboration: scaffolding learning through and in the ZPD

I find the definition of learning provided by the ZPD to be the most compatible with my description of context. The ZPD could be thought of as a context with which productive interactivity can happen, but rather too much is left unspecified for this to be operationalized and integrated. The ZPD does not specify the manner in which the 'actual developmental level and the zone of proximal development' (Vygotsky, 1978) are to be identified, nor does it prescribe the exact nature of the instructional assistance that is to be offered to learners. This need for clarification has been recognized by many researchers, such as Saxe *et al.* (1984), Valsiner (1984) and Wertsch (1984). I find Wertsch's introduction of three additional constructs – situation definition, intersubjectivity and semiotic mediation – particularly useful. A situation definition describes the manner in which a context is actively constructed and represented by those who are operating within it. Development is a qualitative transformation, which will involve a fundamental situation redefinition. Intersubjectivity exists when two participants share the same situation definition and know that they share it. If the child and the adult have different intrapsychological situation definitions then collaboration within the ZPD may require a third interpsychological situation definition. Semiotic mediation provides the means of communication and negotiation to support intersubjectivity and situation redefinition.

The scaffolding metaphor of Wood and the constructs proposed by Wertsch are all useful in pinning down the means by which a ZPD might be created. These have informed my interpretation of the ZPD, which explores the relationship between the identification of a learner's collaborative capability and the specification of the assistance that needs to be offered to the learner in order for them to succeed at a particular task. I refer to this interpretation as the Zone of Collaboration and I introduce two additional constructs called:

1   The Zone of Available Assistance (ZAA); and
2   The Zone of Proximal Adjustment (ZPA).

The ZAA describes the variety of resources within a learner's world that could provide different qualities and quantities of assistance and that may be available to the learner at a particular point in time. The ZPA represents a subset of the resources from the ZAA that are appropriate for a learner's needs. The following scenario, along with the explanation that follows, provides an example:

> A learner is studying numeracy and is trying to solve a homework problem that requires them to divide a number of items into three groups. They have various options available to them: they can watch a video clip that they saw earlier at school and that demonstrates how such problems can be solved; they can use their personal computer tablet to complete an interactive activity that has been designed to develop the appropriate skills and knowledge that they need in order to solve this problem; they can ask a family member or friend for help; they can text a classmate on their mobile phone; or they can send an email to their teacher. Each of these options may also have further choices embedded within them, such as at what level of difficulty they should complete the interactive activity and what sort of help they should ask their mother to provide; that is, the answer or just a hint about how to get started on the problem. There are challenges in this scenario also for those who are charged with helping the learner to learn – teachers, parents and those involved in developing adaptive technology – that are designed to provide timely interventions to support learning.

In this scenario, the ZAA includes: a video demonstration; a personal computer with interactive activities at various levels of difficulty; family members; friends; a mobile phone; email; and a teacher. Part of the aim of the person, people, or technology acting in the role of the learner's MAP (see Figure 2.1 which illustrates these concepts), is to identify and possibly introduce a variety of types of assistance from the available resources. One of the goals for the learner is to express their current understanding and learning needs through their interactions with the elements of the ZAA, including interactions with the More Able Partner. The ZPA is constructed through a negotiation between a learner and their More Able Partners. An impoverished ZAA will limit the possibilities for the construction of the ZPA. However, even if the ZAA offers a rich and versatile range of resources, the success with which a ZPA meets the needs of the learner will depend upon the negotiation between learner and More Able Partners. It is this relationship

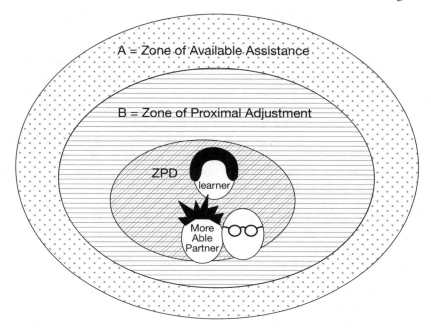

Figure 2.1 The Zone of Collaboration

between learner and More Able Partners that needs to be the focus of scaffolding attention.

Throughout my discussion of context and learning, the active role of the learner has been stressed and I now want to consider the resources that a learner brings to their interactions in more detail, in particular their resources beyond cognition.

Cognition and beyond: motivation, metacognition and epistemic cognition

The Zone of Collaboration describes the learner's world as being full of potential forms of assistance that might act as resources to support learning. The learner as discussed so far has been conceptualized in terms of their interactions and capabilities, with respect to their cognitive development processes. I now consider some of the other resources that a learner might bring to their interactions: their motivation; their understanding of their own knowledge; and their understanding of what knowledge is.

The importance of affect was made clear in Chapter 1. What does this mean? There are a variety of terms that are used to describe the way that a person is feeling. We talk about moods, emotions, affect and motivation, for example. In harmony with previous discussions, my focus is on learning and context. There are a variety of definitions and theories about the way in which learning is related to emotion and motivation. There are theories that consider the relationship between cognition and emotion. Ortony *et al.* (1988), for example, describe emotions as purely cognitive functions determined by a person's goals, standards and attitudes, and Lazarus (1991) suggests that a person's emotions are determined by their goals, their coping potential and their perceptions of the benefits of an action or event for their well-being. There are other theories that consider the manner in which a learner's emotional state can impact upon their cognition. The cognitive-motivational model (Pekrun *et al.*, 2002), for instance, describes how emotion influences a person's motivation to learn, their cognitive resources and their learning strategies. Each emotion can be positive or negative and each can be activating or deactivating. Positive and activating emotions will mostly result in increased motivation and will support learning, and negative and deactivating emotions will mostly reduce motivation and can be detrimental to learning (Balaam, 2009). This model is based upon a control-value theory of academic emotions and as such there will be elements within the learner's environment that will influence their appraisals of their control and the value to them of an activity. An alternative view to these cognitive theories can be found in socially constructed theories of emotion that look beyond the individual and consider the way in which a person's appraisals, of both an event and their response to that event, are socially constructed (*see* Ratner, 1989; Boehner *et al.*, 2007). There are also theories that are based on a sociocultural approach (for example, Denzin, 1984; Boehner *et al.*, 2007) that acknowledge that different environments and cultures will support different learning interactions and, therefore, different appraisals and emotions.

The term 'motivation' is also subject to a variety of definitions and approaches. Bergin *et al.* (1993), for example, define the term 'motivation' as: 'The physiological process involved in the direction, vigour, and persistence of behaviour'. Ryan and Deci (2000) define motivation as 'reason for action' and suggest two aspects to motivation: one is quantitative and underpins the way we talk about the strength of a learner's motivation; the other is qualitative, and describes the orientation of the process. There are theories that draw the distinction between intrinsic and extrinsic motivation (Ryan & Deci, 2000), theories that are concerned with sociocognitive constructs, such as expectancy-value theory (Wigfield & Eccles, 2000) and self-efficacy (Zimmerman, 2000), and there are achievement goal theories that identify the influence of a person's learning goals on the way that they manage their learning interactions (Ames, 1992; Dweck & Leggett, 1988; Meece, 1991).

There is a limited body of empirical work exploring the relationship of a learner's context, their emotions and their learning and two recent studies are worthy of particular note here. The first by Balaam (2009) offers a detailed study of the relationship between the dynamic school context and the emotional experience of learners aged 12–13 years. Balaam introduces two concepts to clarify the relationship between a learner's context and their emotions: the 'wider school context' and the 'task-based context'. The wider school context is defined as 'elements of the learning context not directly available within the classroom environment' (Balaam, 2009: 258); this includes the learner's perceptions of their social interactions with peers and teachers outside the classroom. The task-based context is defined as the 'elements of the classroom context constructed around learning tasks and immediately manipulable by members working within the context (normally the teacher)' (Balaam, 2009: 259). Balaam's findings show that the wider school context has a strong impact on learners' emotional experiences and that this impact varies between learners and over time. The task-based context can also have a strong impact on learners' emotional experiences, an impact that can be seen amongst groups of learners and classes as a whole.

The second study concerns achievement goal theory, which is particularly interesting when considering a learner's context, because it offers an organizational framework with cognitive, affective and behavioural facets through which the learner's context and motivation can be interpreted. Whilst achievement goals have been considered mainly with respect to individual learners, some studies have explored learners as they collaborate and have suggested that mastery-oriented learners are more likely to be supportive in collaborative interactions with peers and to see these situations as offering an opportunity for what Damon and Phelps (1989a), in their study of collaboration, have called 'creative risk taking'. Performance-oriented learners, on the other hand, may see such situations as opportunities to demonstrate their ability or expose their lack of ability. Work by Darnon *et al.* (2006) also suggests a link between achievement goal orientation and a student's regulation of their sociocognitive conflicts with peers.

In work conducted by Harris (Harris *et al.*, 2008) the context-dependent and dispositional factors in achievement goal orientation were explored with learners aged 8–10 years. Children who had been identified as displaying no consistent disposition for either mastery or performance goal orientation were split into two groups and asked to complete a computer-based task in same-gendered pairs. One group was given mastery goal instructions and was told that the object of their task was to work out the best strategy. Mistakes didn't matter, because these would help them to devise the best strategy. The other group was given performance goal instructions and told that the object of the task was to complete as many successful actions as possible, each of which would be counted towards points that would be awarded to the pair. Findings illustrated that pairs who had received mastery goal instructions engaged in significantly more elaborate problem-solving discussion than those who had received performance goal instructions. The performance-instructed children also displayed lower levels of metacognitive control.

Both the work by Balaam and that of Harris support the view that the way in which we design the environments we provide and the resources we make available to learners, such as the task, peers and teachers, will impact upon their emotions, their motivations, their behaviour and their learning. The work by Harris *et al.* also highlights a link between motivation and metacognition. This relationship has been identified by others, such as Boekaerts (2003), who has developed a model that integrates motivation, affect and learning. This model argues for an integration of metacognition through recognition of the learner's cognitive assessment of their own affective state, and reminds us of the sociocognitive theories of emotion and self-efficacy.

Both Vygotsky and Piaget agree that children lack awareness of their mental functions; what one might term 'metacognition'. Metacognition can be broadly referred to as any knowledge or cognitive process that refers to, monitors or controls any aspect of cognition. Scholars such as Flavell (1979) and Kluwe (1982) distinguish between a person's knowledge of their cognitive processes and the processes they use to monitor and regulate their cognition. This latter regulatory process incorporates a variety of executive functions and strategies, such as planning, resource allocation, monitoring, checking and error detection and correction (Brown, 1987). Metacognition enhances cognitive performance, including attention, problem-solving and intelligence (Bruner, 1996) and can increase learning outcomes (Marzano, 1998). Successful students continually evaluate, plan and regulate their progress, which makes them aware of their own learning and promotes deep-level processing (Goos *et al.*, 2002). Metacognition involves the interpretation of ongoing activity (Flavell & Wellman, 1977). Metacognitive judgements are based upon inferences drawn from external cues. This does not result from people 'turning an inward eye on their memories and somehow analyzing them directly' (Kornell, 2009). The inferences learners draw from these external cues can have negative as well as positive results. For example, fluency in processing information can make a learner feel confident and yet that confidence may not be evidenced in learning (Kornell & Bjork, 2008). Learners do not, apply their metacognitive strategies spontaneously across domains and environments (Kuhn, 1999). It is, therefore, reasonable to suggest that learners would benefit from specific support designed to help them to apply their metacognitive strategies appropriately.

Researchers who are interested in the demands that modern technology makes on learners increasingly recognize the need to consider higher-order thinking skills such as metacognition. For example, Luckin *et al.* (2009) stress that learners need higher levels of critical engagement with information and communications technologies. In addition, Buckingham (2007), Jenkins *et al.* (2006) and Green & Hannon (2007) focus on media literacy and learner criticality, which they describe as a set of primarily cognitive skills and practices. Others, such as Van Dijk (2005) suggest that learner criticality involves the development of a metacognitive awareness of technical, cognitive and cultural aspects of technology use.

In the same way that there are multiple theories about how we learn, there are multiple theories about knowledge development and what can be referred to as epistemic cognition. A variety of terms are used: in the psychological literature, for example, these include personal epistemology and epistemological beliefs. There is also a lack of agreement about the relationship between epistemic cognition and learning. There are a variety of theoretical positions, including: developmental theories (Perry, 1970; King & Kitchener, 2004); non-linear models of learners' 'ways of knowing' (Belenky *et al.*, 1986; Kuhn, 1999); multidimensional theories (Schommer, 1990); and contextualized interpretations that link people's meaning-making with their perceptions of their environment (Baxter-Magolda, 2004). Bearing in mind that the objective of my discussions here is to find a way in which epistemic cognition can be interpreted in a manner that can be integrated with a context-based theory of learning, I constrain my discussion to the consideration of work that has an empirical grounding in psychology or education.

Ways of talking about knowledge vary and it's hard to identify a consistent view. For example, learners' conceptions of knowledge are discussed as being absolutist, multiplist or evaluativist (Kuhn, 1999), or as something that can be simple, handed down by authority and certain (Schommer, 1990). A view that I find personally attractive is that suggested by Hammer and Elby (2000): that learners have access to a range of epistemological resources the use of which is context dependent. If one accepts that the basic constituents of the subject that learners are trying to understand vary in the extent to which they are well-defined, one starts to appreciate the problems of trying to define what it means to know something. In ill-defined domains, such as psychology, learners will need to understand how these constituent knowledge concepts have been formed and justified in order to understand more generally the nature of knowledge and the knowledge construction process. In well-defined domains, such as chemistry and physics, learners may be able to appear to know something merely because they are able to apply established rules and theories that one can learn to apply without understanding the justification for why they constitute knowledge. In ill-defined domains there are no such established rules and theories (Avramides, 2009). An excellent review of the literature from psychology that also makes reference to science education can be found in Avramides (2009). This draws the reader's attention to the inadequacy of existing frameworks with respect to three key issues: the manner in which the sophistication of epistemic cognition is defined; the assumptions that are made about the consistency of epistemic cognition across disciplines; and the assumption that is made about the coherence of epistemic cognition, which does not take into account context dependency.

Issues that I see as particularly relevant from this short discussion of epistemic cognition are: the simplicity or complexity of the way in which knowledge is viewed; its relationship to reality as an objective or a subjective entity; the role of authority and the self in decisions about what constitutes knowledge; the certainty with which one can know something; the discipline and context specificity of knowledge; and the importance of the processes of evaluation, judgement and justification.

The learner's resources

The emphasis that I have already placed upon the way in which knowledge is connected and distributed in the world, intentionality and a learner's subjective and intersubjective experiences with the world, mean that I want to integrate the consideration of epistemic cognition with metacognition and motivation. For example, learners' perceptions of what knowledge is, how it is justified and validated, how they come to know something, and how certain this knowledge will be, are all likely to impact upon their assessment of themselves as thinkers. Goal-oriented theories of motivation draw attention to learners' views about why they learn, and what a learner perceives by 'knowing something' will influence their motivations. The processes of cognition, metacognition and epistemic cognition are all part of the same story of a learner's interactions with the world and they need to be considered in terms of their interrelatedness and not as separate entities. The relationships between these processes become even more significant if learners are to benefit from the greater agency in their learning that a range of technological innovations might support. As I noted above, learners do not apply their metacognitive strategies spontaneously across domains and environments, and the same is true for epistemic cognition. And yet in a world where technology enables us to be increasingly connected, we need to understand more about how learners can take the best advantage of their cognitive, metacognitive and epistemic resources. I have suggested that attention should be given to scaffolding the relationship between learner and More Able Partner in their negotiations of the learner's ZPA. I now add to this the need for scaffolding to look beyond the cognitive to encompass the learner's affective, metacognitive and epistemic resources.

At the beginning of this chapter, I expressed the view that the theories that had been encountered in Chapter 1 had offered a limited conception of formal learning and its associated knowledge concepts. This has now been redressed. However, in this process the importance of the physical reality of the world and learners' interactions with it has been a little sidelined. Cole (1996) reminds us that artefact-mediated action involves the existence of both the mediated and unmediated link between subject and object, a point I noted in Chapter 1 and one to which I now return. I suggest that not only has context been undertheorized in the development of technology to support learning, but so too has the unmediated link between subject and object: the root for the spontaneous concepts. All the connections that make up a learner's context are important, they need to be viewed holistically and the connections between the different elements need to be scaffolded.

I have placed an increasing emphasis upon the concept of scaffolding the creation of a Zone of Proximal Adjustment from the resources available to the learner. In Chapter 3 I review the manner in which the scaffolding concept has been used to inform the design and use of technology to support learning.

3   The role of technology

In Chapter 2, I emphasized the Zone of Proximal Development (ZPD) and the concept of scaffolding. I interpreted the ZPD in terms of the Zone of Collaboration and put scaffolding at the forefront of learning. In this chapter, I review the manner in which the ZPD and the scaffolding concept have been used to inform the design and use of technology to support learning. I use this review to develop a definition of what scaffolding means in my proposed definition of context, and what role technology might play in the scaffolding process.

At the start of this chapter, I emphasize once again that my concern is more with learning than it is with education and more with interaction than with technology. Technology is a word that describes a whole range of different devices and applications. In this book I use the word to refer to digital information and communication technologies, including both hardware and software. I am concerned with the interactive possibilities that technologies can contribute to learning and the role they can, and do, play in a learner's context. I am not, therefore, concerned with any particular type of technology. However, when I describe particular examples of technology use, I specify what type of technology I am discussing. In this chapter, the technology almost exclusively comprises software applications developed by research teams across the world.

There have been enormous developments in digital technologies since their first application to support learning, all of which carry implications for the development of a design framework for technology-rich learning. In the early 1970s, the emphasis was on individual desktop computers offering one-to-one experiences between user and technology, where the aim for the researchers developing the technology was to develop a machine that could act as a teacher. The advent of the Internet offered new possibilities for technology to be used as a tool for communication. A brief reflection over the last 15 years reveals a World Wide Web that made the ability to publish available to the masses. It took us from hypertext to multimedia, brought us networking and enabled people to communicate in more places: to socialize, collaborate, co-author and co-publish. The increased availability of digital devices such as cameras and sensors enables us to digitally capture and store more about our environment than ever before and mobile, ubiquitous and pervasive technologies offer multiple choices about how we keep in touch. The landscape today is both very different and constantly evolving.

Smaller and smaller devices are increasingly embedded in the environment, and vast amounts of computing power will be available as and when we need it through 'cloud computing' (a term used to describe the idea that most computing power and resources are not part of the devices that we use, but are available from banks of computers as and when we need them through the Internet). These rapid developments provide an important reason for not constraining the discussion to any particular current technology instantiation. The key aim is rather to consider the interactions that need to be supported and to then consider what role might be played and by what particular type of technology.

Learning, technology and sociocultural theory

The idea of using sociocultural theory, the ZPD or scaffolding to ground the design of educational technology is not new. These theories and concepts have been used in the design of educational interactions involving technology and to inform the design of software, such as Intelligent Tutoring Systems and Interactive Learning Environments.

As I highlighted in Chapter 2, there has been a trend away from theories of learning that see the learner as a lone individual towards theories that recognize the importance of social interaction and that even see learning as a distributed entity. Collaboration is a key ingredient of the ZPD and many education systems now recognize the social and communicative nature of cognitive development (Mercer, 1992), and the potential for developing a 'collective' ZPD through group activities (Moll & Whitmore, 1993). Various researchers have provided evidence of improvements in learners' individual performances when work is completed collaboratively and have thus confirmed the benefits of learning collaboratively (see Roschelle & Teasley, 1995; Underwood & Underwood, 1999). Work on collaborative learning has expanded beyond an interest in the potential of collaborative experience to increase an individual learner's cognitive progress to the exploration of the social processes that mediate collaborative learning. This has led to practical guidelines and principles; for example, principles for group work that can be applied to classrooms (Howe *et al.*, 2000; Howe & Tolmie, 2003). The role that computer technology might play in the collaborative learning process has also been the subject of much attention. There is now substantial theoretically grounded literature about the role of computers in collaborative learning (Crook, 1994; Scardamalia & Bereiter, 1994; Dillenbourg *et al.*, 1995; Roschelle, 1992), and a large body of research that is encompassed by the description Computer Supported Collaborative Learning (CSCL). The primary concern of CSCL is to explore how best to promote productive collaborative interactions with a range of technologies: both through the design of technologies and through the design of educational activities. The central concerns of this community are with: theoretical grounding; the empirical study of collaborative learning processes; the design of computer-based collaborative learning environments; the roles of different participants within a collaboration, such as teachers, learners and mentors; and with the methods that can be used to research these issues.

Of course, not all researchers who use theory to explore computer support for collaborative learning adopt a sociocultural approach. Some researchers (Light & Glachan, 1985, for example) adopt a social-constructivist approach after Piaget and are influenced in particular by the work of Neo-Piagetians, such as Doise (1990; Doise & Mugny, 1984), who expressed the interpsychological processes of interacting collaborators in terms of sociocognitive conflict. Emphasis within this work remains, however, on the individual learner, whose cognitive processes are influenced by the conflicting experiences of collaborative interaction. This contrasts with the sociocultural approach, which holds that it is the interactions between collaborating individuals that catalyse any increase in learning within an individual and within the group. Learning is a process in which a learner's ability to perform with assistance is of more interest than their ability to perform as an individual; and in which participants develop a shared understanding through the use of mediating tools. It is, therefore, the use of technology to support this view of learning that is of interest in this chapter.

I clarify this point, because examples of computers being used to support this sociocultural view of learning are not always explicitly labelled as being influenced by a sociocultural approach. Therefore, whilst I concentrate on examples where the sociocultural roots are acknowledged, I will also include more general examples where computer technology has been used in a manner that is sympathetic to the sociocultural approach. It should also be noted that researchers often mix social-constructivist and sociocultural approaches. In the next chapter, for example, I detail the development of the Ecolab software that is based upon the operationalization of the Zone of Collaboration concept introduced in Chapter 2. It is, therefore, explicitly sociocultural, and yet it involved individual pre- and post-tests to assess each individual learner's cognitive development, which echoes a more social-constructivist ethos. In discussions of educational technology and collaborative, or social, learning one often finds both an identification with the individual learner's cognitive progress, in terms such as 'personalization', and with the sociocultural through acknowledgement of the collaborative co-construction of knowledge (Luckin *et al.*, 2009).

Vygotksy's work emphasizes the importance of language and there are many interesting examples of work that has adopted a sociocultural approach to explore the language, both dialectic and dialogic, between collaborative learners as the locus of knowledge construction. Wegerif and Mercer (1997), for example, developed a methodology for teaching children how to collaborate that used software called Bubble Dialogue. This involved children in creating stories about particular scenarios as a means to practise their collaborative skills. In particular, learners were encouraged to turn away from the computer to engage in discussion before working further on their story. The WordCat software, discussed in more detail in Chapter 4, builds on this work. Research has also provided evidence of a relationship between learners' willingness to engage in argument and discussion and effective collaborative learning (Tolmie *et al.*, 1993). More recently, Sami and Kai (2009) argue that work on meaning-making and dialogue should be expanded to include more attention to action. Collaborative interactions occur through the construction of shared objects, such as artefacts, practices and externalized ideas and representations. This expansion leads them to suggest a trialogical approach as the other end of a continuum from dialogue to trialogue; an approach which acknowledges a wider range of the potential learning resources in the learner's environment.

Within formal education the limitations on the availability of computers has meant that software in schools is often used by pairs of children, even when that software has been designed for an individual learner. This situation can lead to collaboration, as evidenced by O'Malley (1994), Dillenbourg (1999) and Wegerif (2003), and tools have been developed that intend to support pairs of learners in situations where there is one computer, or at least one monitor, per pupil. The Belvedere software, for example, (Suthers & Jones, 1997; Suthers, 2001) provides a graphically rich groupware tool for authoring and conducting complex dialectical discussions over a network. The emphasis is upon argument and the software provides tools that represent a scientific debate graphically and that advise students on ways in which an argument graph can be improved or investigated further. The characteristics of peer learning that differentiate among tutoring, cooperation and collaboration can be identified (Damon & Phelps, 1989b), and these can be used to inform the use of technology. It cannot, however, be assumed that working in pairs will lead to good collaboration (Crook, 1994) or that collaboration will necessarily lead to learning (Dillenbourg, 2002). In order to help support the collaborative process, not just with pairs but with larger groups too, a scripted approach has become popular. These scripts are sets of instructions that have both an epistemic and a social aspect, so that both the task and the ways in which learners interact to achieve its completion are provided for. Micro-scripts act as dialogue models embedded in the environment that prompt learners to respond, and Macro-scripts provide pedagogical scripts through their provision of a model of the sequence of activities for the group (Dillenbourg & Hong, 2008).

In addition to examples where technology has been used to support peer collaboration, there are also examples where technology has been used to embody a collaborative peer. Chan, Chung *et al.* (1992) and Chan and Baskin (1990) cite Vygotsky's (1978) explanation of the ZPD in *Mind in Society* as influential upon their work with Learning Companion Systems. The design of their Learning Companion System (LCS) uses a three-agent model consisting of: human student, collaborative computer instantiated learning companion and computer instantiated teacher. It is the role of the collaborative computer companion to use collaboration and competition to stimulate student learning. The computer teacher offers examples and guidance to human and computer student alike and determines the order and content of topics to be tackled. Chan (1996) has also used this approach to focus on the more global aspects of social learning via the Internet, where a larger ZPD between an individual learner and a virtual learning companion is envisaged. The potential of learning companion systems has increased due to an increasing interest in agent-based research for educational technology, and the idea of a companion as an educational agent is being redefined as a result (Chou *et al.*, 2003).

More generally, within research that considers learning with technology, there is less emphasis placed on the individual as the unit of study and more emphasis placed upon pairs and upon group interactions. Stahl (2009), for example, makes an interesting case for the group as the unit of analysis. He highlights the importance of Vygotsky's work to the field of CSCL and the potential that networked computing technology offers for collaborative learning. He suggests that 'By observing the group practices through which small groups of learners accomplish problem solving and other tasks, we can begin to determine the mechanisms that make knowledge building possible at the small-group level' (Stahl, 2009: 41).

Access to these knowledge-building mechanisms is enabled by the use of technology to record interactions in detail and to support the analysis of this data. This analysis permits the identification of patterns of interactions that are associated with particular group processes. It supports our increased understanding of the group processes that may lie at the heart of individual learning (Stahl, 2009). This proposal seems related to the earlier suggestion by Roschelle and Teasley (1995) that a 'joint problem space' is created as learners negotiate with each other, and that it is this jointly constructed entity that supports their collaborative activities. The move away from the individual learner is consistent with the emergence of theories of distributed cognition as discussed in Chapter 1 (Hutchins, 1995), and has resulted in the use of terminology that was previously reserved for individual cognition being applied to group processes (Dillenbourg, 1999).

Another word that is prevalent within discussions of CSCL, and that has been a part of my previous discussions, is that of 'community'. Research that explores communities can consider: an individual learning within a community; communities constructing knowledge; and communities learning from one another. In Chapter 1, I noted the idea of a Community of Practice as described by Lave and Wenger (1991) and here, too, there are examples where technology has been used to support the creation of knowledge-building communities. Scardamalia and Bereiter (2003), for example, developed one of the early networked learning systems known as Computer Supported Intentional Learning Environments (CSILE). This was subsequently developed into The Knowledge Forum, a community knowledge space through which learners share work and ideas. The software behind the Knowledge Forum provides learners with tools to support construction, sharing, reflection, critiquing and revision. Explicit visual connections are made between different ideas and contributions within the community space. The emphasis is upon the development of community knowledge rather than individual learning. The Knowledge Forum is not the only tool to support the visualization of collaborative constructions. The Belvedere system, which I discussed above when I considered pairs of learners, offers a graphical visualization of scientific argument and enables learners to create connections between a hypothesis and the evidence that supports or does not support it. The introduction of Web 2.0 technologies increases the possibility for networked group collaboration. However, the mere existence of these technologies will not lead to collaboration and learning. In a study of 11–16-year-old learners' use of Web 2.0 technologies to support learning we found little evidence of learners engaging spontaneously in analysis and knowledge construction without contributions from More Able Partners, such as tutors and mentors (Luckin *et al.*, 2009).

The examples I have discussed so far in this chapter confirm that collaboration between learners and other people is a key learning interaction that has well-evidenced benefits. Enough is known about group processes to develop specifications for roles that could be adopted by both people and technology. Technology is not merely used to help people keep in touch with each other as they collaborate, it is used to help individuals, small groups and large communities to engage in knowledge-building activity supported by communication and shared task visualizations. Technology can be used further to assist in the recording and analysis of patterns of interactions that are associated with particular learner and group processes. This positive evidence must however be considered in the light of more cautionary results that highlight the difficulties associated with making collaborative learning happen and the importance of human intervention if we are to engender learning interactions with new technologies.

Technology and scaffolding

Scaffolding through technology has been used to support both collaborative learning and individual progress where the technology plays the role of the learner's More Able Partners (MAPs). Successful scaffolding requires that learners are provided with appropriately challenging activities that are accompanied by the right quality and amount of assistance. The scaffolding approach has been used, adapted and extended to guide the development of a variety of software applications that have attempted to scaffold learners. The first example of this can be seen in the EXPLAIN system developed by Wood *et al.* (1992). This software implemented the contingent teaching strategy to operationalize tutorial assistance using a video-disc system to support young learners in a block-building task called the 'Tower of Nottingham'. The block-building task used in EXPLAIN is a problem-solving exercise which uses procedural skills. An extension of this approach to conceptual skill development was tested through a second software scaffolding system called the Quadratic tutor (Wood *et al.*, 1992; Wood & Wood, 1999).

The essence of the contingent strategy relates to the student's success at the preceding instructional level. Both EXPLAIN and Quadratic use a contingent tutoring approach to support learners as they complete tasks with a clear start and finish. Both software systems implemented Instructional Contingency to provide online help at the learner's request. The software continually monitored learner activity and responded to requests for help based upon the contingent help provision principle: that is, if the help level of the last software intervention had been followed by learner success, then the help level should be reduced; if the help level of the last software intervention had not been followed by learner failure then the help level should be increased. This system activity was supported through the system's maintenance of a rudimentary learner model in the form of a record of the most recent help level offered to the learner, and the learner's subsequent success or failure at the task. The system did not attempt to implement the domain or temporal forms of contingency described in Chapter 2. Learners worked through problems at their own pace and were free to stop a problem at any time (Wood, 2001).

In more recent years, considerable research attention has been given to the roles that technology can play in scaffolding learning. As has been noted by a range of researchers, (Puntambekar & Hübscher, 2005; Pea, 2004), scaffolding is used to describe a wide range of support provided by both humans and technology. One thing that is striking when looking at the range of empirical studies that have been conducted, is the enormous diversity of learners and settings that have been encompassed. These extend far beyond the adult and child interactions studied by Wood and his colleagues. For example, empirical studies have been undertaken with learners aged 5–11 years, studying a range of subjects including science and maths (Holmes, 2005; Butler & Lumpe, 2008). Work has also been completed with learners aged 11–18 years studying maths (Koedinger *et al.*, 1997; Beal & Lee, 2008), science (Azevedo *et al.*, 2005; Puntambekar & Styllianou, 2005) and history (Li & Lim, 2008). There have also been numerous studies with older learners in college and in higher education, including trainee teachers (Oh & Jonassen, 2007); science students (Chen *et al.*, 1992; Crippen & Earl, 2007; Ge & Land, 2004), and technology students (Tuckman, 2007).

The breadth of the settings and approaches is large and it is easy to lose track of the core ideas from the ZPD that influenced the construction of the scaffolding approach at its inception. It is possible to identify some common features amongst all applications of scaffolding within software. For example, they all aim to offer a means of enabling learners to achieve success with a task beyond their independent ability. However, there are also some distinct differences between the ways in which the term 'scaffolding' is applied and used. For example, there is a difference in emphasis between scaffolding that aims to scaffold the task and its circumstances, and scaffolding that aims to provide support to scaffold learners as they tackle challenging activities. Reiser (2004) also draws a distinction between software scaffolding approaches that aim to structure the learner's task and those approaches that shape the learner's performance and 'problematize' the task. This latter approach focuses on the need to challenge learners that is an inherent and important aspect of the ZPD. Reiser acknowledges that the problematizing process is likely to make the task harder for the learner, but that the benefits of engaging learners in the complexity are important. He also envisions the two approaches – structuring and problematizing – working together to scaffold learners.

Scaffolding the learner focuses design attention upon how the learner's role can be simplified and how they can be offered assistance by the system (or their colleagues). This involves diagnosing the learner's needs, providing assistance to support success and reducing this assistance when appropriate to enable the learner to develop. Examples of scaffolding techniques, which place emphasis upon the learner and their role, can be found in the adaptation of Wood *et al.*'s original notion of scaffolding into the contingent teaching approach implemented in the Quadratic tutor (Wood *et al.*, 1992; Wood & Wood, 1999). This provides a series of graded help interventions that support the learner; the system always tries to reduce the amount of help being given and places much emphasis upon this process of 'fading'. More sophisticated knowledge-rich systems have been designed to give one-to-one tuition that involves both instructional and domain contingency (Koedinger *et al.*, 1997). These systems are designed to make decisions about what the learner should do and what feedback they should receive; they rely upon building detailed models of learner knowledge and understanding.

My point here is that there has been a great deal of work done to build software systems that aim to provide interventions to scaffold individual learner progress. These learner-focused instantiations of scaffolding highlight the need for those providing learners with scaffolding assistance to know something about the learners' current understandings of the subject matter being learnt. For technology to provide software scaffolding this has meant systems maintaining a model of the learners. A number of systems have developed effective methods for modelling learners and providing scaffolded, learner-sensitive help (see, for example, Luckin & Hammerton, 2002; Aleven *et al.*, 2004; Koedinger *et al.*, 1997). In addition, finding ways to open up and represent the information maintained by the software to the learner and/or teacher has also proved fruitful (Bull & Kay, 2007). I discuss the nature of learner modelling activity further in Chapter 6 when I explore what is meant by the word 'model' within technology and education.

As I have already noted, the use of technology to scaffold learning has been applied to both individuals and groups, and a further approach to the theme of scaffolding the learner is provided through the use of technology, to scaffold collaboration between learners. Assistance is provided through support for peer collaboration rather than graded interventions offered to an individual by the system. For example, Guzdial *et al.* (1996) build on the view that groups can solve more difficult problems than individuals, as well as problems that require articulation, which in turn encourages reflection. In their system McBagal (Multiple Case-Based Approach to Generative Environments for Learning), synchronous collaboration amongst a group of students using a single computer is supported through the provision of structure, as students brainstorm and plan. A computer environment called CaMILE (Collaborative and Multimedia Interactive Learning Environments) is used to support asynchronous collaboration between students sharing resources as they work separately. Support is structured through prompts to individual students, for the role of their own notes for example. Case libraries are used to support the authentic problem-solving process and modelling and simulation software DEVICE (Dynamic Environment for Visualization in Chemical Engineering) is used to provide students with the sort of modelling tool experts use.

Working as part of a group may involve sharing technology or working at a distance, it may also involve groups of learners each with their own device collaborating in face-to-face situations. Zurita & Nussbaum (2004) and Nussbaum *et al.* (2009) use a scripted approach (Dillenbourg, 2002) to explore small group learning. Mixed ability, randomly selected groups of three learners are required to propose and defend their own ideas, and then to seek clarification and justification for the ideas of their peers. This is a more complex process than mere consensus seeking, it is a process in which the 'epistemic and social components are blended'. The process can be supported through software, called CollPad, run on hand-held computing devices. This supports a sequence of interactions in which learners first tackle a problem individually, then as a small group and finally through a teacher-mediated class discussion. The CollPad software is described as 'a collaborative scaffold that guides and mediates the interactions between students as they work through a structured sequence of information sharing and knowledge construction' (Nussbaum *et al.*, 2009: 148). This approach can be applied to different knowledge domains, because it is independent from the process through which problem representations are generated. The task presented to learners must, however, be appropriate, matched to their capabilities and structured in a manner that means that children must work together in order to complete it. These examples of work that involves collaborative learning is, of course, remarkably similar to that described in my earlier discussions of collaborative learning and technology, and the CSCL tools discussed at the start of this chapter might also be considered under this heading: tools such as CSILE (Scardamalia & Bereiter, 1994), that have been shown to help students explore scientific issues more deeply as they engage in knowledge-building activity. This overlap exemplifies the breadth of ways in which scaffolding is now considered.

Scaffolding the task and its circumstances concentrates on what and how the task, the curriculum or the learning environment can be structured in order to provide assistance. For example, the Virtual Town Hall project (Rosson & Carroll, 1996) offered learners problem examples that were small and simple to start with and gradually increased in complexity as the learner progressed. Scaffolding the task and its circumstances has also been achieved through design attention to the importance of the learning environment, as well as the use of complex authentic problems to ground the learning environment in the learner's experience and prior knowledge (see Guzdial *et al.*, 1996). This sort of task scaffolding is fixed before the learners start interacting with the system. Other approaches to task scaffolding allow interactive flexibility once the learner starts to use the system. The environment can be varied after the interactions have begun, allowing more control to be given to the user (Rosson & Carroll, 1996). In a similar manner, the scaffolding techniques illustrated in the 'Model-It' system developed for 14- and 15-year-olds learning about the ecology of a stream by Jackson *et al.* (1994, 1996) places a great deal of emphasis upon grounding activities in the learner's experience and prior knowledge. Other adopted techniques include using multiple synchronous representations to bridge learners' current understandings to a more expert-like model and enabling learners to interact with a model that they have built themselves.

The Model-It system is also used as an example case study by Soloway *et al.* (1996) in their discussion of Learner Centred Design (LCD). They suggest a design framework of guidelines for scaffolding what they consider to be the four components of a learning environment: the context; the tasks; the tools; and the interface. The model-building and testing with authentic problems approach of Model-It is used to demonstrate an example of scaffolding for the context component. The Model-It system has undergone further development (Fretz *et al.*, 2002) and three types of scaffold are now provided: process structure through task decomposition; support for explanation articulation; and the provision of multiple manipulable representations. More recent work by Quintana and colleagues develops a Scaffolding Design Framework for science inquiry (Quintana *et al.*, 2004; Quintana & Fishman, 2006). In this, the focus is upon the provision of scaffolding support for science inquiry activities without the implementation of automated fading of that scaffolding. The framework is based upon some key scaffolding processes for science inquiry: Scaffolding Sense Making; Scaffolding Process Management; and Scaffolding Reflection and Articulation.

These examples illustrate the enormous shift that has taken place in the ways in which researchers interested in using technology to support learning use the term scaffolding. The core of the carefully structured interactions between a learner and a MAP seen in the original EXPLAIN and Quadratic systems can still be seen in systems such as the cognitive tutors (Koedinger *et al.*, 1997) and the Ecolab (Luckin, 1998). These are at the heart of many of the approaches that focus on scaffolding the learner through specific support interventions, whether provided by a human or by technology. Other approaches that focus on supporting the learner through their problem-solving activities involve using technology to support collaboration between groups or communities of learners, and using technology to visualize or structure the task, the curriculum and the learning circumstances. These encompass a wide range of techniques that include varying the complexity of the task or the environment, offering authentic problems to ground the learner's experience and engage their prior knowledge, and using multiple synchronous representations and visualizations. None of these approaches to scaffolding are necessarily mutually exclusive and are combined within some systems. However, the original focus on the diagnosis of learner need, the provision of assistance and the fading of that assistance, that were essential to the original conceptualization of scaffolding, are absent from many software scaffolding applications. This has had the positive effect of enabling the investigation of technology support for learning across a large range of subject areas, learners and learning environments. It has also had the effect of diluting the original idea and making it hard to gather evidence together that speaks to the same underlying issues.

A further dimension to the use of technology for scaffolding is offered by developments through which researchers have concerned themselves with the potential for scaffolding to be used to support the development of affect and higher-order thinking, such as metacognition. I highlighted the importance of these for learning in Chapter 2 and I, therefore, devote some space here to the consideration of how scaffolding has been applied to the development of these processes.

Along with researchers exploring scaffolding cognition and collaboration, researchers who have studied affect and higher order thinking, such as metacognition, have adopted a broad range of approaches across a range of subject areas. Researchers have explored both the theoretical implications of scaffolding with technology and the empirical evaluation of scaffolding applications. The themes that I have already identified are apparent in this work also. There are researchers who conceptualize scaffolding higher order and affective processes by attending to the learner's role, by supporting collaboration, and by attending to the nature of the task or problem that the learner is being asked to complete. There are examples of scaffolding that involve fading by the technology, and examples where fading is not accounted for.

The Ecolab II system (discussed in more detail in Chapter 4), offers an example of metacognitive software scaffolding to improve young learners' ability to select appropriately challenging tasks and suitable amounts of help (Luckin & Hammerton, 2002). The software offers a simulated mini-world where learners can experiment with the feeding relationships between a selection of animals and plants. The conceptualization of scaffolding in Ecolab II involves focusing on the learner by offering adaptive and fadable advice about what difficulty of task might be most appropriate and what level of system assistance might be the nearest to what that learner needs, in order to complete the task selected. The complexity of the actions that can be completed in the mini-world environment can also be adjusted, providing task-focused scaffolding too. Other systems that model learners' help-seeking behaviour include the approach of Aleven *et al.* (2004), who have developed a cognitive tutor to support help seeking. Their approach to scaffolding involves focusing on the learner and providing fadable scaffolding advice. The difference in their approach to that adopted in the Ecolab II can be seen in their development of an ideal help-seeking model to support the system in detecting when the student deviates from the ideal, so that appropriate feedback can be provided.

Other researchers have considered scaffolding the learner through human tutoring whilst learners use technology. Azevedo *et al.* (2008), for example, summarize a series of their studies that have explored how the use of self-regulated learning can foster and enhance students' learning about complex science topics using hypermedia. They use the scaffolding concept to describe human tutor-facilitated self-regulated learning in which a human tutor following a script prompts students to: activate their prior knowledge; plan time and effort; and monitor their progress towards their goals. This form of adaptive scaffolding provided by the human tutor has been found by Azevedo and colleagues to lead to greater shifts in the learners' understanding, with increased activation of prior knowledge, increased self-regulatory and monitoring activity and greater engagement in help seeking. Hadwin *et al.* (2005) also study human interaction with the aim of informing the design of pedagogical agents that can support self-regulation and adjust to learners' increasing understanding. They study the transition of self-regulatory control from teacher to graduate student during naturalistic instructional conferences and use discourse analysis to develop a portfolio of analysed interactions that provide guidance for computer scaffolds for self-regulated learning. The emphasis within this work is upon the search for ways to gradually fade teacher support in favour of learner agency.

Research that attends to learners' affective states, especially motivation, has received particular attention in recent years from researchers wishing to apply scaffolding techniques to the development of motivationally intelligent systems. The designers of these systems aim to use different scaffolding techniques to engage the learner's desire to learn and to maintain their efforts. As we identify in du Boulay *et al.* (forthcoming) the design of motivationally intelligent systems can be characterized by their consideration of three different issues: first, the data that they use to make decisions about the learner's motivation; second, the reasoning mechanisms that are applied to this data; and third, the ways in which the system interacts with the learner, based upon this reasoning. A novel approach to scaffolding learners in the communication of their feelings to their teacher can be seen in the work of Balaam (2009). The scaffolding concept is also used in work that seeks to explore the relationships between metacognition and motivation (Harris *et al.*, 2009). It should be noted that there is no hard line between approaches that scaffold cognition and those that scaffold metacognition or motivation. The CollPad software of Nussbaum, for example, aims to foster learners' metacognition as well as their collaborative learning.

Scaffolding collaboration can be seen in research where technology is used to support the dialogic interactions that have been shown to be effective for engaging students with higher order thinking (Mercer & Littleton, 2007; Soller, 2002). This builds, for example, on research that has identified relationships between exploratory talk and the development of critical thinking (Wegerif *et al.*, 1999). On occasion, technical support for collaboration is provided, such as the use of discussion constraints and labels (Oh & Jonassen, 2007), and insistence on agreement to foster discussion (Nussbaum *et al.*, 2009).

Distributed scaffolding

There is an increasing recognition of the interactions that occur among the complex environments in which learners work, the nature of the task that learners are completing and the scaffolding that is available. Puntambekar & Kolodner (2005), for example, use the term 'distributed scaffolding' and explore this through classroom-based science learning. The increased complexity that occurs when scaffolding is distributed and the potential for distributed scaffolding to offer learners more opportunities to notice scaffolding opportunities are key findings from this work. Tabak (2004) also explores complex settings and distributed scaffolding and also identifies this positive possibility of increased opportunities for scaffolding. Her vision for distributed scaffolding is that learners can take advantage of different types of support provided by different means in an integrated manner, in order to solve complex problems. This is described as 'synergistic scaffolding' and is illustrated by Tabak through case studies drawn from learners' interactions with the differentiated scaffolding system called BGuILE (Reiser *et al.*, 2001). These case studies lead her to suggest that the design of distributed scaffolding 'should include an attempt to create cohesion and direct interaction between the elements of the scaffolding system' (Tabak, 2004: 330).

This notion of distributed scaffolding is important when considering learners' contexts and the possibilities it offers can be further enhanced through attention to the potential offered by new technologies. Most of the examples discussed in this chapter use rather traditional technologies and yet contemporary technologies that are participatory, pervasive, ubiquitous, environmentally embedded or virtual offer great potential to complete some of the activities that have been described as scaffolding. There has been a limited amount of research exploring scaffolding through wireless, mobile, embedded and ubiquitous technologies. The work discussed earlier by Nussbaum *et al.* (2009) provides one example in which hand-held technology is used to scaffold learning. The Personal Inquiry project (http://www.pi-project.ac.uk/) for example also adopts a scripted collaboration inquiry process to the use of personal mobile technology with learners aged 11–14 years. The scripts provide a template that structures the task and guides the learner's collaborative activity across locations. There are also some heartening examples of large-scale collaborations that use networked technologies to connect learners, teachers and professional scientists in the 'collabatories' created through the Collaborative Visualization project (Pea, 2002). This project is relatively old, having been run between 1992 and 1997, but its underpinning emphasis upon the concept of Distributed Intelligence that is exemplified through the project remains remarkably timely.

Sami and Kai (2009) draw our attention back to the importance of action, which highlights the way in which the majority of the work that has considered scaffolding has focused on interactions with other people and interactions with the task. There is little evidence of work that considers scaffolding learners' interactions with and through their physical environments. Environmentally embedded technologies and tangible technologies, that take the form of physical artefacts with embedded technologies, ought to offer the potential to use technology to scaffold the learner's appreciation of the relationships between the physical reality of their world and their conceptual understanding. There is a growing body of research that is exploring the use of tangible and embedded technologies to support learning (see Stanton-Fraser, 2007; Marshall *et al.*, 2009 for example). There are also some encouraging examples of work that uses modern technology in novel and interesting ways to embed the learners' experiences across a range of the elements of their physical environment. RoomQuake and WallCology (Moher *et al.*, 2005, 2008) provide two such examples through their use of an 'embedded phenomena' representational framework: in which 'dynamic animated simulations are depicted as occurring within the physical space of the classroom, rather than within the confines of a single display' (Moher *et al.*, 2008: 164).

There is, however, very little work that uses tangible technology to scaffold learners in the traditional scaffolding sense and on which we can draw for evidence. In a study that explored the potential of digital toys as learning companions, we found evidence that learners, aged 4–6 years, working in pairs, engaged in greater social interaction when the physical toy was present than when it was absent (Luckin *et al.*, 2003). This suggests that there might be potential for such artefacts to support learning, a sentiment that has been echoed by a range of researchers including O'Malley and Fraser (2004) and Cassell (2004). However, there is little evidence of real learning gains (Marshall, 2007). No frameworks specify the relationships between learning and tangible technology, although work that explores the use of theories about external representations to develop a framework for conceptualizing tangible environments looks promising (Price *et al.*, 2008). An added issue may also be inappropriate conceptualization on the part of technology developers, as noted by Y. Rogers (2006) in her call for a move away from attempts to develop technology to make the environment smart towards developing technology to empower people.

This short review of the ways in which technology has been used to offer scaffolding for learners has highlighted the diversity of approaches that have been labelled as scaffolding. This situation has led some researchers to suggest that we need to look at the ways in which different communities have used the scaffolding concept in order to further develop its theoretical foundations (Davis & Miyake, 2004). It has led others to suggest that we need to look back at the origins of scaffolding and, in particular, to Vygotsky's conception of learning (Pea, 2004; Puntambekar & Hübscher, 2005). There is a growing body of opinion that fading is a fundamental and intrinsic component of scaffolding (Pea, 2004; Lajoie, 2005; Puntambekar & Hübscher, 2005), and that a line needs to be drawn between scaffolding with fading and scaffolding without fading: 'If the support does not fade, then one should consider the activity to be distributed intelligence, not scaffolding achievement' (Pea, 2004: 432).

Learning in the Zone of Collaboration

In my definition of context in Chapter 1 I have stated that learners engage with partial and distributed descriptions of the world that are offered to them through the resources with which they interact. I now suggest that it is the role of the more able participants to scaffold a learner's construction of a narrative that makes sense of the meanings distributed amongst these resources. Through this scaffolding the learner at the centre of their context internalizes their interactions and develops increased independent capability and self-awareness.

I therefore propose that we need to:

1) Refine what we consider to be scaffolding and revisit its roots in the ZPD. Scaffolding involves the evaluation of learner need, and the offer of challenging tasks that are accompanied by the provision of assistance and the withdrawal of that assistance in order to engender learner development. This assistance may be provided through particular help interventions offered to a learner as they complete their task. It may also be offered through altering the complexity of the task or the environment with which the learner interacts. Other contingencies for scaffolding may also be identified through further implementations.

2) Broaden the scope of learner activity in a similar manner to that proposed by those who favour distributed scaffolding, but taking away the classroom boundaries and considering the learner and their interactions more holistically. In Chapter 2, I offered the Zone of Collaboration as an interpretation of Vygotsky's ZPD and introduced the Zone of Available Assistance (ZAA) and the Zone of

Proximal Adjustment (ZPA). I defined the ZAA as the variety of resources within a learner's world that could provide different qualities and quantities of assistance and that may be available to the learner at a particular point in time. I described the ZPA as a subset of the resources from the ZAA that are appropriate for a learner's needs. It is the learner's interactions with the resources in their Zone of Available Assistance that should define the starting point for the consideration of scaffolding. The scaffolding process should support the construction of the ZPA and should maintain the interactions that develop this as a dynamic entity centred on the learner.

3) Explore and refine how we can integrate scaffolding to support the relationships between the resources that a learner brings to their interactions.

These proposals will involve designers of technology-rich learning environments in supporting activity across multiple locations and with multiple people. It will also require mixed methods of human and computer scaffolding as proposed by Pea (2004) that encompass learning that occurs naturally, as well as learning that is officially orchestrated. The scaffolding assistance will, therefore, be provided by a range of different people and artefacts, the connections between which need to be recognized as part of the wider task environment in a meta-scaffolding process. This means orchestrating the fading of the whole environment as well as the components within an individual artefact (Puntambekar & Hübscher, 2005).

Part 2
The Ecology of Resources model and design framework

4 Software design and the Zone of Proximal Adjustment

In Part 1 of this book, I explored some of the literature about the nature of context, learning and educational technology. I identified the Zone of Proximal Development as a particularly important influence and presented the Zone of Collaboration as an interpretation of Vygotsky's theory. I also highlighted the potential offered by the scaffolding concept of assisted learning interactions and proposed that a clarification and refinement of this concept is needed. In this chapter and the one that follows, I draw together these theoretical foundations and combine them with evidence from empirical studies through which I have explored the role of technology to scaffold learning.

This empirical story starts with the tightly focused learner modelling and software scaffolding found in Intelligent Tutoring Systems and considers what we can learn from the development of these systems, which is relevant in a world of pervasive and ubiquitous technologies. My focus progresses from modelling and scaffolding learners' interactions with domain knowledge through technology, to modelling and scaffolding learners' interactions with some of the multiple resources available to them. The aim is to explore how to help both learners and their More Able Partners (MAPs) to seek support appropriately from their environments. I use the empirical examples of scaffolding to develop the Ecology of Resources as a way of characterizing a learner, and the interactions that form that learner's context.

Theoretical Underpinning

The concepts of the Zone of Available Assistance (ZAA) and the Zone of Proximal Adjustment (ZPA) discussed in Chapter 2 highlight the importance of interactions between learners and MAPs. MAPs need to identify and possibly introduce a variety of types of assistance from the available resources and find out enough about the learner to ensure that the resources selected for use are those that are most likely to meet the learner's needs. This may mean providing information so the learner can assess their own learning needs, including making it clear which resources might be most suitable for them. In other words, this enterprise is not always about MAPs driving learning interactions, sometimes it is about MAPs making it possible for the learner to drive their learning interactions. A teacher, parent or peer, can fulfil the role of the MAP; indeed, anyone who knows more about what is to be learnt than the learner themself. In this chapter, we will see that technology can also fulfil some elements of the MAP's role.

Empirical grounding

The series of research studies that I discuss here involve the development and evaluation of educational technology. In each of these empirical case studies, I will draw attention to the manner in which this work gradually progresses in the following dimensions:

1 From a desktop or laptop screen-based computer to a combination of multiple computer-based technologies;
2 From a single user to multiple learners;
3 From a single formal education location to encompass a range of locations;
4 From single to multidimensional learner modelling and scaffolding that involves metacognition and affect, as well as cognition;
5 From a small, tightly focused part of the knowledge domain to a broader range of subject matter.

Ecolab I and II

The Ecolab I software provided 10–11-year-old children with a simulated ecology laboratory environment and an artificial collaborative learning partner that offered adaptive assistance based on a detailed learner model. It was built as a research tool to investigate how the ZPD could be used to inform software design. The Ecolab was designed for a single learner to use on a laptop or desktop computer. It needed no connectivity beyond this machine. The software constructed a software-based model of the learner and scaffolded their interactions with timely interventions. Initially, in the Ecolab I software, this learner model represented the system's interpretation of the learner's understanding of a small curriculum of domain knowledge. Subsequently, in Ecolab II, this model also included the learner's ability in two metacognitive processes: help seeking and task selection.

Ecolab I: the original system

The original Ecolab system, called Ecolab I (Luckin, 1998; Luckin & du Boulay, 1999) was a software environment into which a child could add their selection from a range of different organisms. The child could then explore the feeding relationships that existed between the organisms that they had selected. The overall motivation presented to the learner was that they could explore which sorts of organisms can live together and form a food web. Ecolab I operated in two modes: 'build', which allowed the child to add the plants and animals they had chosen; and 'run', which enabled them to activate these organisms. If the child selected an action that was not possible they would be guided towards a possible alternative so that the effects of the selected action could be completed. The child controlled the software through mouse-driven commands selected from a series of menus.

The full complexity of the relationships between the Ecolab I organisms was not offered to a new learner straight away, but could be introduced through four phases of relationship complexity. In each of these phases the action commands available to the learner through the menus were appropriate to the complexity of the relationships that could be simulated in the Ecolab I. For example, in phase 1, the relationships that the child could explore were those between an animal and the food that it eats, the commands available were therefore the 'eat' and 'eaten by' commands. The second phase of complexity allowed the formation of food chains. The third and fourth phases allowed the formation of food webs and the exploration of relationships between the different members of the web. The system could switch between these four phases from the less to the more complex, or in reverse from the more to the less complex. Finally, the child could view their Ecolab I simulation from four different perspectives or views: a picture of the organisms in their habitat; a diagrammatic food web; a block graph illustrating the energy level of each of the organisms; and a textual description of what had happened in the Ecolab I simulation to date. The choice of view used was largely, though not completely, under the child's control and they could use the mouse to click on organisms to find out what they ate and what they were eaten by. Figure 4.1 illustrates the Web and Energy views from the Ecolab II interface, which is in essence the same as for Ecolab I.

The Ecolab as a More Able Partner (MAP)

In addition to this variably complex simulation that the child could build and activate, the Ecolab I software acted in the role of the MAP and could offer the child assistance or collaborative support in two ways:

1   Five levels of graded help specific to the particular situation. The higher the level of help, the simpler the action required by the child and the greater the control taken by the system, resulting in there being less scope for the child to fail (Wood, Wood & Middleton, 1978). If the child attempted to complete an action that was incorrect, for example giving the command for a caterpillar to eat a thistle, the system would offer help in the shape of a hint. The level of hint offered was decided by the system based upon its model of the learner. If the level of help offered to the child was insufficient, then the level could be increased gradually until the system completed the particular activity for the child. An example of the lowest level hint would be: 'Caterpillar does not eat thistle, try again'. The highest level hint would be 'Thistle is not the right sort of organism. Let's try rose leaves' followed by the system completing this action for the child.

2   Variation in the difficulty level of the activities the child was asked to complete using the Ecolab I software. There were 144 individual activities that could be offered to the child. Three levels of Activity Differentiation were possible,

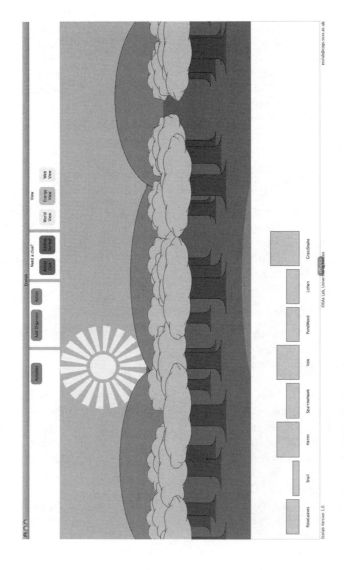

Figure 4.1 The Ecolab Energy view interface

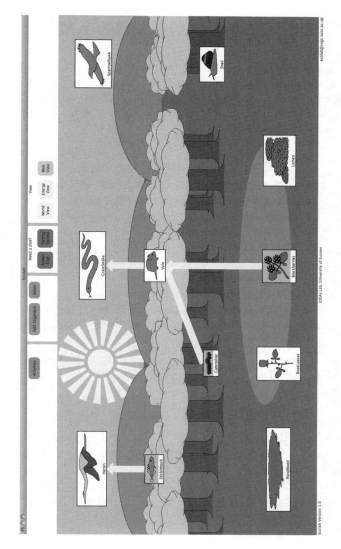

Figure 4.2 The Ecolab Web view interface

from 0 (the hardest) to 2 (the easiest). The variations in difficulty were based upon adjustments to the level of refinement that the child was asked to cope with, and the use of specific good exemplars to direct activity, as well as partial completion of tasks to help reduce the possibility of confusion (Griffiths & Grant, 1985). This meant, for example, that when the child was offered an activity about energy transfer the instructions could be varied from 'Use the "action" button to explore how you can reduce the energy levels of the animals and plants you have chosen' to 'Use the move command from the "action" button to explore how you can reduce the energy levels of [names of organisms in the child's simulation]'. Activity Differentiation was presented to the child through different levels of challenge: an activity with a level three challenge was more difficult than level two, which in turn was more difficult than level one.

Ecolab's knowledge of food chains and webs

The Ecolab I software needed a representation of knowledge about food chains and webs to underpin both the flexible complexity of the simulation environment and the provision of collaborative support to the learner. The structure of the content knowledge representation in the Ecolab I software was informed by work done by educators who had identified potential difficulties and made suggestions about the order in which concepts should be introduced (Griffiths & Grant, 1985; Lumpe & Staver, 1995). It was also informed by the requirements of the age-appropriate UK school curriculum for the Ecolab I users. The content knowledge was also simplified in some instances to respect the age of the children for whom the system was designed. The knowledge was represented as rules about feeding relationships and was organized in a structure adapted from the Genetic Graph (Goldstein, 1982) and is illustrated in Figure 4.3.

Each of the rules was used to describe a particular node in the graph structure, and sets of nodes were grouped to correspond with the phases of complexity of the Ecolab I simulation. Each of these phases is associated with a subset of actions made available through the menu commands. For example, the menu commands available in phase one are: 'move', 'be eaten', 'be a predator', 'be prey' and 'eat'. This knowledge structure supported the ways in which the Ecolab I software could be presented to the child with varying degrees of complexity as described above. Each of the activities that a child could be asked to complete was associated with one of the rule nodes. The activities at any rule node could be offered at any of the three levels of Activity Differentiation.

Ecolab's knowledge of the learner

The final component that enabled the Ecolab I software to operate in the manner described was the model that the system built of the learner who was interacting with it. This was needed by the system in order to enable it to make decisions

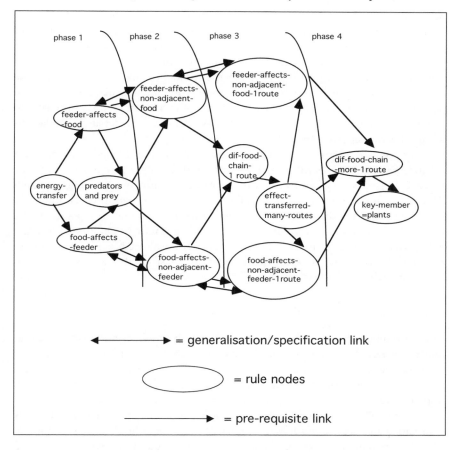

Figure 4.3 Knowledge representation: rule nodes

about what level of simulation complexity the Ecolab I software should offer to the child, which activity, what level of difficulty, and how much support should be provided in order to ensure that the learner was successful when interacting at a node. For each learner who used the Ecolab I software, a model of the knowledge structure of rule and concept nodes was created. This was used to maintain a dynamic model of the learner's progress. As the learner interacted with the software, two values were calculated and added to each of the nodes in this learner model. One value represented the amount of support that the system had given the learner in order for them to complete their most recent activity, and was a combination of the Activity Differentiation and help level. The second value represented the extent to which the child had demonstrated the understanding of a rule as interpreted by the system from their assisted performance. Each of the node links in the learner model was also described by a probability value that represented the prerequisite relationships between the nodes in the four phases of rule complexity. Bayes Theorem was used to create a Bayesian Belief Network from the learner model through which the two values at each of its nodes could be percolated throughout the entire model. This meant that at any time when the learner was interacting with the Ecolab I software the system would have a value associated with each node in the learner model that could be used to make decisions about the extent to which that node represented a rule that was within the child's independent ability. From this value the level of help that the system should offer the child for the next activity was deduced. The detailed calculations within this model can be found in Luckin (1998).

A key point of progress was the realization that, in order to base a system upon an interpretation of the ZPD theory, it required finding a way to quantify how much help had been given to the learner. Wood's contingent tutoring approach (Wood & Middleton, 1975) was useful in categorizing help interventions into five levels and into three different types: Domain, Task and Temporal. In the Ecolab I software these were incorporated into the Activity Differentiation and help provision scaffolding techniques. A more sophisticated learner model than that used by Wood was developed to underpin decisions about how much help should be offered in any intervention.

Learning with and from the Ecolab I software

In the original version of the Ecolab I software the sophistication of the learner model was varied in order to create three system variations, referred to as: NIS (No Instructional-Intervention System); WIS (Wood-inspired Instructional System); and VIS (Vygotsky-inspired Instructional System). The VIS system variation implemented the learner model and associated scaffolding as I have already described it. The NIS system variation made no decisions for the child and simply maintained and presented a record of the rule nodes that the child had attempted. The WIS system variation recorded the attempted rule nodes and, in addition, kept track of the level of help that the child had used. This information was used by the WIS system to generate suggestions to be made to the child about what they should try next, and to apply a contingent strategy to the selection of the next help level. In all other respects the systems were identical.

The Ecolab I software was evaluated by a class of 30 children (20 boys and 10 girls) using a 'pre-test, system use, post-test' paradigm. Groups of children, who had been matched on the basis of ability, used the Ecolab I software for three sessions resulting in a total interaction time of one hour and twenty minutes for each child. Figure 4.4 illustrates the mean changes in pre-test (T1) and post-test (T2) scores recorded for learners using the three versions of the Ecolab I software.

This suggests that if the test scores are considered to be a reflection of the children having learned something while using the software then all three system variations appear to have supported some learning. The test used was designed to enable an evaluation of the learning gains, with different complexities of relationships represented by the different phases in the Ecolab simulation complexity. An analysis of learning gains for learners, using the different

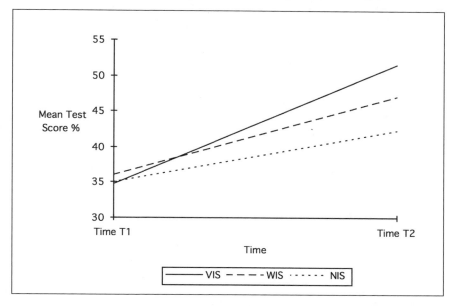

Figure 4.4 System variation by time interaction

system variations over the four categories of Ecolab complexity, is illustrated in Figure 4.5. This analysis suggests that for the small user group evaluated in the study, the system variations that provided more guidance to the learner, which were VIS and WIS, supported learning gains with the more complex feeding relationships.

In addition to this type of quantitative analysis based on learning gains, each child's interactions with the Ecolab I software were logged. For each child a summary record of their interactions was produced from these logs so that the software features the child actually used could be evaluated, as could any relationship between these and any gains in learning as recorded by the post-test. This analysis revealed that learners who used the WIS and VIS system variations made greater use of all the different types of available assistance, whereas learners using the NIS system variation did not. It is also interesting to note that the children who achieved above average learning gains when using the Ecolab I software came from all ability groups and were users of all system variations. Within their interactions, the following common features were found:

- 85 per cent interacted with the Ecolab I software in more than one phase of complexity;
- 92 per cent used a high level of system help intervention and/or Activity Differentiation, and 76 per cent used an above average amount of help and/ or Activity Differentiation;
- 69 per cent had both interacted with more than one phase of system

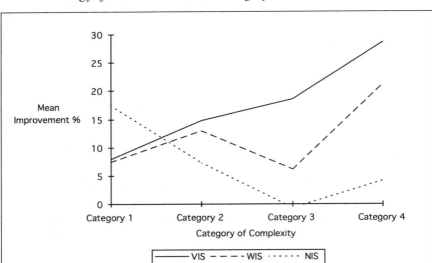

Figure 4.5 System variation by category interaction

complexity and had used above average levels and amounts of help and/or Activity Differentiation.

A full analysis of the Ecolab I data can be found in Luckin (1998) and Luckin & du Boulay (1999). The points I want to make here by reporting some of these data and findings are twofold. Firstly, the Ecolab I software demonstrated that software could be used to offer learners a variety of different types of assistance that could be described as the ZAA of the system, and, secondly, that learners benefit from guidance about how to select the most appropriate quantities and qualities of assistance to meet their needs.

The ZAA and ZPA in the Ecolab I

In the Ecolab I software the resources available to the learner (ZAA) were those within the software itself: that is, the animals and plants that could be placed in the child's simulated world; the flexible complexity of the different phases of the simulation environment; the actions that could be completed; and the different views that the child could use to look at their simulation. The underlying knowledge of food chains and webs used by the software was organized in a manner that reflected educational requirements about the concepts to be learnt and which ones might be particularly problematic. This was in effect the curriculum as studied through the child's interactions with Ecolab I. The MAP's role was also played by the VIS and NIS versions of the software through the selection of different levels of help and different levels of Activity Differentiation. Decisions about how to target the assistance offered by the MAPs were based upon a detailed, dynamic model of 'beliefs' about the learner's ability to solve problems, that was based upon the rules in the curriculum and the amount of assistance they would need from the system in order to achieve success.

The available assistance within the Ecolab I software was through the software scaffolding techniques, that is the Ecolab ZAA could be targeted for a particular learner to form the interactions of their ZPA. These were partly in the control of the learner, and partly in the control of the software. The learner could decide upon the animals and plants to be added to their simulation, the actions they wanted to complete with those animals and plants, and the view they chose to look at their simulation. They could also select the initial activity they wanted to complete. This meant that a child could select an activity that required them to use the most complex phase of simulation right at the start, or they could pick an activity that took them to the simplest phase. After this initial selection, the system would then take over decisions about how the activity and phase might be changed in the light of the learner's performance with the activity they first selected. Obviously, the manner in which the learner could access the resources within the software was constrained by the way in which the software was written, in terms of the underlying knowledge representation, the learner model and the interface.

Ecolab II

Findings from the Ecolab I evaluation demonstrated that offering learners a combination of challenging activities and appropriate support could improve test scores, which may indicate learning. A further important finding from the Ecolab I evaluation was that the increased sophistication within the VIS learner model did not result in more effective learning interactions for all learners. Help-seeking behaviour amongst learners became an important factor and I wanted to explore how this aspect of metacognitive awareness might be scaffolded through software. I have already discussed the nature of metacognition in Chapter 2. The aim for Ecolab II was to develop an environment that could provide metacognitive support to help learners improve their help-seeking and task-selection skills and, through this, their performance in learning about food chains and webs.

The original version of Ecolab I provided 'help' at the domain level, that is at the level of individual actions, such as when an animal moved or ate another animal or plant. This help was available when the learner was completing these specific actions and made an error. Ecolab II was designed to combine aspects of the original VIS and WIS system variations of Ecolab I. However, rather than just offering a learner a suggestion about what to do next, as the WIS system variation had done, Ecolab II offered different qualities and quantities of prompt to try to get the child to consider what they should do next: be it selecting a task or selecting how much help to ask for.

Metacognitive learner modelling and scaffolding

In addition to the different levels of help that Ecolab I offered learners when they were trying to complete actions within their simulation, Ecolab II also offered learners:

1 Feedback on their progress through the rule nodes in the Ecolab;
2 Additional help at four points during their interactions with Ecolab II:

    a   when the child selected what they were going to learn about;
    b   when the child decided what level of challenge to choose;
    c   when the child needed help at the domain level;
    d   during interactions, as a reminder to check their progress.

The help for points 2 a–c above was available in three levels. For example, for 2c, when a child needed to select help at the domain level, the following hints were available:

Level one. Don't forget that the Ecolab can help you;

Level two. Why not ask for more/less help (the system model of the learners is used to select either more or less help)?

Level three. Try Level X help (where X is the level of help as indicated by the system's model of the learner).

In order for the Ecolab II software to be able to offer this type of assistance, additions were made to the learner model. A third value was added to each of the rule nodes in the learner model structure described earlier. This value was used to represent how aware the child was of their own learning needs and was based on a combination of their use of the metacognitive scaffolding hints and on their performance with the activities. This value was used to decide upon the level of the next metacognitive prompt offered to the learner and to make recommendations to the learner about how much domain level help to request. The Ecolab II interface is illustrated in Figure 4.6.

Learning with Ecolab II

Two evaluation studies were conducted with the Ecolab II software. In both cases the same paper pre-test and post-test was used as in the original Ecolab I evaluation study. The first study involved a class of 32 children (16 boys and 16 girls) aged 9–11 years and is reported in Luckin and Hammerton (2002). Of the 32 children who started the study, only 26 completed all the sessions between, and including, the pre- and post-tests. As with the analysis of Ecolab I, learner interactions with Ecolab II were logged and analysed to explore how learners had used the features of Ecolab II. With both Ecolab I and II systems learners who tackled more than one phase of Ecolab simulation complexity performed well at post-test. An odds-ratio analysis illustrated the consistency of these results between Ecolab I and Ecolab II. Children who both interacted with different phases of simulation complexity and completed an above average number of actions were 11.4 times

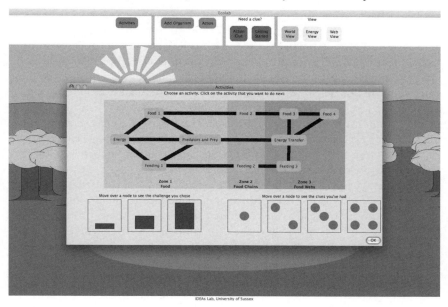

Figure 4.6 The Ecolab II interface with Curriculum and Progress screen

more likely to be amongst the learners achieving above average learning gains with Ecolab II, and 12.4 times more likely with Ecolab I. Another consistency between Ecolab I and II was seen in the high percentage of children with above average learning gains who used a high level (level three domain help or above; level two metacognitive help or above) and an above average amount of system assistance. The children who achieved above average learning gains when using the Ecolab II software exhibited the following common features:

- 73 per cent used a high level of system assistance and 82 per cent used an above average amount of system assistance;
- 64 per cent had interacted with more than one phase of system complexity and had used above average levels and amounts of system assistance.

A second evaluation study was conducted at a different school and involved a class of 26 children (11 boys and 15 girls) aged 9–11 years. The learning interaction analysis once again confirmed the relationships between learning gain and the learners' willingness to take on a challenge, and learning gain and the use of help. The children in this study who achieved above average learning gains when using the Ecolab II software exhibited the following common features:

- 87 per cent used a high level of system assistance and 62 per cent used an above average amount of system assistance;
- 62 per cent had interacted with more than one phase of system complexity and had used above average levels and amounts of system assistance.

Ecolab II built on the findings from Ecolab I and tried to support learners to be better at seeking appropriate help. Evaluations of the Ecolab II software demonstrated that it is possible to develop learner models and scaffolding techniques that can support learners in their selection of appropriately challenging tasks and suitable quantities and qualities of help. The numbers involved in these studies are, of course, small, although each extra study adds more evidence to support the assertion that this type of scaffolding approach can be effective. Further studies that have compared Ecolab II with more recent versions of the Ecolab, that have been designed to explore motivational scaffolding using the same paper-based test, have also demonstrated a positive relationship between learning gain and the use of system assistance.

Rebolledo-Mendez (2003) developed a system called M-Ecolab that monitored learners' levels of effort, independence and confidence to build a model of the learners' motivation. Scaffolding consisted of providing levels of motivational feedback by suggesting to, but not directing, the learner when to ask for more challenging tasks, when to put in more effort or when to select more or less help. M-Ecolab built on each previous Ecolab system and maintained the original domain level scaffolding mechanisms. The results of a pilot study investigating the effect of motivational scaffolding in M-Ecolab showed that learners with greater learning gains requested a higher level of help (Rebolledo *et al.*, 2005). The results of a second evaluation showed a significant difference in learning gains between different ability groups and once again illustrated the relationship between learning gain and the use of a higher level of system help and taking on more challenging tasks (Rebolledo *et al.*, 2006). A further study explored the deployment of different scaffolding strategies according to different goal orientation styles (Martínez-Mirón, 2007). Two new versions of the Ecolab II software were implemented. One version included system feedback that emphasized a mastery goal orientation (moEcolab), the other a performance goal orientation (poEcolab). An empirical evaluation study with learners aged between 9 and 11 years found evidence that performance goal-oriented feedback provided by the system affected the way children interacted and learned from the system.

The ZAA and ZPA in the Ecolab II

The resources that make up the ZAA of the Ecolab II software were very similar to those found in Ecolab I software, with the addition of metacognitive help. The software maintained increased information in the learner model; that is, information about the learner's use of metacognitive help, in order to inform the scaffolding that it offered the learner. This scaffolding was offered through the provision of increased information (see Figure 4.6 on page 65) and through suggestions made to the learner about how much help they should use and what level of task difficulty they should attempt. In Ecolab II there was a move towards decreasing the control taken by the system for the assistance offered to the learner and increasing the information provided to learners about the ZAA to support their own decisions about the assistance they needed to use in the construction of their ZPA.

Moving beyond the confines of a single software application

Supporting peer collaboration: the Riddles Project

The Ecolab II software illustrated that young learners' help-seeking and task selection behaviour could be supported by metacognitive scaffolding. Another project that also looked at supporting learners in their development of meta-level skills was the Riddles Project. The Riddles Project team explored the use of external representations of language ambiguity in riddles and stories to scaffold reading comprehension for children aged 7–9 years. Several multimedia software applications were developed as part of an iterative participatory design process. The contribution that the Riddles Project makes to the empirical grounding of the Ecology of Resources model is twofold. First, and similar to Ecolab II, it demonstrated that young children can be supported through technology to increased metacognitive skills (Pearce *et al.*, 2005; Kerawalla *et al.*, 2008). In this instance, the metacognition was in the form of metalinguistic awareness (Yuill *et al.*, 2009). These findings, along with those from Ecolab II, join a growing body of evidence, as highlighted in Chapter 3, that technology can be used to support learners' metacognitive needs.

The second way in which the Riddles Project informed the Ecology of Resources model was through the interface that was developed to support pairs of learners working collaboratively. It is this collaborative working aspect of the Riddles Project that I focus on here. The Ecolab I and II software applications had involved individual learners interacting with a piece of software that aimed to offer those learners all the resources and assistance they needed to complete their activities. However, as I have already stressed, the development of networked and pervasive technologies provides the possibility for technology-rich learning experiences to extend beyond the confines of a single piece of software. The Riddles software offers a first step to the consideration of scaffolding learning beyond the software alone. The Riddles software was developed to support pairs of learners interacting at a single machine. For each learner the ZAA offered by the Riddles software, therefore, encompassed the learner's interactions with a peer, as well as the learner's interactions with the resources offered from within the software itself. Responsibility for constructing the interactions of the ZPA for each learner in the pair became a collaboration between learners and system. The system offered activities and also structured the manner in which the learners could interact with the software and how they should interact with each other around the software. The manner in which children actually supported each other was of course not within the control of the system.

The Riddles Software

Previous research (Yuill, 1997) had indicated that children with poor text comprehension skills often also had poor awareness of language, and that engaging children in metalinguistic discussion could enhance their text comprehension. The Riddles Project team explored the design of an interface that would encourage 7–9-year-old children to practise their collaborative and discussion skills. Early classroom observations of children using shared computers with a single mouse to complete an activity originally designed for a single user had indicated that, in this situation, children often behaved in a cooperative rather than a collaborative manner, and one child tended to dominate the other. The primary objective of the interface developed for the Riddles Project software was to overcome this and support collaborative interactions between children. The design was called Separate Control Of Shared Space (SCOSS) (Kerawalla *et al.*, 2008). The SCOSS interface differed from a single-user interface in the manner in which it gave each child simultaneous, but separate, control of their own area of the computer screen. Each child had their own mouse that they could use to manipulate screen elements in their own area of the screen and *only* in their own area of the screen. These screen elements were to be used by each child to construct a representation of their current understanding of the task that they had both been asked to complete. When both children were in agreement the representations in their area of the screen would be identical, when they disagreed their representations would differ. The shared screen area therefore represented explicitly the state of agreement between the pair of children. In situations where there was disagreement these differing representations could be used as a resource for discussion between the pair.

The way that this interface could be used is best explained by means of an example. One of the software applications that implemented this interface design was for a word categorization task based upon Cartwright (2002). The software was called WordCat. It presented children with 12 words that they were asked to sort into four groups according to two rules:

- A 'letter' rule; for example, that the word contained a particular number of letters; and
- A 'type of thing' rule; for example, that words represented food or animals.

In collaboration with each other, the children had to work out how the two rules applied to different sets of 12 words. Each word was presented in a 'word pool' box and each child used their mouse to drag the word into one of four different coloured boxes. If the two children agreed about which of the four boxes to place the word then they could select the 'agree' button on their screen and a new word for them to categorize would appear in the 'word pool'. Each of the four coloured boxes could contain three words and when three words had been correctly allocated to a box the words changed colour to match the background of the box. Once this had happened the words could no longer be moved. Figures 4.7 and

4.8 illustrate the SCOSS interface design and the WordCat word categorization task.

A comparative evaluation of a SCOSS interface version of the WordCat software and a single-user interface version was conducted with 64 children aged 7–9 years in 32 pairs. The single-user interface offered the pair of children shared access to a single representation of the task. The SCOSS interface offered each child access to their own representation of the task as described above. Both versions of the software offered the child their own mouse. The children were allocated blindly to a partner of the same sex, but of a different level of ability based upon their earlier individual performance on a WordCat task. All children received 'Talk Lessons' resourced by those developed by Dawes *et al.* (2004) to prepare children for their collaborative use of the software (Kerawalla et al., 2005). They then took part in a session with the WordCat software that lasted 30–40 minutes with an initial practice session followed by three 'rounds' (sets of words) of word categorization using WordCat.

As reported in Kerawalla *et al.* (2008), these sessions were video recorded, transcribed and analysed leading to the following findings. Children using the single interface were observed to behave in unproductive ways, including one partner dominating the interactions, one partner undoing the work of the other and pairs operating in organized or spontaneous turn-taking. Children using the SCOSS interface used their separate spaces to express agreement and disagreement.

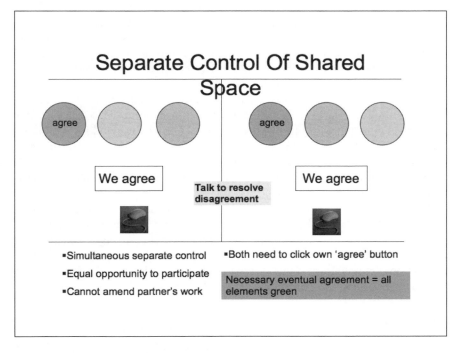

Figure 4.7 The SCOSS interface design

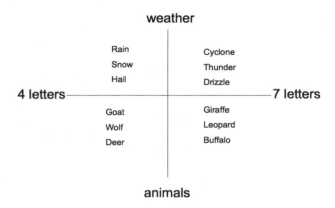

Figure 4.8 The WordCat Software Word Categorization Task

They did not always talk about their actions, but there were examples of productive collaborations supported by the interface.

It was clear that the SCOSS interface on its own could not correct poor collaborative skills, such as one child simply copying the other or working in parallel. However, the SCOSS interface forced the children to consider each other's actions, because if their actions resulted in disagreement then the children could not both select the 'we agree' button on their separate areas of the screen. The SCOSS interface also detailed the actions that each partner had completed that illustrated the child's beliefs about which rules should be used to categorize the words. This enabled the individual partners' contribution to the collaborative enterprise to be recorded and made clear. This feature offers the potential for representing this behaviour back to learners and for building a model of this behaviour in the system that could underpin software scaffolding to support collaborative performance and increase each partner's meta-collaborative awareness. The findings from this study were subsequently successfully applied to a different task (Yuill *et al.*, 2009).

The development and evaluation of the SCOSS interface illustrated that children can benefit from having structured collaborative interactions with technology. This suggests that technology can play a useful role in supporting and scaffolding interactions between learners around technology and not just in scaffolding interactions between learner and technology. This is consistent with other research evidence as discussed in Chapter 3.

The ZAA and ZPA in the Riddles WordCat software example

In the Riddles WordCat software the resources available for the child from within the software were more limited than in Ecolab. However, the software attempted to engage the child with resources outside the software, namely their partner. This meant that the ZAA taken into account by the project was a combination of resources, both provided and supported by the software. The development and evaluation of the SCOSS interface illustrated that technology can play a useful role in structuring and scaffolding collaborative interactions between learners as they use technology. The use of the SCOSS interface illustrated that its design could influence the manner in which the resources provided by the software were made available to the learners. Each child could engage with the words and categories in the WordCat software, but could not interfere with the resources being used by their partner. The interface design also influenced the learner's interactions with resources outside the software, namely their partner. It provided support for learners to collaborate, but without further scaffolding, the interface alone could not ensure that learners did collaborate, nor could it influence the quality of this collaboration.

Interactive toys in the CACHET project

The second example of a project that explores how learning might be scaffolded outside the confines of a learner interacting with a single piece of software and through a single screen based interface is a project that explored interactive toy technology. The CACHET project (Computers and Children's Electronic Toys) provided some confirmations that the nature of a learner's interactions with technology impacts upon their interactions with their wider environment. In particular, it illustrated that the form of these operational interactions and the technology interface through which they occurred could impact upon the child's interactions with other resources in their environment, including people. The CACHET project had no aim to develop technology. Its brief was to explore the potential of commercially produced digital learning toys for 4–6-year-old children in homes, after-school clubs and at school. The project was interested in the role that these toys might play in children's learning with technology. A particular focus of these explorations was on the manner in which the toys and the software that was supplied with them offered help to children who used them. This situation led to our asking: 'What happens when the helper is taken out of the box?' This alluded to the fact that the toy was outside the confines of the desktop computer box. This feature enabled us to explore whether the existence of a toy interface would make any difference to the nature of the interactions that would occur between children and the software, and between children and other resources outside the desktop computer, such as other people.

Interactive Toys and Help-seeking

The interactive toys used by the project were freestanding character-based soft toys about 30 cm tall, equipped with motors to support movement and a ROM chip that enabled them to respond to input stimulus. The toys could move and produce canned speech from a digitized vocabulary of more than 4,000 words when sensors placed within the toy's body were stimulated, for example by a child's squeeze. The toys could also be 'linked' to a desktop computer through a purpose-built wireless unit, which meant that accompanying software on the computer could send a message to the toy that would also result in some movement or speech by the toy. The software included games to support basic language and number skills, a painting application and some puzzles. As children used the software the toy provided feedback and gave encouragement. If the toy was not present it was represented by an on-screen icon of the toy, which provided the same feedback. The children who used the toys and software were, therefore, interacting with the individual artefact of toy and computer, and were also party to interactions between them. Figure 4.9 illustrates the toys used by the project.

If the child wanted help from the toy when they were completing an activity with the software, they could request it by squeezing the toy's ear. If children experienced difficulty completing the software activity then the toy might suggest that they 'squeeze my ear for a hint'. If the toy was not present when the software was being used then an image of the toy would appear on the top right-hand corner of the computer screen. The toy's icon head and eyes moved from side to side as if to follow the child's use of the software and it could be clicked on with the mouse to elicit the same help as would be offered by the toy when its ear was squeezed.

One of the games that children could play with the software was a hide-and-seek game called 'Where's Pal?' This offered a cartoon representation of the Roman Colosseum as a 5 x 6 array of windows on the computer screen. The instructions given to children were that the dog character called Pal was hiding behind one of the windows of the Colosseum and that the child needed to find the dog by clicking on the window where he was hiding. If the child's selection of a window was unsuccessful and they did not find Pal, then they were given feedback. This feedback varied in sophistication depending on the level of difficulty at which the game was being played. On the easiest level, the square glowed red, green or blue depending on how close the child's selection was to Pal's actual hiding place. The child was also given an audio prompt such as 'You're very close/far away from Pal's hiding place.' Children could also get extra help by squeezing the toy's ear or clicking on the on-screen toy icon. These actions resulted in a hint such as 'Why don't you try a window lower down,' accompanied by one of the appropriately located windows flashing and buzzing conspicuously. The advice offered by the character, whether in the form of the toy or on-screen icon, was not always correct, which meant that children were left with the task of deciding whether or not to follow the advice.

As reported in Luckin *et al.* (2003) a study was conducted in a school with 24 children of 4–6 years of age (12 male and 12 female). One group of 12 children (composed of 3 pairs and 6 individuals) played the 'Where's Pal?' game with the toy present, and a second group of 12 children (3 pairs and 6 individuals) played the 'Where's Pal?' game without the toy being present, therefore seeking and receiving hints via the on-screen icon. The children's interactions were video recorded and dialogue and behaviour were transcribed and coded to explore their

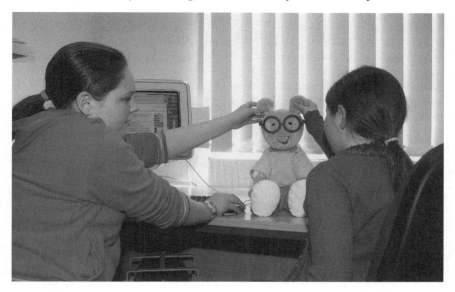

Figure 4.9 The Arthur character soft toy being used with accompanying software

help-seeking activity, acceptance of the help offered and success at implementing it. The actions of the adult researcher were also analysed with respect to the assistance they offered to the children using the technology.

Analysis of the incidence of actions in each of these categories illustrated that, when the toy was present, there were significantly more incidences of: children successfully implementing the help they were offered; children actively seeking help and the researcher actively engaging with the children to prompt or assist in their use of the software. Whether the toy was present or absent made almost no difference to the number of times children refused or ignored the help they were offered. (The details of these results can be found in Luckin *et al.*, 2003.) This small study illustrated that there was a difference in behaviour amongst children when the toy was present, as opposed to the icon of the toy on the screen. They engaged in more interactions not just with the software, but also socially with other children or adults. In the group where the toy was present, there were more than twice as many interactions between peers and over three times as many interactions with the researcher. These results do not imply that the toys were effective as helpers: the point here is that the interactions around the technology between people were influenced by the interface through which interactions with the technology could happen. The nature of the interface also influenced the extent to which learners initiated help-seeking interactions.

The ZAA and ZPA in the CACHET example

In some ways the resources offered by the 'Where's Pal?' game were similar, though far less sophisticated, to those offered by the Ecolab software. The child was set a task to complete using the technology and help was made available by the technology. The quality and quantity of help provided by the technology itself was impoverished, but the manner in which the toy technology influenced the interactions between resources outside of its control was interesting. The increase in social interactions when the toy was present, as well as the software on the desktop computer, demonstrated that the arrangement of the resources within a setting impacts upon the way that the resources are used to support learning within that setting. The ZAA taken into account by the CACHET project was made up from resources within the software and resources outside the software: the toy, the children's peers and the researcher. The situation without the toy was similar to that for the Riddles learners, except that the interface made no attempt to support their collaboration. The selection of the resources that would contribute to the interactions of the learner's ZPA was done by the child, the software, their peers and the researcher. This selection was not the result of an explicit ZPA construction task, but was the result of the interactions in which learners engaged. The influence of the toy on these social interactions suggests that beyond the virtual world of the software, the role played by the technology and the way in which this role is implemented can contribute to the ZPA construction process.

The studies discussed in this chapter add to the contribution made by the literature and are formative in the development of the Ecology of Resources model. They illustrate that the design of technology can influence a learner's interactions with the resources in their environment beyond those provided solely by the technology. This suggests that technology can have a role in supporting learning interactions across a range of resources and that, as designers, we need to understand more about the nature of these interactions. We need to expand our understanding of the contingencies around which scaffolding interventions can be designed and we need to develop appropriate scaffolding techniques. We also need to understand more about the role that technology can play with respect to the learner's MAPs. It is also interesting to note the impact of the learner's wider environment and culture on their interactions with, and around, the software. It was necessary to offer the learners, who took part in the WordCat study, lessons about working together before they used the software, because early pilot work had indicated that the skills they brought to the study were cooperative rather than collaborative (Kerawalla *et al.*, 2005). It is also important to note that all the studies discussed in this chapter have taken place in formal institutional environments, which bring their own particular and individual cultures.

In the next chapter, I will look beyond the classroom and consider empirical evidence about learners' interactions across locations.

5 Modelling a learner's context

This chapter extends the enterprise of charting the empirical landscape that I started in Chapter 4. I explore evidence from studies conducted across multiple locations and consider some of the potential afforded by wireless, mobile and ubiquitous technologies. These technologies bring with them the opportunity to link a learner's experience across multiple locations. I discuss the Homework project and the associated HOMEWORK software. This project explored how technology could be used with 5–6-year-old children to support their interactions with a variety of other people as well as with a variety of other resources across a range of locations. At the end of the chapter I integrate the theoretical and empirical grounding and present the Ecology of Resources model of context.

Looking beyond the single user, single system, single location paradigm

The Homework project was a collaboration of academics, film producers and broadcasters[1], parents, teachers and children, and was based on an earlier version of the Ecology of Resources model called the Broadband Learner Model (Luckin & du Boulay, 2001). The focus for this Broadband Learner Model was also on modelling the learner and their interactions and its aim was to build a model of the learner's interactions that could take into account their interactions across multiple locations and with multiple other participants. In particular, the model aimed to support the development of technology to link each learner's experiences at school with their experiences outside of school, so that knowledge learnt at school was also relevant for outside school too and not seen as something that was only for formal school education.

A model to Scaffold Learning between school and home

The Broadband Learner Model (Luckin & du Boulay, 2001) was the starting point for the Homework project team's desire to design a framework that could be used to develop technology that would bridge the gap between home and school, by providing scaffolding support for learners and their parents. This Broadband Learner modelling approach grew out of discussions about the need to find a way to develop scaffolding and learner modelling techniques that could accommodate a wide 'band-width' of participants, senses, devices and contexts. The term 'Broadband' was influenced by, but not synonymous with, the term as it is applied to network connection speed. The concept of the Broadband Learner Model was defined as: a learner model created through the use of networked technology to link a learner's educational experience across time and location. The concept was based upon the ZAA and ZPA used for the Ecolab I and II software and was based on the belief that the ZAA could be provided by a combination of software and other resources available in the learner's environment, such as people. The role of the More Able Partner (MAP) in helping the learner to select resources that form the interactions of the learner's ZPA was to be fulfilled by a collaboration between the software and other people identified as potential sources of assistance.

The HOMEWORK system was developed incrementally and interactively with learners, teachers and parents. Each interaction gave the design team a clearer understanding of the interactions that made up the learning contexts of the children, who the system was developed to support. It is described in some detail in Luckin *et al.* (2006). Here, I describe the system that was the product of this development and use the empirical data it enabled the researchers to collect to demonstrate how it led to the evolution of the Ecology of Resources model of context.

The HOMEWORK system was an interactive mathematics education system for children aged 5–7 years that used a combination of interactive whiteboard and Tablet PC technology, plus some bespoke software, consisting of lesson planning, control and home use components. The system contained a rich set of multimedia and associated interactive numeracy resources. Teachers used the software to link these resources into lesson plans. In the classroom, the interactive whiteboard was used for whole-class activities and each child also had their own Tablet PC for individual and small group activities. The teacher could control the classroom activity from their own Tablet PC and could allocate new activities or send messages to individuals or groups of children in real time. When planning each lesson the teacher could also decide upon homework activities and allocate them to individual children's Tablets as appropriate. After school, the children took their Tablet PC home with them and used it at home or elsewhere; individually or with parents. At home, in addition to homework activities set by the teacher, the Tablet provided access to the resources the learner had used in class that day, the resources that they had used in previous sessions (irrespective of whether the child was actually in school or not) and information for parents about the learning objectives to which these activities related. There were also links to other relevant fun activities and a messaging system to support parent and teacher communication. Figures 5.1 and 5.2 illustrate the use of the HOMEWORK system in the school classroom and at home, while Figure 5.3 illustrates the Tablet PC interface seen by the child and their family when the Tablet was outside the classroom.

Figure 5.1 HOMEWORK in use in the classroom

Figure 5.2 HOMEWORK in use in the home

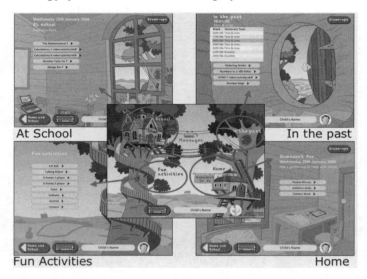

At School   In the past

Fun Activities   Home

Figure 5.3 The HOMEWORK system home interface

How the HOMEWORK software was used

A version of the HOMEWORK system was evaluated with a class of 30 children aged 5–7 years, over a four-week period in Spring 2005, and a slightly updated version of the system was used with a different class of 32 children aged 5–7 years, from the same school, for just over two weeks in January 2006. Multiple data sources were collected during both of these evaluations. These included: logs maintained by the system; diaries maintained by parents; interviews with parents; and questionnaires completed by parents. The details of the study design, data sources and system version are presented in Luckin *et al.* (2006). In the current chapter, I discuss the findings from the project to illustrate how they influenced the empirical grounding of the Ecology of Resources model. In particular, I focus upon the data that illustrate how the Tablets were used by children and their families outside the classroom. It is these data that can offer valuable information about the child's wider learning experience across multiple locations and with a variety of other people. Initially, I offer a description of how the HOMEWORK system was used by all participants to illustrate how often, in what location, and with whom the technology was used. I then explore the use of specific system features that were introduced to support building a relationship between the child's in-school and out-of-school learning. Finally, I offer a detailed study of one child and their family to illustrate the role that technology can play in a child's learning, both inside and outside school.

When, where, how often and with whom the HOMEWORK System was used

In both evaluations, the system was used for three, hour-long mathematics lessons per week. The teacher would use the lesson planning features of the system to organize each session and would select the content they wanted the class, small groups or individual children to use. The resources associated with this content could then be allocated to the interactive whiteboard or to the children's Tablet PCs, as appropriate. The teacher could also allocate homework activities to the Tablets for each child. The interface that the HOMEWORK system offered the teacher to support lesson planning is illustrated in Figure 5.4. The classroom lessons usually consisted of an initial session during which the whole class watched a short *Number Crew* video on the interactive whiteboard and completed some interactive activities as directed by the teacher, with individual children being called to the whiteboard to complete a particular action. After this, children would go to their individual seats and use their Tablet PCs to complete the activities that had been preselected for them by the teacher. The teacher could take control of one, some or all of the Tablet PCs if they wanted to send a particular message to members of the class.

During both the 2005 and 2006 evaluations of the Homework system, log data were collected from the Tablets. These data were particularly useful for highlighting how the Tablets were used when outside the classroom, where there

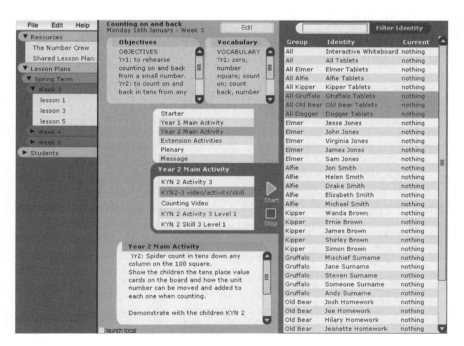

Figure 5.4 The HOMEWORK lesson planning interface for teachers

was no researcher or teacher to observe what was happening. The logs indicate that, in 2005, the average home session length was 31 minutes and the average number of times the Tablet PC was used at home was four times per week. In 2006, the Tablets were used, on average, slightly less than once a day for the equivalent of 25 minutes a day. However, there was great variability in both session length and in the total time children spent using the Tablets during the research period. The diaries maintained by parents in both the 2005 and 2006 studies indicate that the most common time for the Tablet to be used was weekday evenings (after 5.30 pm). In 2006, the most common time for using the Tablets was during the daytime at weekends. In both studies, the least popular time was before school. These diaries also reveal that the Tablet was most often used at a table located in a communal space such as a lounge, dining room or kitchen, followed by the bedroom and, occasionally, in a car or somewhere else. The diaries also reflected that Mum was the person who most frequently helped children with their Tablet activities, with Dad, siblings and other family members being the next most frequent helpers.

The HOMEWORK system as a tool to support parental engagement

The 'History' facility built into the home interface of the Tablet was intended to support parents who, during the participatory design process, had asked to know more about what their children had done at school so they could follow their child's activities over time. It enabled families to view any activity and rerun any media that the child had used on their Tablet PC, either at school or at home. Discussions in interviews and focus groups with parents reveal that the use of this 'History' facility was family specific and often depended upon parents' perceived need for it; for example, if their child was finding something particularly difficult. The following statement made by a parent during interviews as part of the 2005 study illustrates this well:

> I think I'd probably use information from history if we had a problem, if we ran into a problem with a particular homework, to see when he'd covered it and how they'd covered it and perhaps re-visit it ourselves and then if we still had a problem, we might well go back to [teacher's name] or speak to whichever teacher.

There was also evidence that the use of the 'History' facility might be developed through increased familiarity:

> I think if [the Tablet] was to become part of the homework routine then we probably would get into the habit of reviewing work that's been done at school [using the history], get the hang of it ourselves, feel confident about it and then try and help [child's name] with her homework.

In the 2006 study, parents could access information that had been created specially for them by pressing the 'Grown-ups' button on the interface, as illustrated in Figure 5.5.

This button offered information about the objectives of the activity, the vocabulary used and suggestions about how the parent might help their child, as illustrated in Figure 5.5. Once the button had been selected, 'Grown-ups' information was displayed until the button was switched off. The log data from the Tablets reveal an interesting pattern of use of this facility. The number of Tablets on which the 'Grown-ups' button was selected fell, as did the number of times the button was selected. The first three days when the Tablet was taken home were a weekend and in this period the 'Grown-ups' button was selected at least once on 76 per cent of the Tablets, and the mean number of times the button was selected was 5.6. During the following week the button was selected at least once on 54 per cent of the Tablets, and the mean number of times the button was selected was 2.1, and in the second week the button was selected at least once on 38 per cent of the Tablets and the mean number of times the button was selected was 1.6. Figure 5.6 illustrates this change. There were only three Tablets on which the 'Grown-ups' button was never selected, and none of the Tablets on which the 'Grown-ups' button was selected in the second week were Tablets on which the button had not been selected previously.

However, the mean length of time during which the information was on-screen during each of these selections changed little over the study period, as illustrated in

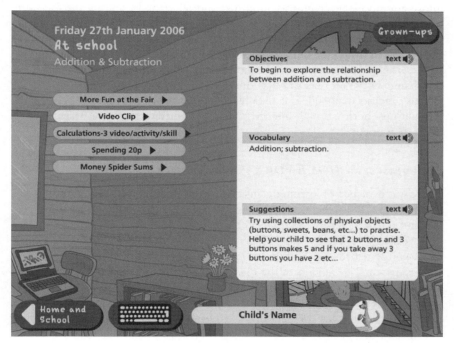

Figure 5.5 Help provided through the 'Grown-ups' button

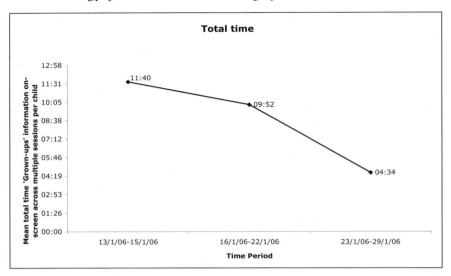

Figure 5.6 Number of times the 'Grown-ups' button is selected

Figure 5.7. During the first three days, the mean length of time during which the information was on-screen was 3 minutes and 50 seconds. During the following week, the mean length of time during which the information was on-screen during one of these selections was 3 minutes and 12 seconds, and during the second week the mean length of time during which the information was on-screen during one of these selections remained at 3 minutes and 12 seconds. Figure 5.7 illustrates the change in the number of selections.

This suggests that while not all families found the information provided by the 'Grown-ups' button useful, but those who continued to select this feature did so more than briefly.

The impact of the HOMEWORK system on learning

There was evidence of learning gains during the time the HOMEWORK system was in use. In 2006, these can be seen in the changes in children's scores in a pre-test and post-test set by the teacher. The mean scores for the youngest children (5–6 years of age) increased by 17 per cent and for the older children (6–7 years of age) by 26 per cent. In addition to these test scores, in both the 2005 and 2006 studies, parents' comments in the diaries they maintained and during interviews also suggest that children's learning may have benefited during the Homework project studies. For example, from diaries maintained by parents in 2005: '[Child's name] found using her Tablet PC very enjoyable, helpful, fun and in using it, it meant that she was able to be more independent and was able to work and learn without any distractions, sitting where was quiet.'

In the interviews with the class teacher, in both 2005 and 2006, there are

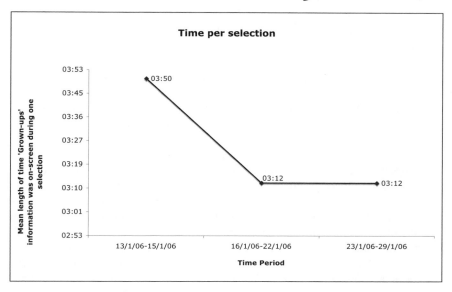

Figure 5.7 Length of time 'Grown-ups' information on-screen per selection

reports that reflect the teacher's belief that children are learning through their use of the HOMEWORK system. For example:

> I've certainly noticed people like [child's name] seems a lot more confident with her mental arithmetic. I don't know if that's as a result of using the Tablet at home and in school or whether Mum's been doing extra things with her, I'm not sure.

Family case studies

To explore more about the nature of the way in which the system may have supported learning, and the range of interactions that the HOMEWORK system was able to support I discuss one family's use of the system in more depth. I present this as an extract from a narrative about a learner – Alison, and her family – and the way that they used the HOMEWORK system through the Homework Tablet. The narrative is constructed from the data logged by the Homework Tablets and the entries made in the diary kept by the family. The timings for the length spent on activities are rounded down to the nearest minute. On occasions, where there is insufficient data to be sure who is using the Homework Tablet, this entry is described as the Homework Tablet being in use without stipulation of the user's identity. The '…' symbol indicates where there is a day's entry in the full narrative that is not part of this extract.

Alison's Story
In 2005, Alison is 6 years old. She has two sisters, Catherine and Elizabeth. Alison

and her sisters live with Mum and Dad and they took part in the Homework project during April and May of 2005. The Tablet was brought home for the first time on Wednesday 20 April.

...

The next time that Alison brings her Homework Tablet home is on Friday 22 April. Alison uses her Tablet on the lounge floor at about 4.30 pm and works with Mum. When the Homework Tablet comes home again on Monday 25 April, Alison has dancing club so is unable to work with her Tablet.

...

On Wednesday 27 April, there are some new homework activities for this week that are based on adding up to ten: these are called the 'Octopus Game'; 'Ten-Thing Bowling'; and 'Crew Calculations Skill Activity 5'. This last activity gives the child a chance to achieve a certificate. At about 6.30 pm, Alison uses her Tablet on the lounge floor, helped by Mum. Everything is working fine and she spends ten minutes working with the *Number Crew* and has a brief look at task 1 of the homework. She then gets distracted and runs off to play. Later on, at around 8 pm, she sits down again, this time by herself on the lounge floor, to work out how to do the task and completes it on her own in about 15 minutes.

Alison is shown how to use the camera on her Homework Tablet by Miss Green and is able to try this out at home on Thursday 28 April. Alison spends just over 25 minutes taking pictures of herself and Mum. She also plays the Ink Ball game for three minutes, which is one of the fun activities included on the Homework Tablet and then spends ten minutes completing a *Number Crew* calculation exercise. She plays a video and then spends a couple of minutes completing *Number Crew* Activity 6 at level 1, before moving on to the skill activity that is part of this week's homework, involving adding and subtracting numbers 9 and 11. Alison completes this activity at levels 1 and 2, with each level taking between two and three minutes. When she views her progress chart, it indicates she has achieved her Skill 5 certificate, so this homework activity is complete. Alison finishes working with her Homework Tablet at about 8.15 pm, after reviewing the pictures she had taken earlier and taking one more photo of the cat.

...

Monday 2 May is a Bank Holiday and Alison uses her Homework Tablet today after lunch at about 12.20 pm. Alison writes and draws in Windows Journal for about 20–25 minutes. She wants to show her Homework Tablet to Grandpa at 6.30 pm, but the batteries are flat so they have to be charged. Later this evening, at around 8.15 pm, Alison does one of the homework activities in her bedroom on her bed. Dad works with Alison who completes the 'Ten-Thing Bowling' Activity, as illustrated in Figure 5.8. Alison then does level 2 of the Skill 5 homework activity for about five minutes and finishes this session by watching some *Number Crew* videos with Dad.

...

When the Homework Tablets come home on Wednesday 18 May, Miss Green has set some new Homework activities. This week there is a *Number Crew* Activity called 'Daily Routines', another one about shapes and a digital camera homework activity that requires Alison to take pictures and tell a story. Alison uses her Tablet on her bed this evening, at about 8.30 pm, working with Dad while Mum is helping one of her sisters. Alison's computer is slow to load, which leads to too much button pushing and it runs slowly. Alison and Dad eventually get into the activity, 'Daily Routines' (illustrated in Figure 5.9), and they detach the Tablet screen from the case and keyboard in order to work on this activity. Alison does this for about 15 minutes and gets about half way through. She then watches a *Number Crew* video before her session ends at 9 pm.

On Thursday, Alison takes her Tablet home for the final time. Alison uses her Tablet with her Mum and Elizabeth at about 5.15 pm, while they watch sister Catherine take part in a karate lesson, so they use the headphones. Alison spends a few minutes writing in the Journal and they then watch two videos and complete activities 8 and 6 before watching another video and stopping at 5.50 pm.

At the end of the study, Mum took part in a focus group and an interview. Her reflections were that Alison had enjoyed having the Tablet. There was a drop-off after the initial excitement and Mum found that they went through phases of using the Tablet a lot or not much. The formal homework activities took longer than paper activities: 30–40 minutes instead of 15–20 minutes. Sometimes Alison found it hard to understand what to do and Mum had to try and work it out and help her. Mum didn't look at the Tablet much herself, as is reflected in her lack of access of the 'History' and 'This Week at School' facilities. Mum said she might ask Alison what she had done in school and Alison would show her the videos and activities from class, but she did not go into the Tablet much herself, as she was not sure which parts were for her and which were for the teacher. She

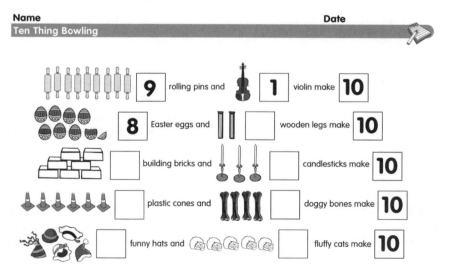

Figure 5.8 Homework activity: 'Ten-thing Bowling' partially completed by Alison

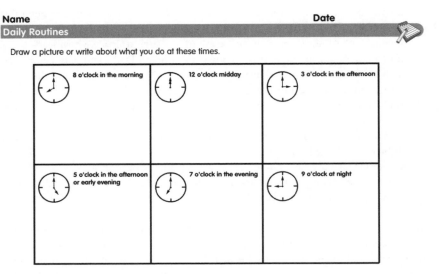

Figure 5.9 Daily Routines Homework

did, however, feel that she knew more about what Alison was doing in class as a result of Alison showing her the Tablet.

Summary of HOMEWORK system use

To summarize, the data discussed illustrate that teachers were able to use the HOMEWORK system for mathematics lessons and could see benefits in the system for children and their families. This is summed up well in a statement from an interview with the class teacher, who took part in the 2005 evaluation:

> Yes I think it's great, before I was only able to issue homework that was either worksheet based or activity based, or physical where they've brought something in. The fact that they've got a camera to use, access to videos and activities, it's really exciting. It's opened up a link as well between home and school ... the parents have been happy that they can see what we do at school as well. It's a good thing.

Families used the system at home and accessed it, on average, for slightly longer than the system was used by children in school. There is still a considerable amount of formality in the way the technology was used at home. Most incidents of use occurred at a table in a communal living space. The Tablet was reasonably small and mobile so could have been used in a wide variety of places and yet it was only in a minority of cases that families elected for this flexibility. The prominence of use in spaces where other family members may also gather, is interesting and the data illustrate that families did take advantage of the fact that the Tablet enabled the system to be used in more than one location. This possibility is also borne out in the evidence about family members working with children using the technology. Whilst Mum was consistently the most frequent helper, Dad was involved in approximately half as many help episodes as Mum, and other family members and friends were also involved on several occasions. During the participatory design process, families had reported that they wanted to know more about what their children were doing at school and to have information designed for them about how they could help their children. This was provided within the software and was used by the majority of families. The way in which it was used depended upon individual families and their needs. The design of the system enabled flexible use that allowed individual preferences to be met. There were also indications that the continuing existence of such facilities might have become part of family routine had the system continued to be available. Finally, there are multiple sources of evidence that suggest that children learnt while the HOMEWORK system was in use.

Alison's story offers an unusual and valuable insight into technology use out of school. It illustrates that she made use of the flexibility offered by the technology and used her Homework Tablet in a variety of locations, including the lounge, her bedroom, the garden and at her sister's karate club. She worked on the floor, sofa, at a table or on her bed, and at many different times throughout the day, from just after 8 am until after 9 pm. She could choose when and where to work on her numeracy within the constraints negotiated with her family. Sometimes she worked on an activity for a minute or two and on other occasions for much longer. Alison worked on the homework activities set by Miss Green, but did much more besides and clearly enjoyed herself, provided that the technology was working properly. She was able to choose what she wanted to work on, could show it to her friends and other family members and, in so doing, behaved independently. The numeracy activities sometimes offered Alison the opportunity to record information about her life outside school; for example, the 'Daily Routines' activity. Alison could also use the camera to capture information about her home for use with her numeracy activities.

Alison's mother reported that Alison's interest in numeracy had increased, that she enjoyed the activities and regarded them as play. The whole family was able to, and did, get involved with the numeracy activities available through the Homework Tablet. Mum, Dad and sisters worked with Alison during the study. They could do this in a way that fitted in with family life. After the study, Mum reported that she had an increased awareness of the numeracy that Alison was working on at school.

This brief overview paints a very positive picture of technology supporting learning at school and at home. It is true to say that across all the data sources analysed, the positive feedback greatly outweighed the negative. However, there were, of course, some less positive findings that need to be taken into account. For example, the technology was a research prototype and constantly under development, which meant that the kit had to be taken into the school and set up at the start of each evaluation study. There were some teething troubles with the classroom network and the speed of data transmission to Tablets once the lesson plans had been constructed. The parents also reported some technical difficulties, although these were minor and included issues such as some of the text on the screen being a little small and the batteries, that operated the pens used with the Tablets' touch screens, having a short life. The aspects of the system that could be viewed as very positive could also have their downside. For example, the increased independence of children with the Tablet also led to some parents feeling 'shut out' from their child's learning. In some instances, children felt very strong ownership of their Tablet PC and did not want to share it with other family members. Parents reported that siblings got involved more often, which was good except on the one occasion where there was a problem with jealousy and a fight ensued! Primarily, however, the point of my discussion of the Homework project findings in this chapter is not to provide evidence that it was a successful research project, but to illustrate how the results of this project influenced the construction of the Ecology of Resources model.

Homework summary and contribution to the Ecology of Resources model

The aim of the HOMEWORK system development process was to build a model of the learner's interactions that could take into account their interactions across multiple locations and with multiple other participants. In particular, the technology was developed to help link each learner's experiences at school with their experiences outside school, and to help provide conceptual coherence, so that the knowledge learnt at school was made relevant for home, too, and not seen as something that was only for formal school education. The system also extended the application of the scaffolding concept beyond the learner to explore the possibility of scaffolding parental interactions with their children, and help family engagement and communication with the school.

In terms of the ZAA and ZPA concepts, the HOMEWORK system aimed to enable designers to expand their knowledge of the resources available to a learner, both within and outside the software. As I stressed in earlier discussions about the role of the MAP, the process of selecting resources to enable the construction of a ZPA is a negotiation between learners and MAPs. In a situation such as that described by the Homework case studies, it is clear that in the out-of-school environment there may be various people who play the role of the MAP at different points during the learner's interactions. Likewise, in the school environment, there will be the teacher, classroom assistant, peers, other teachers and parent helpers, each of whom may also fulfil the role of the MAP at different points in time. The HOMEWORK system was designed to support both the child's learning and to support those in the position of the child's MAP. It also had a part to play in the negotiation of the learner's ZPA with, and between, those playing the role of the child's MAP, through, for example, the provision of information for parents and teachers about what each MAP had done with the learner at home and at school. The data gained from the Homework project are helpful in providing a starting point for working out how best the technology can support this negotiation. For example, the information for 'Grown-ups' supports communication between teacher and parent to engender continuity of language in the way that the activities are discussed with the learner. The ability to replay and review completed activities offers each person acting as the learner's MAP the ability to see what the child has done when either working alone or with another. In addition to supporting other MAPs, the system itself had a role to play as a MAP through the carefully designed scaffolding provided for learners.

At the start of the Homework project, the system's modelling was focused on the learner and attempted to 'model' the learner's wider experience through their interactions at different times and in different places. So, for example, the system model could differentiate between what activities the learner worked on at school and what they worked on outside the school classroom. In theory, this richer learner model could be used to individualize the nature of the content that was offered to the learner. In reality, this individualization remained in the hands of the teacher. Information gained through analysis of the data collected by the project supports the idea that, in the future, the model may be to offer each person who becomes a MAP an opportunity to adapt their actions in the light of the evolving learner model, and to contribute to the evolution of that model. The model may then become a tool to support the negotiation of the resource selection between the different people and technologies playing the role of a MAP, as well as between those MAPs and the learner.

The Homework project also highlighted the manner in which each learner's HOMEWORK Tablet was personalized from the first moment of use. Each Tablet was physically personalized by the learner, who decorated the bag in which it was carried, and each was digitally personalized, as the child completed the class-based activities selected by the teacher, the homework and the activities selected by the learner themselves or members of their family. As time passed, each Tablet became increasingly personalized and represented an individual learner's interactions across multiple locations and with multiple people. This confirms the fact that the experience a learner has, when using a particular piece of content, is part of its personalization for that learner. So whilst two learners may both watch the same video clip or complete the same worksheet in their homes, their experience of this will be different owing to the interactions that surround their experience, such as the conversations they have with their sibling about the video clip or the comment that Mum makes whilst they are completing the worksheet. There can be no assumptions made about content that works well in school working equally well, or in the same way, when this same content is used outside school. The content needs to be adapted if the learning interactions we want learners to engage in are to be integrated both inside and outside school.

The physical artefact of the learner's HOMEWORK Tablet represented a form of digital and physical personalization as it travelled to and from school. Had the same content been available online and accessible by devices within the family home there may well have been less personalization. Such family devices are most often shared and, even if the learner can have their own storage space on such devices, the level of device personalization and the experience is not the same. The interface on the Tablet was specifically designed for the learners and limited their options. It was easy to use and resulted in few problems for the children or for their families. The children's ownership of the device was strong and their independence increased with use.

Empirical grounding summary

The projects I have discussed throughout this and the previous chapter have explored the use of a range of technologies to support learning; from single use software such as Ecolab I and II to systems that used multiple technologies such as the HOMEWORK system. The locations where learning was studied started with the school classroom and extended into the home and its environs. The initial examples considered a single learner and a software application that was designed to play the role of the MAP for that learner. Subsequent examples have considered more than one learner and more than a single piece of software and indeed more than a single person playing the role of the learner's MAP. The opportunities for technology to scaffold the learning process have moved beyond the concepts of the domain to encompass meta-level scaffolding. And the nature of the domain studied has expanded from extremely small, tightly focused areas of the curriculum, such as word categorization, to the consideration of broader areas within numeracy. My aim in exploring these projects, and doing so at such a level of detail, was to extract the findings from these projects that have influenced the construction of the Ecology of Resources model.

The Ecology of Resources model

In Chapter 2, I introduced the concepts of the ZAA and ZPA to describe existing resources that can be used to support learning, and I have used these concepts to frame my discussions of the empirical work. I now present the Ecology of Resources model as a way of characterizing a learner and the interactions that form that learner's context.

The Ecology of Resources model is a development of the ZAA and ZPA concepts and I return to these for a moment by way of clarification. Figure 5.10 shows a snapshot of a learner's ZAA, the smaller dots in the outer rectangle represent the world of possible types of assistance; the dots within the circle inside the rectangle are the types of assistance currently available to the learner at the centre of the figure. The types of assistance with which the learner is interacting are represented by the larger dots linked to the learner by double-headed arrows: these are the types of assistance the learner is using to support their learning. I refer to these types of assistance as 'resources', each of which is potentially interconnected, as symbolized by the connectors between the resources. The interactions between this network of resources and the learner comprises the learner's Zone of Adjustment; the extent to which this resource selection from the ZAA is a Zone of *Proximal* Adjustment is as yet unknown. Figure 5.11 is a simplified representation in which the learner in the centre interacts with all of the resources that are interconnected by the outer circle. Once again, this outer circle represents the Learner's Zone of Adjustment.

Within the resources of the ZAA there will be a wide range of categories, including people, technologies, buildings, books and knowledge. It is useful to consider the different types or categories of resource that might be available in order to help us identify them and the relationship they bear to the learner and to each other. Figure 5.12 offers a representation of the resources available to the learner with some suggested categories.

The Ecology of Resources model has the learner at its centre. One of the resource categories that the learner needs to interact with comprises the 'stuff that is to be learnt': the knowledge and skills that are the subject of the learning. This is represented by the 'Knowledge and Skills' label in Figure 5.12, but it is important to stress that this label encompasses skills, such as carpentry, as well as knowledge of 'scientific' concepts, like the mathematics, that were part of the HOMEWORK system. The nature and variety of knowledge and skills is huge and the Ecology of Resources model is not prescriptive about what type of knowledge or skill can be included. Some domains are more well defined (such as chemistry) than others (such as psychology) as are their underlying concepts. Jonassen (1997) makes the interesting observation that well-defined problems are common in education, but rare in the real world. The building blocks of the domain that learners are presented with will vary in their level of definition according to the discipline. In less well-defined disciplines students will need to understand how the knowledge concepts have been formed and justified in order to understand the nature of knowledge and the knowledge construction process more generally. This impacts on the way that students will reason about a problem. Knowledge can also be tacit and implicit, experiential and craft based, for example. I see no reason why any form of knowledge or skill cannot be included within an Ecology of Resources model. However, most of the empirical examples upon which I draw involve the type of knowledge concepts found in formal education, which is a limitation.

A second category of resource is that represented by the 'Tools and People' label in Figure 5.12. This category includes books, pens and paper, technology and other people who know more about the knowledge or skill to be learnt than the learner does. The last category of resource is that represented by the 'Environment' label. This category includes the location and surrounding environment with which the learner interacts: for example, a school classroom, a park, or a place of work. In many instances, there is an existing relationship between the resources within these three categories: Knowledge and Skills, Tools and People and Environment. For example, the book resources appropriate for learning French are located in the Language Learning section of the library and formal lessons probably take place in a particular location in school. Hence, in Figure 5.12, the categories of resource surrounding the learner, and with which they interact, are joined together. In order to support learning, the relationships between the different types of resource with which the learner interacts need to be identified and understood. They may need to be made explicit to the learner in order to build coherence into the interactions.

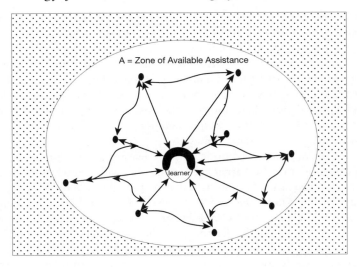

Figure 5.10 The resources and interactions of the Zone of Available Assistance

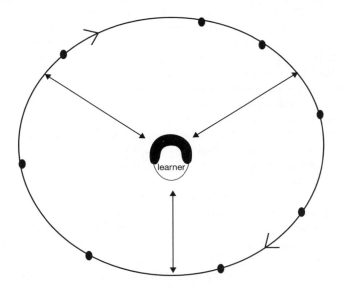

Figure 5.11 A simplification of the resources and interactions of the Zone of Available Assistance

For example, if I wish to teach French conversation to an evening class, which involves how to order a meal, I may choose to provide a menu and to organize the room like a restaurant. I will also need to ensure that the language concepts I introduce are relevant to meal ordering.

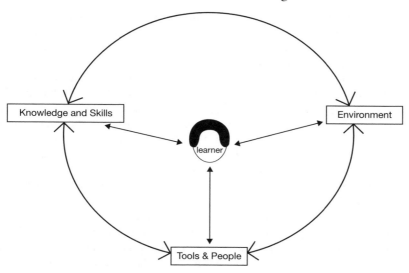

Figure 5.12 The resource elements in the Ecology of Resources

The Ecology of Resources filter elements

This language learning example highlights another factor that needs to be taken into consideration. I mentioned that I might organize the room in a particular fashion. This is an example of the way in which a learner's interactions with the available resources are often filtered by the actions of others – in this case, me as the teacher – rather than experienced directly and unimpeded by the learner. For example, the subject matter to be learnt is usually filtered through some kind of organization, such as a curriculum, that has been the subject of a process of validation by other members of the learner's society. This resource filter is stronger for subjects such as mathematics and other formal educational disciplines than for more grounded skills such as farming. However, even with skills-based subjects there is, to some extent at least, still some formalization of what is recognized as the accepted view about the nature and components of the skills that need to be mastered. The Tools and People that may be available to the learner are also organized or filtered in some way. For example, a teacher taking a French conversation evening class is only available during that class, or perhaps at some other times via email. The Tablet PCs the children used in the Homework project were not always available: there were school and home rules and protocols that restricted the learner's access to this resource. Finally, and again as reflected in the French conversation learning example, a learner's access to the Environment is mediated by that Environment's organization. This resource filter is more obvious in formal settings such as schools, where timetables and regulations have a strong influence on the ways in which learners interact with their environment. These filter elements have been added to the model illustrated in Figure 5.13.

In the same way that there may already exist a relationship between the different resource elements in the outer circle of the figure, there may also exist a relationship between the filter elements. For example, the organization of the numeracy curriculum in the Homework project example influenced the teacher's choice of resource for their lesson plan as well as the nature of the technology that was to be used by learners; that is, the interactive whiteboard or the Tablet PC. The layout of the classroom was also influenced by the nature of the resources being used, such as a floor space near the interactive whiteboard large enough to seat the whole class. These relationships are illustrated through the connections between the filters in Figure 5.13. Once again, the coherence of the learner's experience can be enhanced through careful consideration of the existing relationships between the filter elements and between the individual resource elements and their associated filter.

In both Figures 5.10 and 5.11 (page 92) the arrows that link the different elements in the Ecology of Resources represent an *influenced by* relationship. All arrows are bi-directional indicating that each element has an influence upon, and is influenced by, the element to which it is linked. The strength of this influence may, of course, vary and on occasions it may be limited in its impact. For example, the way in which mathematics knowledge is organized and validated has a great influence upon a learner's interactions with those mathematics knowledge concepts in school. However, a learner's interactions with the mathematical knowledge concepts at school have little influence upon the way in which that mathematics knowledge is organized and validated. On other occasions, the link between learner and knowledge organization may be stronger. For example, a group of friends might invent a use for a word, attaching a meaning to it,

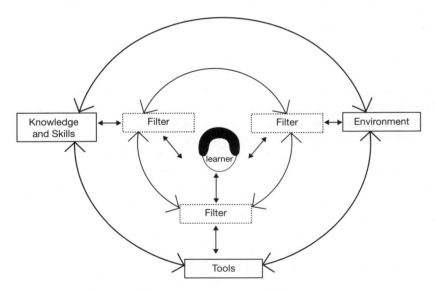

Figure 5.13 The resource elements and their filters

adopting it and imitating it, so the word becomes part of the linguistic knowledge of that group and may rapidly spread beyond.

There are also relationships and interactions between the elements that are part of the same category. There are four types of these relationships:

- *influenced by relationships* as discussed already;
- *vomponent relationships*, in which one element is part of another, such as the different components of the Tablet PC;
- *typology relationships*, in which one element is a type of another; for example, a child's bedtime is a type of home 'rule';
- *social relationships*, such as those among family members, friends or communities.

The relationship between resource elements in different circles of the Ecology of Resources model is also one of influence; in particular, the constraining influence of the filters on the availability of a particular resource element. So, for example, the relationships between the Knowledge and Skill resource element and its filter is one in which the Knowledge and Skills filter element constrains which Knowledge concepts are presented to the learner, and in what way. In return, the activity of creating a curriculum and of organizing knowledge may influence changes in the underlying knowledge concepts.

The learner's culture and history

All of the elements in any Ecology of Resources bring with them a history that defines them, as well as the part they play in the wider cultural and political system. Likewise, the individual at the centre of the Ecology of Resources has their own history of experience that impacts upon their interactions with each of the elements in the Ecology. The existence and the importance of this wider cultural perspective are discussed further in Chapter 6.

The role of the More Able Partner and the formation of a Learner-Centric Ecology of Resources

In Chapter 2, I highlighted the role that the Zone of Proximal Development (ZPD) plays in the crystallization of the internalization process. The subset of interactions that represent the Zone of Proximal *Adjustment* (ZPA) within a learner's Ecology of Resources is aimed at supporting this crystallization. The role of the MAP is of particular importance in this process: it is played by one or more of the resources with which the learner interacts within their Ecology. The MAP is responsible for working with the learner to ensure that an optimal subset of resources from the ZAA is pulled together, so that the learner's interactions with this subset of resources form a ZPA centred around the needs of the learner. The role of the MAP can be fulfilled by technology, as was the case with the Ecolab I and II software, or it can be played by a peer, supported by the technology, as was the case with the Riddles WordCat software. It may also be taken by a combination of different people and technologies, as was the case with the HOMEWORK system example.

The Learner-Centric Ecology of Resources represents the instantiation of a ZPA for a learner from amongst the ZAA identified in the Ecology of Resources model. The Ecology of Resources model can be used to describe individual learners and groups of learners as a way to understand the learning context for which technology is to be developed, deployed and/or used. However, the formation of the Learner-Centric Ecology of Resources represents the instantiation of the model for a particular learner and as such this instantiation can have only one learner at its centre. The same is true for the Zone of Proximal Development (ZPD): the concept can be applied to multiple learners, but each learner will have their own individual ZPD. I return to this subject of the learner at the centre of the Ecology of Resources in Chapter 7, when I describe the Ecology of Resources design framework.

At the start of Chapter 4, I explained that I would focus on pulling together the theoretical foundations outlined in Part 1, using the empirical foundations from my own work to explain the grounding of the Ecology of Resources model of context. I have given examples of the way in which technology can be used to scaffold learning in a variety of situations, to build up an account of the relationship of learning, technology and context. I have used the concepts of the ZAA and the ZPA to frame discussions about each of the empirical examples given and these concepts form the basis of the Ecology of Resources model. I have also framed these discussions in terms of the relationships between the learner and the systems and people that can play the role of a MAP. In particular, I have focused on the task of targeting a ZPA to meet the needs of a learner, as well as the negotiations that need to take place in order to achieve this effectively.

6 The Ecology of Resources method
Models and participatory design

After illustrating its theoretical and empirical foundations, I presented the Ecology of Resources model in Chapter 5. In this chapter, I discuss alternative models used in educational technology and computer science and position the Ecology of Resources model with respect to these. I also discuss the process of participatory design in preparation for Chapter 7, in which I present the Ecology of Resources design framework. First, I consider the meaning of the word 'model' within computer science and education and discuss the way that educational researchers interested in the use of technology apply the terms 'theory' and 'model'. I expand on my discussions in Chapters 3 and 4 about the activity of modelling within computer science with respect to learner modelling within software systems. My intention is to position the Ecology of Resources model within education and computer science rather than review or critique the different modelling approaches across the multiple disciplines where models are used. Second, I explore the type of methodology that would support using the Ecology of Resources model, including a discussion about participatory design as a method to encourage learners and teachers to find out more about the influences within and on their ecologies of resources.

The word 'model' occurs frequently in everyday and academic life: organizational model, funding model, mathematical model, data model, and object-oriented model to mention just a few common examples. The ways in which the word 'model' is used varies enormously across and within different disciplines, as does the nature of what a model represents and its relationship to reality. For example, in engineering a model might represent a replica of a physical artefact such as a bridge or housing estate. On other occasions, the word 'model' describes a smaller version of some object: a model village, aeroplane, or car, for example. The relationship of the model to reality can vary from an exact replica at a different scale to a representation that is similar enough to reality to be recognizable, but makes no claim of a closer relationship with reality than that recognition.

In the social sciences, such as psychology and education, the word 'model' is used to explain different human behaviours and processes, for example David Marr's model of visual processing or Craik and Lockhart's levels of processing model of memory. These models help explain how a process works or how something is structured, but the extent to which they claim to be an exact representation of the reality of structures and interactions in the brain varies. For example, a large body of work has arisen from the proposal of Johnson-Laird (1983), which suggested mental models as internal representations of the reality that people use to reason about the world.

This type of psychological model can also provide the basis for a computational simulation that can be 'run' to produce a resultant output. This output can represent the current state of some aspect of a particular person or process, provide insight into the process being modelled, or evaluate the usefulness of the model itself. The ACT theory of 'adaptive control of thought' (Anderson 1976, 1983), for example, attempted to combine such psychological theory building with a computational paradigm. The resultant ACT* star model underpinned one of the early intelligent tutoring systems (ITSs) and was further developed and extended into GRAPES (Anderson *et al.*, 1984) and COGNITIO (Chan, Chee & Lim, 1992).

The word 'model' is also used to describe some ideal version of a particular object, for example the model answer or model school. In this case, the model is intended to act as an example for people to aim towards. The large variety of ways of using the word 'model' and the range of models that exist as a result is far beyond the scope of this book. However, some key issues span discussions across disciplines. For example, it is possible to differentiate between models by considering the relationship between the model and what it represents in reality, the purpose for which the model is developed, and the nature of the people who will use the model.

Models in educational technology

The Ecology of Resources model is grounded in the work of Vygotsky and, in particular, in an interpretation of Vygotsky's Zone of Proximal Development. Therefore, I start by discussing the relationship between theories and models in education and technology. As identified in Chapter 2, there are many and varied theories about learning and teaching and a number of reviews have considered the relationship between educational technology, theories, and models. These offer a more detailed analysis of a fuller range of models than I will consider here (see, for example, Beetham, 2004; Dyke *et al.*, 2007; Mayes & De Freitas, 2004; Thorpe & Lea, 2002). The aim of this discussion is to identify the relationships between theories and models in education and technology and specify the nature of the relationship between the Zone of Proximal Development and Ecology of Resources model.

The terminology of theories and models is used inconsistently within educational technology literature. What some readers might consider a theory is described as a model, while some models read more like a discussion of a theory. For example, John Keller's ARCS model of motivational design (Keller, 1987) is described as both a theory and a model. Both theories and models can be thought of as abstractions that generalize away from the specific details of a situation. Is there a difference in the abstractness of educational technology theories and models? For example, are models less abstract than theories? The word 'model' can certainly be used to describe a specific instance, for example a computer-based model of a particular learner at a particular moment in time during their interactions with an ITS. The model is the software system's representation of that learner with respect to the features that the learner model is designed to represent. In that instance, the model is not abstracted away from a particular learner to learners in general; it is, however, abstracted away from the full detail of that learner and focuses only on the features that are designed to be modelled by the software system.

Conole *et al.* (2005) consider the relationship between theories and models in their work on the development of learning activities. They too note the inconsistent use of terminology and highlight the complexity of the relationship between theories, models and the development of learning activities. They suggest that the array of theories available to practitioners is confusing and that 'mediating forms of representation' are needed to help practitioners select from this confusion to create specific learning activities. The term 'mediating forms of representation' encompasses a variety of forms, including models, use cases, patterns, guidelines, case studies, and narratives. Here the word 'model' is used to denote 'an abstract representation which helps us understand something we cannot see or experience directly' (Conole *et al.*, 2005: 8). The model is a tool to help make accessible to practitioners a theory or a group of theories. The difference in the level of abstraction between theory and model is also apparent in the discussions of Conole *et al.* This is further clarified in the distinction they draw between 'theoretical positions' that are underpinned by a particular 'theoretical perspective' and that can in turn underpin more than one 'theoretical approach', which in turn can underpin more than one 'mediating form of representation'. In practice, the alignment between position, perspective, approach and mediating form is seldom simple, and consequently the same model can be aligned with different theoretical perspectives by different authors. Conole *et al.* cite as an example Laurillard's conversational model (Laurillard, 2002), which is aligned with their own situative perspective as well as with the cognitive perspective by Mayes & De Freitas (2004). I would add that these differences in the certainty with which some models can be aligned with the specified theoretical categories are also related to the closeness of the coupling between model and theory. On some occasions, the model is so tightly coupled to the theory that there can be no question as to its alignment, for example Papert's (1980) implementation of Piagetian learning theory and the creation of learning environments such as LOGO. On other occasions, a model may be associated or informed by a range of theories and, therefore, loosely coupled and open to different alignments. For example, Sharples *et al.* (2007) espoused a theory of mobile learning which was informed both by the conversational framework of Laurillard and by Engeström's activity systems theory.

By taking the distinction drawn by Conole *et al.* (2005) and applying it to the Ecology of Resources model, it might be said that (a) the Ecology of Resources model is a 'mediating form of representation' and (b) its theoretical approach is the Zone of Proximal Development, its theoretical position is sociocultural, and its theoretical perspective is social constructivist. These labels might vary a little; for example, at another level, it may be that the theoretical position is the Zone of Proximal Development and the theoretical approach is scaffolding. But it remains clear that the Ecology of Resources model is closely coupled to the Zone of Proximal Development and the work of Vygotsky, and that it could not be aligned other than with a social constructivist perspective. It is not as closely coupled to its theory as Papert's LOGO work is to the work of Piaget, but it is unquestionably an interpretation of the Zone of Proximal Development and intends to offer a translation of that theory to be used by practitioners. In this sense, it is less abstract as a model than the theory it translates.

In a similar manner to Conole *et al.*'s discussion of the difficulties faced by practitioners using educational theories to inform their development of learning activities, Fitzpatrick (2003) in the study of computer-supported collaborative work (CSCW) highlights difficulties facing designers when using models produced by social scientists. Although working in a different discipline to Conole *et al.*, she too calls for 'shared abstractions' (Fitzpatrick, 2003), which can be likened to the notion of a 'mediating form of representation'. Fitzpatrick suggests that one source of this difficulty can be found in the different ways social science and computer science communities use models. Social scientists' goals are description and analysis, whereas computer scientists aim to generate a design that can be implemented in a software system. Education modelling is more concerned with creating models that permit the description and analysis of learning and teaching interactions. In educational computer science, the concern is models that can help develop technology software systems and/or be used as the basis for representing learner behaviour or characteristics when interacting with or through technology.

The Ecology of Resources model needs to bridge the divide between the social and the technical. It needs to be able to be a descriptive mechanism that permits analysis and a generative tool to support software system design. It also needs to be represented at an appropriate level of abstraction so that it can be shared. However, unlike most models discussed by Fitzpatrick, the Ecology of Resources model relates to a particular theory of learning and as such must be capable of being translated into an accessible and appropriate form for those using it as a shared abstraction. In short, it must be an interdisciplinary tool.

Beetham (2004) adopts this concept to distinguish between different types of models. The author defines a model as 'a representation with a purpose' and suggests there are five types of models, including: (a) a 'practice' model, described as an approach to learning and teaching; (b) a 'theoretical' model, described as empirically grounded and associated explicitly with a particular theoretical perspective; and (c) a 'technical' model, described as offering a way of structuring information. The descriptive or generative nature of these model types varies, with the 'technical' model more closely aligned to computer science approaches.

Another interesting intersection between social and computer science approaches is using modelling languages as abstractions that can be shared and that support the process of design, for example pattern languages in computer science (Gamma *et al.*, 1995), learning design (Goodyear, 2005), and the unified modelling language (UML; Booch *et al.*, 2005) and its extensions used in software engineering and requirements engineering.

As discussed, it is possible to differentiate between models by considering the relationship between the model and what it represents in reality, the purpose for which the model is developed, and the identities of the people using the model. All models for developing educational technology discussed so far relate to teaching and learning, and all intend to be useful in the real world. However, few would claim to be faithful representations of reality. Within education, Brewster (2009) draws on work from the philosophy of science, especially the DDI (denotation, demonstration, interpretation) approach of Hughes (1997), to help discuss the relationship between models and reality in education. Brewster uses this approach to substantiate the critique of Laurillard's conversational framework, which Brewster describes as 'an idealized abstract representation' and suggests such models are useful for understanding how a software system operates in an ideal situation, but not for planning real world interactions. This highlights something of a conundrum for those wishing to develop models useful for producing technology-rich learning applications in the real world. How much of reality can and should we model? In some senses, an abstraction will always be idealized simply because the aim of an abstraction is to lose some of the detail and complexity of the real world. Any model that is a faithful representation of reality in all respects is impossible because it itself would be reality. The key to this conundrum might be choosing which aspects of reality to remove from the process of abstraction. However, this relates to the foci of attention of the models. I will return to the issue of planning for real world interactions when discussing participatory design later in this chapter.

Modelling the learner

Chapter 3 discussed ways in which software has developed to adapt to the needs of the learner or group of learners. Such models are implemented within the software program code and represent the designers' beliefs about what information about the learner needs to be collected and processed and what output needs to be produced to determine how the software reacts. The word 'model' is used to describe both the structure and code that exists in the software system before use and the instances when that model represents the learners who use the software system. When the word 'model' is used in relation to the empirical work discussed in this section, it refers to the structure and code that exists in the software system before use. One of the purposes of this uninstantiated version of the model is to structure the collection of data about specific learners.

The relationship of learner models to theory varies. In many cases, the types of software systems that have learner models are designed according to a particular belief about how people learn. Decisions about which features need to be included in the learner model are informed by the features of a learner that are important for that theory. The way information is captured by the learner model is processed by the software system to enable it to make a decision about its interaction with the learner and informed by the particular learning theory. For example, Vygotsky's Zone of Proximal Development has been used to inform the development of several educational software systems and learner models. The Ecolab I and II learner models (model being used here to mean the structure and code that exists in the software system before use) have resulted from an interpretation of the Zone of Proximal Development. The Quadratic tutor (Wood *et al.*, 1992) operationalized the contingent tutoring approach to scaffolding, which is another interpretation of the Zone of Proximal Development. In contrast, the Model-It system (Jackson *et al.*, 1996) was based on the scaffolding approach, but excludes a learner model that operationalizes the associated theory. In these examples, the coupling of theory to model exists to different extents. Not all learner models are based on, or informed by, a theory. Sometimes learner models are deployed merely to collect data about how a learner has used the software system. In addition to situations where the theory informs the model, it is also possible for the model to inform the theory, as is the case with grounded theory, for example.

The purpose of learner models and the detail of their intended relationship to reality vary greatly. In some cases, such as those where biometric data are used to build the learner model, the model intends to be an accurate representation of the learner's state on the measures selected. For example, the AutoTutor (http://www.autotutor.org/) is an ITS offering learners an animated agent that holds a conversation with them in their native language about scientific reasoning across a range of subjects. There are several different versions of the AutoTutor, one of which includes tracking technology for facial expressions and body posture, which is used to evaluate the learner's emotions (D'mello & Graesser, 2007). Body movement and facial expressions have also been used by Dragon *et al.* (2008) to explore the relationship between these physical behaviours and changes in emotional valence, arousal, and on-task behaviour. Other software systems have used heart rate and galvanic skin response readings to contribute to models of learner self-efficacy (McQuiggan *et al.*, 2008). Electromyography (EMG), which records the activation signal of muscles, has contributed to a model of learner emotion during interactions with an educational computer game (Conati & Maclaren, 2009), while electroencephalography has collected brainwave readings to explore the relationship between changes in brainwave activity and learner affect when completing a test (Heraz & Frasson, 2009).

In other cases, learner models can be based on a learner's own reports of their feelings at a particular moment in time (Craig *et al.*, 2004; Beal *et al.*, 2006). However, here the relationship of these data to how the learner really feels may bear little relationship to reality because the learner is unable to interpret their own feelings or does not wish to reveal the truth. Multiple data streams have also been used to combine both self-report and biometric data to build a learner model (Kapoor & Picard, 2005; Kapoor *et al.*, 2005).

Some models may strongly relate to reality for a small part of that reality but because the software system is only modelling a particular part, its relationship to reality more holistically may be poor. For example, a model may accurately reflect a learner's success in completing a set of mathematical calculations or physics problems only in a particular setting. The Andes ITS developed by Van Lehn and colleagues at the University of Pittsburgh (Van Lehn *et al.*, 1992, 2005) is a mature software system used by hundreds of university physics students. It has been through a series of evaluations since 1999 to demonstrate its efficacy. The Andes tutor focuses on the homework that students complete and replaces pencil-and-paper problem-solving homework with computer-based problems. As students complete the problems, the Andes tutor offers feedback tailored to the individual student using a model within the tutoring system software. A key component of the Andes system is a problem-solving module that generates all acceptable solutions to a problem so that it can attempt to recognize the plan used by the student. This problem-solving module has the necessary understanding of the rules of physics to solve any problem the students tackle. These rules are based on a cognitive model of knowledge acquisition that has been developed by analyzing protocols of physics students completing example problems. The Andes tutor also has an understanding of the different abstract plans an expert might use to solve such problems. All this means that when the Andes module is given an initial description of the problem and a problem-solving goal, it can produce a graph of the solution space that encompasses all acceptable solutions to the problem along with the abstract plans for generating those solutions. The Andes student model strongly relates to the reality of a particular learner's performance with particular physics problems under laboratory conditions. However, the relationship of this student model to the reality of that same student's understanding of these physics concepts as applied to other problems, or when completed under different conditions, is less strong.

Similarly, the Pump Algebra Tutor (PAT) tutor was developed by the Carnegie Mellon University Advanced Cognitive Tutor Centre. This tutor combines an ITS with a maths curriculum to help students model real-life problems using algebraic representations. The curriculum helps students draw on their existing maths knowledge as well as their common sense to solve formal maths problems. Therefore, it helps students see the relevance of their maths learning beyond the classroom. PAT maintains a cognitive model of the processes of successful and near-successful student performance instantiated as a system of if–then production rules that can generate the multiple possible solution steps that a student might take, including correct and incorrect options. The student model is created by processes of model tracing and knowledge tracing which match student actions to those generated by the software system. Like the Andes tutor, this model is used to understand how the software system will help the learner and is based on research into mathematical cognition. However, in this instance the model is designed to encompass the informal routes that a student might use to construct mathematical knowledge and is intended for use outside the laboratory. It is already used in schools in the US and Europe with considerable success in increasing test scores. The relationship of this model to reality is again strong with respect to its intention to model the cognitive processes of the students learning maths. However, the model is constrained to the particular maths problems that the software system can offer, although it does attempt to extend beyond formal maths formulations to include the informal knowledge students bring to their interactions. Both the Andes and PAT tutors are based on the ACT theory (Anderson 1976, 1983) and aim to instantiate that theory.

Learner modelling continues to evolve as researchers develop new techniques supported by increasingly sophisticated technologies. The increase in digital information available for some elements of subject content in an educational system has grown enormously and has resulted in the development of meta-tagging as a way of describing pieces of information. There has also been growth in approaches exploring ways in which pieces of information can be used as 'learning objects'. Large schemas of meta-tag descriptors have been constructed to describe these content elements and learning objects. If the descriptors are compatible, the aim is to build software systems that can access all the content elements with compatible description formats to find those most suitable for a learner or group of learners. The size of the content elements varies from a single word of text to a movie clip. This proliferation in digital content tagging has been accompanied by an increased focus on ways in which a software system's model of the learner, sometimes now referred to as their 'profile', can be constructed to match learners' needs to appropriate content elements. This work is increasingly linked to developments in the semantic web (Aroyo *et al.,* 2006; Brusilovsky & Peylo, 2003; Brusilovsky *et al.,* 2007).

In addition to this increase in the range of subject matter information available, there has also been a parallel increase in the available information about learners' behaviour with technology. The range of learner interactions with or through technology with other people can be recorded and made available for data mining techniques. This has produced a new interest in educational data mining to ensure the development of technologies capable of taking advantage of this increased information. Data mining techniques are used to build models from large data sets to make predictions, for example, about the features of particular maths problem statements that encourage learners to 'game' the software system (Baker *et al.,* 2009) or about the effectiveness of particular combinations of problem types and tutoring approaches (Feng *et al.,* 2009).

Some learner models, such as those in AutoTutor, Andes, Ecolab and PAT, are kept private from the learner, while others are open to the learner and even other people. These open learner models vary but their main aims are summarized by Bull and Kay (2008) as

> promoting learner reflection through confronting students with representations of their understanding, facilitating planning and/or monitoring of learning, facilitating collaboration or competition amongst learners, supporting navigation, the right of access to information stored about oneself, learner control over their learning, trust in the learner model content, and assessment.
>
> (pp. 7–8)

Most open learner models are part of an ITS with an underlying modelling approach. However, some simply allow the learner to view the software system's model, some allow learners to edit the model, and others allow the learner to share the model with other people. The nature of the model's relationship to reality is affected by the approach underlying the ITS; however, the ability of others to view and edit the model opens up the potential of extending the model to represent the reality of a particular learning activity for a particular learner. Kay (2009) recently proposed an important extension to this open learner model approach. Kay recognized the potential for change brought by pervasive and ubiquitous computing and offered a vision of a lifelong learner model, which is controlled by the learner but exists independently of particular applications and technologies. The author identified technical issues, such as interoperability and the huge quantities of interaction data available for analysis, as well as human concerns, such as control, privacy, and augmented cognition, as the key challenges that need to be addressed to fulfil this vision. This vision is also compatible with the Ecology of Resources model.

Learner modelling is not limited to modelling individual learners. As discussed in Chapter 3, there is enormous interest and active research in the field of computer support for collaborative learning. The work of Soller (2002, 2007) offers a computer science modelling approach to collaboration that complements the examples cited in Chapter 3. There are, however, fewer attempts to build computational models of collaboration or adaptive software systems to support collaboration.

These learner modelling examples illustrate that while the general aim of learner modelling is to develop models that are useful for building software systems to help people learn, researchers set about this task in different ways. Learner modellers attempt to represent the learner's cognition, metacognition, and emotions. They use different methods for collecting data about these aspects and different computational techniques to represent and manipulate this information. However, one common trait across all these examples is that they are designed to collect real-world data.

There is little common ground between the discussions of models in the educational technology literature and those concerned with the design of adaptive software systems, such as ITSs. In the educational technology literature discussed earlier, there is little or no mention of building computational models for learners and little or no acknowledgement of developing adaptive software systems such as ITSs and interactive learning environments. Likewise, in adaptive software system design models there is little discussion about the educational technology practice literature, learning technologists, their role, and the models that describe their practices. One community primarily helps practitioners use technology to develop technology-enhanced learning activities, whereas the other develops technologies that can contribute to helping learners learn and/or teachers teach. The Ecology of Resources model aims to appeal to both these communities.

Modelling learning and teaching interactions

When it comes to models that focus on teaching and learning interactions there is greater overlap between those who use technologies to support learning and those who build technologies to support learning. Across both communities, there is a common interest in the underlying theories of learning and teaching interactions.

From a computer science perspective, software systems that are designed to teach a particular subject need some mechanisms for making decisions about what teaching actions to adopt. Initially such teaching 'expertise' was somewhat crude and consisted of a set of rules that helped the software system decide which set of teaching tactics to use with a learner at any particular point in time. After a series of somewhat critical reviews in the 1980s (Ohlsson, 1987, for example), greater attention was placed on ways software might 'teach', including exploring ways human teachers behaved and developing software systems to model such activities (du Boulay & Luckin, 2001).

The advent of the Internet and more recently Web 2.0 technologies has influenced teaching modelling. Teaching tactics that can be generally applicable beyond a single domain. Tactics that offer support for groups of learners collaborating either face-to-face or electronically and tactics that support distance learning are now the focus of research attention, for example Salmon's e-moderating approach (Salmon, 2004) for an educator's perspective and De Bra *et al.* (2003) for a computer science view.

The representations below are frameworks rather than models and have been selected because they are recognized as mediating representations from within educational technology and computer science research. They also offer a useful comparison with the Ecology of Resources model.

Laurillard's conversational framework

Laurillard's conversational framework (1993, 2002) is widely cited within the educational technology literature. Laurillard interprets phenomenographic research on student learning and describes the teaching and learning process as essentially dialogical with the one-to-one teacher to student situation framed as the ideal. Certain characteristics are specified as necessary to the learning process, which must be:

1   discursive, with the teacher providing an environment in which they and the students agree goals and make their conceptions available to each other;
2   adaptive, with the teacher using her own conception and that of the student to specify the focus of the learning dialogue;
3   interactive, with the teacher providing meaningful feedback; and
4   reflective, with the teacher supporting the student in linking the feedback to each task action.

Laurillard is particularly concerned with higher education students and the types of knowledge their studies involve. She recognizes the distinction drawn by Vygotsky between spontaneous and scientific concepts and describes teaching as 'mediating learning', which involves constructing 'environments which afford the learning of descriptions of the world'. Communication is through symbolic representations of the world. Educational media can be classified into the discursive, adaptive, interactive, and reflective categories identified above as necessary for learning. These media can also be classified as narrative, interactive, adaptive, and communicative in line with their 'logistical properties'. In evaluating different types of educational media, Laurillard assesses each according to what they contribute to the discursive, adaptive, interactive, and reflective learning categories. Laurillard concludes that university teaching should not rely on any individual learning technology, but should balance multiple media types according to their pedagogic value. This approach is more usually known as blended learning. Laurillard's conversational framework is used as a vehicle for planning technology-enhanced learning and has been proposed as a potential 'generic framework[s] for e-learning activities' (Laurillard & McAndrew, 2002). However, it has not been widely tested, as highlighted by Brewster (2009), who suggests that the conversational framework would be improved if it depicted 'non-idealized contexts'.

The Scaffolding Design Framework

My second selected model that is cited in the education and computer science literature is the scaffolding design framework for science inquiry (Quintana *et al.*, 2004; Quintana & Fishman, 2006). This addresses the need for a theoretical framework to define the 'rationales and approaches to guide the design of scaffolded tools' (Quintana & Fishman, 2006). The aim is to provide a way of describing successful scaffolding approaches to guide the design process. The theoretical basis for this is a combination of the original work by Wood *et al.* (1976), as discussed in Chapter 2, and cognitive apprenticeship (Collins *et al.*, 1989), cognitive modelling (Anderson, 1983) and situated cognition (Lave & Wenger, 1991). The wide range of approaches to scaffolding highlighted in Chapter 3 is also acknowledged by Quintana *et al.*, who focus on the provision of scaffolding support for science inquiry activities without implementing automated fading of that scaffolding. The scaffolding design framework is based on the identification of difficulties that learners encounter, the provision of assistance by a More Able Partner (MAP), the potential for multiple MAPs to provide different types of assistance, and the provision of temporary assistance that fades away when no longer required. The framework is organized into three types of process:

- scaffolding sense making, for example through bridging learners' understanding of scientific concepts by using familiar concepts;
- scaffolding process management, for example by structuring a complex range of tasks that learners face when taking part in science inquiry activities; and
- scaffolding reflection and articulation, for example by prompting learners to articulate ideas at particular points in the inquiry process.

Quintana and Fishman (2006) also discuss the importance of supporting teachers through the science inquiry process and offer a tool called 'knowledge networks on the web' (KNOW) to provide scaffolding to teachers involved with scientific inquiry curricular. They make a similar observation to that made in Chapter 5, i.e. that software can link human and technology scaffolding activity.

The central concern of using technology to offer appropriate support for learners and teachers involved in complex learning activities transcends the scaffolding design framework and the Ecology of Resources model. There are, however, some clear differences between the scaffolding approach proposed in the scaffolding design framework and that adopted within the Ecology of Resources. The main difference relates to the emphasis within the Ecology of Resources model on MAPs, learners, and technology working together to choose the optimal resources for assisting learning. This is complemented by the emphasis on quantifying assistance to support the evaluation of learner progress to make decisions about when and how to remove assistance.

Scaffolding is one of the few theories to appear in learner modelling literature in computer science. It is also a theory that has prompted researchers to take a broader view beyond a particular educational sector, such as university students, and a particular subject area, such as science. The Ecology of Resources model aims to extend the way we think about scaffolding beyond single locations, devices, and people.

Modelling the Learner's Context

As discussed in Chapter 1, context has been discussed and modelled outside educational technology but little work has explicitly attempted to model a learner's wider context and the role of technology. Some work within the open learner modelling community has considered lifelong learner modelling (Kay, 2009), while some has considered the use of mobile technology to model mobile learning behaviour (Sharples *et al.*, 2007). However, I now return to computer science and to an example taken from the field of CSCW because it is an attempt to capture the complexity of the real world in an abstraction that can be used to support the design of technology. It is about the workplace rather than education, but acts as a useful touchstone for modelling the complexity of a learner's context.

The locales framework

The locales framework (Fitzpatrick, 2003) was motivated by the author's desire to find a way of understanding the requirements of complex social situations and design software systems to support such situations. The framework is a shared abstraction and a common language for both those who want to understand the complex social world of work and those who want to design technology support. The framework is built on the premise that designing a socially embedded system is a 'wicked problem'. Wicked problems are not clearly defined and nor do they have a definite solution; a 'good enough' solution is the realistic goal' (Fitzpatrick, 2003). There is clearly a similarity here between the locales framework and the Ecology of Resources. Fitzpatrick suggests that there is a co-evolution of problem definition and solution when wicked problems are involved and when there are no clear rules for deciding when the solution has been reached. This type of problem is common in social situations, such as learning. The aim of the locales framework is to support both the increased understanding of complex wicked problems and the system design for wicked problem solutions. The work is clearly relevant to the development of technology-rich learning environments. It is also an interesting example of increasingly common situations where taking an interdisciplinary approach is fruitful. Fitzpatrick's work is aimed largely at the CSCW community, yet it possesses clear and useful parallels to education.

Fitzpatrick's work is both theoretically grounded in other work from within CSCW and empirically grounded in Fitzpatrick's experience of system design and workplace study. It is based on a metaphor of 'place' in recognition of the way people construct 'places' through their interactions with spaces (also described as sites) and things; the resources (also described as means) through which people achieve their work. This leads Fitzpatrick to define the unit of analysis as the 'locale', which is defined as

> the place constituted in the ongoing *relationship* between people in a particular social world and the 'site and means' they use to meet their interactional needs, i.e., the space together with the resources available there, resources including whatever constitute the 'things' involved in the accomplishment of work, be they objects, artefacts, tools, features, mechanisms, and so on.
>
> (Fitzpatrick, 2003: 90)

The locales framework has two organizing principles that aim to enable its application at any level. First, centre which is defined as 'an attractor that relates together, and give sense to, the relevant people, site and means around it' (Fitzpatrick, 2003: 93). The principle of centre enables the framework to recognize the concept of a boundary effect without needing to introduce the notion of a physical boundary. Second, perspectives where everything within a social world is defined from a particular perspective. A two-phase approach to working with the locales framework is also suggested. The first phase aims at understanding the current state of the locale(s) of interest. This involves using the framework to organize and structure existing data, as a heuristic to instigate the process of collecting data, or help people articulate their own locales as part of a participatory design process. The second phase is concerned with the future and the way in which the spaces and resources of the locale(s) can be evolved. Its focus is on how the spaces and resources can support a locale and designing support that is grounded in an understanding of the interactional needs of the social world supported by the current locale. The emphasis of the locales framework is on place and work, whereas the emphasis of the Ecology of Resources is on interaction and learning. There are however, some useful similarities.

Mobile learning and context

Sharples *et al.* (2007) offer an interesting model of context to discuss a theory of mobile learning that encompasses portable technology and the mobility of people as they learn. They suggest that traditional classroom learning is built on the illusion of a stable context. However, as already highlighted in Chapter 1, the concept is not static: it must take into account the history of the learner and MAPs and recognize ongoing development and change. They suggest that mobile learning removes the fixed elements of the learner's situation that allow this classroom illusion, 'creating temporary islands of relatively stable context'. Learning is 'characterized as a process of coming to know through conversation across continually re-constructed contexts' (Sharples *et al.*, 2007: 231).

Sharples *et al.*'s model is built on the belief that learning is driven by conversation. They propose that Laurillard's conversational framework can be used more broadly with other age groups and settings. An adapted conversational framework stresses that conversations take place at the level of actions, involving the performance of an activity, and at the level of descriptions, when learners and MAPs talk about their actions to make sense of them. Sharples *et al.* state that each individual member of such conversations is located in some physical reality and, therefore, in addition to a need for the constant negotiation of the language of communication, there is also a need to constantly negotiate the context of these conversations. To this end, they propose a model of context and learning called the 'activity system of mobile learning'. This model is based on activity theory and has two layers of tool-mediated activity: the semiotic, which uses cultural mediating artefacts, and the technological, which uses devices as the mediating artefacts in a human technology system. The two layers can be considered separately, for example the semiotic in discussions about activities with educationalists and the technological in discussions about system designs with software and hardware developers. The two layers can also be superimposed 'to examine a holistic system of learning as the interaction between people and technology' (Sharples *et al.*, 2007: 232). The framework is intended to set up a continual dynamic in which the two layers move together and apart to drive analysis and develop new ways of interacting with technologies and of learning in parallel.

The Ecology of Resources model draws on learning from modelling activity within educational technology and computer science research. My aim is for it to bridge the divide between the social and the technical and be used both as a descriptive mechanism to permit analysis and as a generative tool to support system design. It represents a purpose that can be shared and interactions that make up a learner's context. It models part of a learner's reality with respect to supporting the interdisciplinary enterprise of developing technology-rich learning activities. This includes both the design and the evaluation of technologies. Therefore, it aims to support social scientists and computer scientists. The Ecology of Resources model is coupled to an interpretation of Vygotsky's Zone of Proximal Development and is learner centric. It is about identifying the complexity and interrelatedness of learner interactions.

We know little about the relationships comprising a learner's context. I hope that the Ecology of Resources model will motivate further investigation and provide the basis for a framework for further work to be conducted. The Ecology of Resources model is neither idealized nor intended to be a complete and faithful representation of the objective reality of a learner's context. Decisions about what detail to include and exclude will be motivated by the design problem under attention. The aim for those using the Ecology of Resources model should be to construct a 'good enough' representation of a learner's context that is appropriately detailed to usefully underpin the process of scaffolding learner progression.

In this chapter, I have separated my discussion of models of learners, models of the teaching and learning process, and models of the learning context. However, with respect to the Ecology of Resources model this distinction is artificial. The Ecology of Resources model provides a means to characterize a learner through the interactions that form the learner's context. It integrates learner modelling and learning context modelling in the sense that the learner is modelled with respect to the interactions that constitute their context. The extent to which we will know enough about the interactional parameters of a learner's context to develop a dynamic instantiation capable of being run in software is an open question. Presently, we can use the Ecology of Resources model as a template of a representation to be used and shared with and by learners, and that has the potential to support an open learner modelling approach.

Designing technology-rich learning

The Ecology of Resources model provides an understanding of the different resource elements and interactions contributing to a learner's context for learning. When using this model to support the design of activities and technologies to engender learning, practitioners need to be able to identify the potential forms of assistance which make up the resource elements of a learner's ecology and to explore the relationships and interactions between these elements. This requires a detailed knowledge of learners' environments and the people, tools, and subject matter they are likely to interact with. The learner and all of these resource elements will also be subject to cultural, social, and political influences that need to be encompassed in the design process. This knowledge can only be gained by using participatory design methods involving the beneficiaries of the design activity in the design process. I will develop the Ecology of Resources model into a design framework in Chapter 7. This design framework adopts an iterative and participatory methodology to capture rich information about learners' experiences and interactions necessary for the design process. In the remainder of this chapter, I will consider what participatory design is and why it is important for the Ecology of Resources model.

Involving users in design

The nature of design and the act of designing are complex. It is an enterprise engaged in by multiple disciplines across the arts and sciences and is the subject of multiple viewpoints. There is, for example, a stark contrast between the formality in engineering and industrial design (Roozenburg & Eekels, 1995, for example) and the creative individualism within certain, though not all, of the arts. Irwin (1991) provides a good account and history of this debate. There is insufficient space in this book to consider the range of opinions about what constitutes design, how design should be, and who can participate in the design process. Therefore, I will discuss the beneficiaries of the design process and consider how they can be engaged in the design process.

This book is concerned with increasing understanding about how technology can be used and developed to enrich learning by highlighting the range of interactions that make up a learner's context. It is concerned with both designing the learning activity, including the technology to be used, and designing the process through which that activity and its technology are designed. This recognition of the importance of the process is reflected in the work of, for example, the Design Council (www.designcouncil.org).

User-centred design is a widely accepted term for the collection of approaches to the design process that includes the participatory design approach that the Ecology of Resources model requires. In my discussions about design, however, I talk in terms of 'beneficiaries' and their role in design. I use the word 'beneficiaries' in preference to 'user' because I want to emphasize that the people I wish to engage with are those whose lives could be improved by the activity and/or technology being designed. They should be active participants in the design process. As highlighted in Light and Luckin (2008), the desire to move away from the word 'user' is commonplace among those wishing to engage in inclusive design processes. Indeed, the passivity and lack of agency associated with the word 'user' has sparked heated debate (Suchman, 1987; Thimbleby, 1990; Laurel, 1991). There is a wide literature of books, journals, and conference proceedings that discuss the reasons for and the methods by which the needs of beneficiaries can be incorporated into the design process (Norman & Draper, 1986; Carroll, 2002; Preece *et al.*, 2002). This body of work illustrates the two main motivations for engaging with beneficiaries. First is the business case motivation, which helps avoid disastrous outputs from the design process and tackles the evolving, changeable, hard to predict consumer environment, and second is the social motivation of developing a more egalitarian process (Light & Luckin, 2008).

The process of participatory design is difficult to define and manage. I share the view of Reymen *et al.* (2005) in believing that it is the responsibility of those with experience and training and who initiate the design process to find ways in which beneficiaries can effectively participate. The skills and experience required evolve over time with a certain recursive flavour revealing itself as the process of design fleshes out the design space that must be encompassed (Dorst, 2003). This means that a process involving beneficiaries in a real way is time consuming and requires careful communication and facilitation, motivated participants, sensitive management, and an open attitude to ownership.

An increasing amount of work on developing technologies to support learning is conducted in collaboration with a wide range of beneficiaries using a variety of participatory design methods. On the occasions when participatory design is used for developing educational applications, it is also referred to as learner-centred design. This term evolved from a series of articles in the 1990s (Soloway *et al.*, 1994) that encompassed work closely related to the field of human computer interaction and work from the user-centred design movement (Druin, 2002; Scaife & Rogers, 1999). A brief history of learner-centred design can be found in Good and Robertson (2006). The participatory or learner-centred design approaches can be used to develop software, such as Ecolab I and II, that aims to react 'intelligently' towards the learner through techniques from artificial intelligence and can be used for less adaptive applications.

The social imperative of the participatory design process and the associated desire for equality is exemplified well in projects that use such approaches with disadvantaged learners. This includes learners with profound and multiple learning disabilities who have been involved in the specification and validation of system requirements (Williams & Minnion, 2007; Williams, 2006). Work at locations such as the Rix Centre (http://www.rixcentre.org/) has developed techniques such as 'Talking Mat' interviews. These use symbols and drawings to capture the views of learners and have contributed to the development of a personalized learning environment for people with learning disabilities (http://www.rixcentre. org/appleproject/index.htm). Disadvantages can sometimes be social rather than physical or psychological and once again participatory design approaches have been used to capture aspects of a learner's wider world within the design of technology. For example, work in UK online centres has indicated a clear role for participatory methods and resulted in the community development model of learning (Garnett & Cook, 2004). Day & Farenden (2007) and Day (2008) have also demonstrated the benefits of using participatory design to develop community engagement and emphasize that it takes a great deal more than simply finding ways of engaging in dialogue with the community.

Increasingly, technology can expand our understanding of the world, for example by scientists building a clearer picture of issues such as climate change and biodiversity and those who see the potential of e-science to support learning such as Woodgate and Stanton-Fraser (2005) and Underwood *et al.* (2008). Technology can, for example, support scientific inquiry activities that are interdisciplinary, collaborative and inherently participative. This increased possibility for the participation of multiple people in generating scientific data also offers the possibility of more people becoming involved in designing ways for technology to help people learn more about science (Bugscope, http:// bugscope.beckman.illinois.edu/, for example). The benefits of the participatory design approach include motivating people to get involved in contributing to and learning about science. The pace of technology change and the potential this affords for beneficiaries to adapt technologies to meet their needs can be seen in developments commonly referred to as Web 2.0. The term is used here to refer to the way the Internet supports social activity and new forms of user involvement and participation. Web 2.0 technologies enable beneficiaries to take greater control of the way they use technology and how those technologies develop. These technological developments enable beneficiaries to participate in creating content and tools for learning.

The Ecology of Resources model recognizes that learners and those who work with them bring a personal history that defines them and the part they play in the wider cultural and political system. The role of participatory design methods is to support the capture of these influences in the design process. The increasing development of technologies that can be part of, or even embedded into, a learner's broader environment offers opportunities to collect new sources of data to increase our understanding of the range of interactions that make up a learner's context, which subsequently feed into the participatory design process. A well-designed participatory process can take advantage of these new opportunities for data collection and use them to influence both future technology design and the purpose it intends to fulfil. In the next chapter, I present a design framework that uses the Ecology of Resources and participatory design methods to guide the development of learning activities and technology.

7 The Ecology of Resources design framework

In Chapter 5, I presented the Ecology of Resources as a way of characterizing a learner in terms of the interactions that form a learner's context. It offers an interpretation of Vygotsky's theory in the form of an abstract representation that can be shared by practitioners, technologists and beneficiaries as they explore the potential learning benefits afforded by the wide range of available resources, in particular technologies. It represents the learner holistically with respect to the interactions that make up their context.

The model is based upon identifying the forms of assistance available to a learner that make up the resource elements with which that learner interacts. The identification of these resource elements enables us to recognize a learner's ZAA and in particular the resources that may play the role of the learner's More Able Partner (MAP). The Ecology of Resources model introduces the concept of filters as elements that can influence the availability of some of the resources within a learner's Zone of Available Assistance (ZAA). These filters may need to be given special consideration by learners and those playing the role of a learner's MAP, and therefore they need special consideration in the design process. Once we have identified a learner's ZAA and their potential MAPs we are in a position to explore how the learner and their MAPs can work together to select and shape the subset of the ZAA that will form the elements with which they will interact in the formation of their Zone of Proximal Adjustment (ZPA). During this process of identifying the learner's ZAA and their potential MAPs, the role that technology might play can also be identified.

The Ecology of Resources model could be viewed statically as merely a snapshot of the set of elements that describe a learner's ZAA and that can be 'optimized' by design and/or by practice. The model can also be seen, however, as the basis for a dynamic process of instigating and maintaining learning interactions in technology-rich environments. The objective of the framework presented in this chapter is to support the dynamic process of developing technology-rich learning activities. The aim of the Ecology of Resources framework is to map out the complexity of this design process so that it can be conducted with an enhanced awareness of the complex nature of the learner's context. This does not mean that the entire complexity can be taken into account within the process, but that a greater understanding of the complexity enables the process, and the resultant technology-rich learning activities, to be more effectively situated. In particular, the design process supported by the Ecology of Resources framework will identify the ways in which technology, people and the learners themselves can best support learning.

I describe the people using the framework as a design team but it may well be that those who wish to use the Ecology of Resources framework do not see themselves as a design team per se. My use of the word team is not meant to suggest that design skills are essential; it is used merely as a collective way of describing the different types of people who might find the Ecology of Resources framework a useful tool. It also highlights the expectation that users and beneficiaries will be involved in the design process. Within the Ecology of Resources approach there is also an assumption that the design team wish to engage users and beneficiaries in a participatory design process that will be iterative, with cycles of design evaluation using increasingly sophisticated versions of activities and technologies. If the Ecology of Resources approach, by which I mean the Ecology of Resources model and its associated design framework, is to be useful to a design team, the overarching aim of their design process must be to engage with the learner's context as part of the design process.

In my description of the design framework that follows I use the Homework project that I described in Chapter 5 as an example. The use of the Homework project for this example enables the descriptions of each phase in the design process to be based on real data. At the end of the chapter I describe a further case study as a contrasting illustration. These examples are by no means exhaustive; they merely scratch the surface of possible ways in which the approach might be deployed. Examples of design problems might include the development of:

- A particular technology: a piece of software or hardware. In this example, the role of the Ecology of Resources design framework could be to develop a functional specification for the technology based on the particular relationships within a learner's Ecology that need to be supported. The desire to build an interface to support collaborative learning as part of the Riddles Project is an example of this type of problem.
- Ways in which a range of technologies might be used together, which might for example involve developing the software infrastructure to support this use. In this example, the role of the Ecology of Resources design framework could be to develop a clearer picture of the way that learners use the different technologies to interact with a variety of people across multiple locations and how the technologies might most usefully interact with each other. The Homework project is an example of this situation.
- A single activity, or indeed a course of study in which technology is to be used, but there is no intention to develop the technologies themselves, rather to decide which technologies to use and when to use them. In this example, the role of the Ecology of Resources design framework could be to support decisions about what role technology might play in this learning activity. The South Downs Learning Centre project, which forms

the case study at the end of this chapter, is an example of this type of design problem.
- A learning activity with a focus on a particular community, subject or exhibit. In this example, the role of the Ecology of Resources design framework could be to develop a clearer understanding of the people who are likely to take part in the activity or visit the exhibit.

As part of these design activities we also need to consider the resources that learners bring to their interactions. By this I mean the cognitive, affective and physical capacities and capabilities of a learner. I include this within my discussion of the framework below. In the third and final section of the book I also revisit this issue of the learner's resources and how they can be developed for best support of learning in our technology-rich world.

The learner at the centre of the ecology

By definition a Learner-Centric Ecology of Resources can have only one learner at its centre. The characterization at the heart of the Ecology of Resources model can of course be applied to any learner, however, and could be considered in terms of a prototypical learner or a particular category of learners whose resource elements and potential interactions will be identified through the participatory design process. The Ecology of Resources as a model only becomes centred on a particular learner once that learner engages in the activity that is the subject of the design process. This can be likened to the way in which a software learner model can be designed to include particular parameters and characteristics about a learner. The model only becomes a model of a particular learner once these parameters and characteristics have been instantiated with values that relate to that particular learner. This is not to say that a learner's interactions as identified through the Ecology of Resources approach did not exist before the design process was applied, but merely that their representation in the Ecology of Resources model did not exist.

Collaboration is at the heart of the Ecology of Resources model, in particular the collaboration between a learner and a MAP. There may however be many others with whom the learner interacts, perhaps as part of a group or community. Indeed, without the existence of the other resources with which that learner interacts there would be no Ecology of Resources, and many of these resources can of course be other people. If the situation that is the subject of the design is for a group of learners, then it may be that, for the purposes of design, the Ecology of Resources model for each learner is remarkably similar. It is still the case, however, that each individual group member will have their own individual experiences and it is this that is represented in the learner-centredness of the Ecology of Resources approach.

The Ecology of Resources design framework

The Ecology of Resources framework offers a structured process based upon the Ecology of Resources model of context, through which educators and technologists can develop technologies and technology-rich learning activities that take a learner's wider context into account. The process is iterative and has three phases, each of which has several steps. Each phase and step is intended to be completed as a collaboration between beneficiaries and designers through a participatory design process. The purpose of each of the phases is briefly introduced here and each phase is then discussed in more detail.

1 Phase 1: Create an Ecology of Resources model to identify and organize the potential forms of assistance that can act as resources for learning.
2 Phase 2: Identify the relationships within and between the resources produced in Phase 1. Identify the extent to which these relationships meet a learner's needs and how they might be optimized with respect to that learner.
3 Phase 3: Develop the scaffolds and adjustments to support learning and enable the negotiation of a ZPA for a learner.

The Ecology of Resources approach is not prescriptive about the exact manner in which these iterations are completed, how many iterations are needed, or exactly how the users and beneficiaries should be engaged. One design need may require particular attention to the early steps in the design process, and several iterations that focus only on the early steps of Phase 1. This might be the case when little is already known about the learners, for example. On other occasions, when the participatory design team is well established and much is already known about the learners, then the early phases and steps may be negotiated relatively quickly.

Phase 1 Creating an Ecology of Resources model

The Ecology of Resources model as described at the end of Chapter 5 draws attention to different categories of resource element and identifies the existence of filter elements to highlight where and how the learner's interactions with an element are constrained. The purpose of Phase 1 of the design process is to construct an Ecology of Resources model representation for a particular design need. The seven steps within Phase 1 each contribute to this enterprise.

Step 1 – Brainstorm the potential resources in an Ecology of Resources

The starting-point for the design process and for this design step is that there is a design problem that can be seen in terms of a learning need. This might, for example, be a concern to develop some learning activities that will use technology appropriately to increase people's knowledge of everyday French so that they can converse on holiday, or it might be a concern to develop some technology to support the teaching and learning of numeracy amongst 5–7-year-olds, as was the case for the Homework project team. Different design teams will enter the process with more or less well-formulated design needs and Step 1 makes no assumptions about the extent to which the design need is well formulated. Design teams whose design need is already well formulated may well progress through the early steps more rapidly.

The objective of Step 1 is to identify the potential forms of assistance that might be available to the learners who are to be the beneficiaries of the design process. These will form the resource elements in the outer circle of the Ecology of Resources model and will form an initial specification of the learner's potential ZAA. In this step there is no requirement to divide these resources into the categories of Knowledge and Skills, Tools and People, and Environment. These categories can, however, act as a useful guide when one is trying to identify as many forms of assistance as possible. I use the Homework project as an example throughout this description of the design framework and in Step 1 the list of possible resources would include the following:

> Numeracy concepts, UK curriculum, Weight, Mass, Learner's peers, Learner's family, Books, Paper, Teacher, Teaching assistant, Pens and pencils, Calculator, Time, Classroom, Posters on the wall of the classroom, Scales, Textbooks, Interactive resources, School, Home, School library, Community library, After/before school club, Garden, Car, Satellite, TV, TV set-top box, TV programme, Interactive whiteboard, Home computer, Home Internet, Gaming device

Step 2 – Specifying the focus of attention

First attempts at Step 1 are likely to lead to many possible resource elements and decisions needing to be made about which ones the design team should focus on. Deciding upon the focus of attention for the design activity helps to restrict and focus the design process. For example, in the Homework project, the design need was helping teachers to produce multimedia lessons and linking learning in and out of school. The initial thought was that this would be delivered by interactive TV technology. Other known constraints may also be introduced at this step. In the Homework example, we knew that we would be using digital content from a popular TV series called *Number Crew* and that we would be developing additional content as needed.

There are two reasons for not making the focus of attention Step 1 in the framework. The first is to ensure that at least in the first iteration of the design process consideration is given to as broad a view as possible of the learners' Ecology of Resources. This may be particularly important in engaging beneficiaries in the design process for the first time. It also means that for future iterations in the design process there already exists a wider set of elements that the team may subsequently decide to include. The second reason is to deal with the possibility of multiple foci of attention. It may be, for example, that the design team wants to focus on two different communities of learners or two different subject areas, but wishes to see them as part of the same overall enterprise. Alternatively, it may be that there has to be some prioritization of a particular focus for the current iteration of design. In either case the different foci of attention need to be linked and to draw upon subsets of the same Ecology of Resources. It may be helpful to think of these different foci as different facets in the Ecology of Resources representation.

The output from this design step will be to prune the resource elements identified in Step 1 as the learners' potential ZAA. In the Homework example this would mean pruning the list and excluding, for example:

> Scales, Textbooks, School library, Community library, After/before school club.

It may also be possible to add some new resources to the list, for example:

> *Number Crew* TV programmes, *Number Crew* CD-ROM activities.

In later iterations of the design process further resources can be weeded out and others introduced. For example, the following technologies were all weeded out in later design iterations of the Homework project:

> Satellite, TV, TV set-top box, TV programme, Home computer, Home Internet, Gaming device

and these were added:

> Tablet PC, Wireless classroom network.

Step 3 – Categorize the resource elements

Steps 1 and 2 will have produced a list of potential forms of assistance that are appropriate resource elements for the particular focus of attention identified by the design team. The objective of this step is to complete an initial categorization of the forms of assistance into the resource category elements of: Knowledge and Skills, Tools and People, and Environment. The categories offer a useful way of thinking about the resources with which a learner may interact and the potential assistance that these resources may offer. It is the *role* that a particular element plays that is important, and that can help in making decisions about the nature of the category to which an element belongs for the purposes of development and discussion. This categorization process helps to expose the relationships between resource elements and filters and may also result in some changes to the forms of assistance previously identified. In the Homework example, an initial model at this phase is illustrated in Figure 7.1.

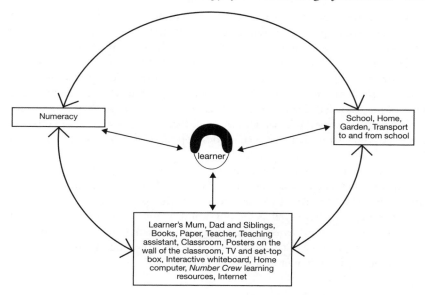

Figure 7.1 An early design iteration of an Ecology of Resources model for the Homework project

Step 4 – Identify potential resource filters

At Step 4 in the design process the question to be addressed is: what, or who, might constrain a learner's access to the resources identified so far? It is important to stress that filtering is not necessarily negative. In the Homework project, it can, for example, be extremely important that the manner in which the number concepts are introduced to learners is organized in some way that has been informed by our understanding about how these concepts are learnt: learning about addition before multiplication, for example. The filters are also important for the design process: if the filter is restricting access to a form of assistance in a negative way then the design process can try to ameliorate that. Alternatively, if the filter is not restricting access and the learner is overwhelmed, then the design process may need to adjust and strengthen the filter. The design process might, for example, address the manner in which a filter can be altered through the role of the MAP and through the way that the technology is introduced, used and designed. At this stage it may be that some of the items identified at Step 1 as potential resource elements are in fact filters. For example, 'time' was identified at Step 1 for the Homework example. This could have referred to learning about telling the time, or it could refer to the time available for a learning activity to be completed. In both cases 'time' might be categorized as a resource element. It is more likely, however, that time will also act as a filter that constrains the availability of resources, and that it will always need to be included as such at some stage in the design process.

In the Homework example the organization of number concepts within the UK curriculum (see http://curriculum.qcda.gov.uk/), the manner in which numeracy knowledge is assessed and the prevalent trends in thinking about how mathematics is best taught are all likely to form a filter for the number concepts to be learnt. This particular filter will also influence the manner in which the teacher and the teaching assistant interact with these numeracy concepts. It is therefore a generic filter of the Knowledge and Skills resource category. This filter can manifest itself, for example, in the way in which books and software have been organized and designed, the lesson plans the teacher develops and the homework that children are set.

The filter element for the Tools and People category in the Homework example will include: family and social norms and relationships at home, and the way that the teacher manages access to the interactive whiteboard, and other computing resources in the class, as well as the physical proximity of a tool to a learner. The filter elements for the Environment category will include: the school timetable, rules, distance, room allocation, and the 'rules' of the household at home, such as bedtimes and where work can be done.

Step 5 – Identify the learner's resources

In the same way that the world in which learners interact offers many forms of assistance that can act as resources for learning, the learners themselves will bring a variety of resources to their learning interactions. These resources will influence the nature of the interactions that learners have with the world. Learning within the Ecology of Resources framework requires the internalization of learners' interactions in the world. This internalization will involve the resources that are already part of the learner's knowledge and skill repertoire as well as the learner's physical attributes and their past experience. It is these types of learner resource that we need to identify in Step 5. The range of potential learner resources is vast, and could, for example, include the learner's linguistic competence, existing knowledge of a subject, confidence, comfort with the environment, metacognitive awareness, and visual acuity.

Those readers familiar with learner modelling may like to compare this part of the process with the decisions they make about what aspects of the learner to model. The sociocultural grounding of the Ecology of Resources means that in all instances the social interactions between learner and others are of concern. In the Homework example, our primary concern was also cognitive with respect to learners' knowledge and understanding of numeracy concepts. It was therefore these resources with which we were primarily concerned. The learner resources that were of interest in the Homework project included: Mathematics current attainment level, Reading age, Confidence, and Collaborative skills. The full detail of the data recorded in the learner model for the Homework system can be found in Luckin *et al.* (2006).

If by contrast we had been exploring the design of an activity to support physical education, then the physical skills resource repertoire of learners would be of particular interest. I return again to the subject of the learner's resources in the third and final section of the book.

Step 6 – Identify potential More Able Partners

Step 6 involves clarifying which of the resources already identified are potential MAPs for the learner and are therefore resources that can help in the negotiation, maintenance and development of the learner's ZPA. It is important to consider as wide a range of resources as possible here, as there can be many. It is also important to note that there may be a lack of suitable MAPs, a gap that may indicate a potential role for technology. In the Homework example a variety of resources can be identified: human, physical and digital. It is likely that family members and school staff may all play the role of MAP at one point or another. Technology too can also play that role at times, for example through software that is designed to offer scaffolding interventions. If, as in the Homework example, more than one resource is identified as a potential MAP, then the overall design enterprise will need to consider how the interactions between individual MAP resources can be supported and made coherent with respect to the learner. Here again there may be a clear role for technology in supporting communication between different MAP resources and offering a shared representation of the learner's progress. The completed activities on the Homework tablet offer an example of such a shared representation, a representation that might also be enhanced through commentary from learners and MAPs. For each potential MAP that is identified, the following characteristics also need to be identified:

- The extent to which a resource is likely to be aware that they are a MAP for the learner and consciously to opt into this role or to be content to be explicitly allocated this role. This is described in Table 7.1 as an explicit or an implicit MAP.
- The nature of the MAPs' relationships with the learner and the known constraints on their interactions with the learner. These constraints are additional to those that may already have been identified within the Tools and People filter of the Ecology of Resources.
- The resources the MAPs may bring to their interactions with the learner that are of particular relevance for the focus of attention of the design process.

In the Homework project the MAPs that can be identified would include those illustrated in Table 7.1.

There is the added issue of the extent to which the learner is aware that someone or something might potentially act in the role of a MAP and be a source from which assistance can be sought. The existence of a potential MAP may need to be pointed out to a learner; this may be another role that can usefully be performed by technology.

Table 7.1 Potential MAPs in the Homework project

Name	Explicit/ Implicit MAP	Relationship and Constraints	Resources
Parent	Explicit	Frequent, informal interactions constrained to time out of school	High familiarity with learner; Social skills; Numeracy knowledge and skills
Friend	Implicit	Frequent or infrequent interactions, constrained by others, such as teacher or parent	Some familiarity with learner; Some numeracy knowledge and skills
Teacher	Explicit	Frequent, formal interactions constrained to time at school	Some familiarity with learner; Social skills; Numeracy knowledge and skills
Technology	Explicit	Frequent interactions if personal to the learner constrained by power and access	Numeracy activities Information storage and retrieval Visualization Communication functions

Step 7 – Iterate through Steps 1–6

The possible elements of the learners' Ecology of Resources have been identified through Steps 1–6 of Phase 1 and restricted to those that are relevant for the current design focus of attention. These elements now need to be described in greater detail so that the extent to which they may or may not act as forms of assistance for learners can be assessed and the appropriate adjustments and scaffolding interventions can be designed. It is important that these descriptions are produced in a form that is accessible to all those who are part of the participatory design process, both to support the design process itself and for possible later use by learners and MAPs during the learning activity.

Phase 2 Identify the relationships within and between the resources and filters of the Ecology of Resources produced in Step 1

Identifying the elements that make up the resources and filters of the Ecology of Resources is important. It is, however, the relationships and interactions between resource elements and between learner and resource elements that are the key to the design process. The activities and technologies being developed through the design process need to support the optimization of these interactions. It is therefore to these relationships that we pay particular attention here. These relationships are complex. Each category of resource element, and therefore each element in that category, is potentially related to every other element, as well as to the learner. As described in Chapter 5, the nature of the relationship represented by the arrows in the Ecology of Resources model is one of influence. One element influences a second and that second element is influenced by the first. There are also relationships between the elements that are part of the same category. These relationships are of four types:

- influence relationships as already discussed;
- component relationships in which one element is part of another;
- typology relationships in which one element is a type of another;
- social relationships such as that between family members, friends or communities.

The creation of the Ecology of Resources model representation as part of a particular design process requires the identification of the elements, their categories and the relationships between and within the element categories. For example, if we look at the Homework project we can develop an initial representation of the different resource elements as illustrated in Table 7.2. This is not an exhaustive representation, but rather a starting-point for further elaboration in subsequent iterations of the design process. A subset of this model is illustrated in Figure 7.2.

As explained earlier, the relationship between the different resource elements of the model is one of influence. For example, starting with the elements in the same outer circle of the representation the Numeracy concepts studied influence the resources that are selected. The manner in which the teacher 'filters' the resources available to the learner through their selection of which resources they load onto the learner's Tablet PC is influenced by the addition components of the curriculum and this will 'filter' or influence the way that the teacher selects content and sets homework. The manner in which the home is organized 'filters' the learners' access to its resources and constrains the length of their interactions with the tablet and therefore the length of time that these numeracy activities might be engaged with at home. The relationship between resource elements on different circles of the representation is also one of influence, in particular the constraining influence of the filter elements on resource elements.

The example so far is still rather abstract and is described at a high level of granularity. This would be appropriate for the initial iterations of design, but as work progresses the level of granularity will become more fine-grained. I therefore also include such an example in Table 7.3. This is taken from the family story case study described in Chapter 5 and looks in particular at the Ecology of Resources for Alison on 4 May as described in this excerpt:

> On Wednesday 4 May the Homework Tablets come home again and there are some new homework activities: '10p in Different Ways', 'Double Ice Creams' and 'Numbers in Your Home', which uses the Tablet camera. Alison spends just over 35 minutes at about 6 pm working at the lounge table with her sisters and Mum. They begin with the '10p in Different Ways' homework sheet, which takes about 10 minutes. They then move onto the 'Numbers in Your Home' homework

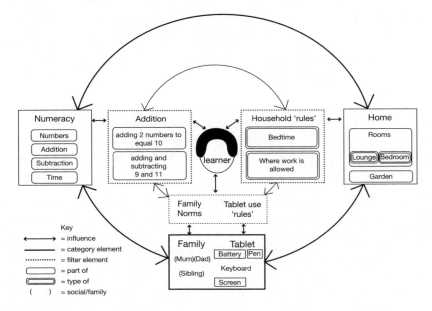

Figure 7.2 Excerpt from the Ecology of Resources model for Homework

activity and spend about 15 minutes doing this. Mum says Alison's camera worked well at capturing the family dartboard and that they managed to use the touchpad fine.

Decisions about granularity are not prescribed in the framework and will depend upon the purpose and iteration of the design activity.

Phase 3 Developing the scaffolds and adjustments

In many ways Phases 1 and 2 of the framework represent the journey from a state of knowing little about a learning design need to being able to map out the elements and interactions of a learner's ZAA. This process is useful in its own right. In order to support learners and MAPs in their negotiation and shaping of a ZPA, however, the relationships identified in Phase 2 need to be explored to identify opportunities for adjustments and scaffolding to support the interactions of the learner's ZPA. The process continues the iterative approach of Phases 1 and 2 and will involve the design team in both the fine-grained analysis of the details of a particular element and interaction, and also the consideration of how this particular element and interaction fits into the totality of the learner's Ecology of Resources. Once Phase 3 is completed for the first time, the design process may well begin again at Phase 1 until the design team believe that they have achieved their objectives. At each Phase in the design process a role for technology may be identified. It is likely, however, that in Phase 3 this will be of particular

Table 7.2 Phase 2 Homework Ecology of Resources

Resource Element	Filter Element
Knowledge Numeracy The *component* parts of numeracy knowledge include the following: – Counting – Addition – Subtraction	Filter: Curriculum UK National Curriculum at KS 1 and 2 The *component* parts of this curriculum include the following: – adding 2 numbers to equal 10 – adding or subtracting the numbers 9 and 11
Influences	*Influences*
Tools and People The *types* of resource include: – Human Resources – *types* might include: School Staff, Friends and Family. School Staff *components* might be Teacher, Teaching Assistant. Friends and Family *components* might include: Mum, Dad, Sibling – Physical Resources – *types* of physical resource include: Paper, Pen and Homework Tablet PC-Constituent parts of the Tablet PC – Digital Resources – *types* of digital resources include: *Number Crew* Activities, *Number Crew* Videos, Homework Activities One Human Resource might also *influence* another.	Filter: Administration The *types* of administration of Human Resources include: Contracts of employment with working hours and contact time. Family and *social* norms and relationships The *types* of administration of Physical Resources include: Classroom and/or home systems. In the class the teacher will constrain access, at home parents may do likewise The *types* of administration of Digital Resources include: the software on the Tablet, the selection of content made by the design team, and by the teacher
Influences	*Influences*
Environment The *component* parts of the environment may include: – School The *component* parts of the school may include: Classroom, Library, – Home The *component* parts of the Home may include: Rooms, Garden, Objects The different *types* of Room may include: Dining Room, Bedroom – Between Home and School The different *type* of environment may include: Sports Ground, Library	Filter: Organization The *types* of constraint on the school environment may include; Timetable, school rules, room allocation The *types* of constraint on the home environment may include: The 'rules' of the household, such as bedtimes, where work can be done The *types* of constraint on the between home and school may include: The 'rules' of a club or the library

Table 7.3 Phase 2 Homework Ecology of Resources detailed example

Resource Element	Filter Element
Knowledge Numeracy The *component* parts of numeracy knowledge include the following: – Counting – Addition – Subtraction	**Filter: Curriculum** The *component* parts of the curriculum for this week include: Solve numerical problems by recognizing simple patterns or relationships, generalizing and making predictions Understand the relationship between addition and subtraction, using number bonds to ten
Influences	*Influences*
Resources – The *types* of resource include: – Human Resources – *types* include: Family – types of Family include: Mum and Siblings. School Staff – *types* include Teacher, Teaching Assistant, Parent Helper – Physical Resources – *types* of physical resource include: Homework Tablet PC – Constituent parts of the Tablet PC include: Camera and Touchpad. Dartboard – Digital Resources – *types* of digital resources include: Homework Activities: Numbers in your home, *Number Crew* 10p in Different Ways, Double Ice Creams, Picture of Dartboard	**Filter: Administration** The *types* of administration of Human Resources include: Family and *social* norms and relationships The *types* of administration of Physical Resources include: 'rules' of the home The *types* of administration of Digital Resources include: The software on the Tablet, the selection of content made by the teacher for this particular learner
Influences	*Influences*
Environment The *component* parts of the environment include: – Home The component parts of the Home include: Rooms and Objects The types of Room include: Lounge The types of Object include: Table (lounge) Dartboard	**Filter: Organization** The *types* of constraint on the home environment may include: The 'rules' of the household, such as bedtimes and where work can be done

The *influences* labels appear between the columns: *influences*, *influences*, *influences*.

relevance, when decisions need to be made about how any identified adjustment and scaffolding are to be affected.

Both the term 'adjustment' and the term 'scaffold' refer to the identification of ways of supporting a learner's interactions and both are intended to engender learning. At the end of Chapter 3 I clarified scaffolding as involving the evaluation of learner need, the provision of assistance and the withdrawal of that assistance in order to engender learner development. It requires a quantification of the quality and/or quantity of assistance that is offered to a learner. Quantification is required in order for assessments to be made about when and how much assistance to remove during fading. It also provides a way of describing a learner's collaborative capability in terms of what the learner can do with a particular specification of assistance. In this way, a learner's development can be tracked through the patterns of assistance that they use.

This interpretation of scaffolding requires that the MAP resources have the ability to provide and fade different qualities and quantities of assistance for a learner, according to their perception of learner needs. The decision to provide or remove a particular type of assistance might be made by technology, as was the case with the Ecolab software. Such decisions would be based upon a model of the learner's understanding. These decisions could also be reached through negotiation between MAP resources, which may include both technology and human partners. This negotiation could also include the learner and be based upon information maintained by the technology about the learner's interactions. The MAP might also make decisions alone. The Ecology of Resource design framework does not specify by whom or how the scaffolding should be provided. What it does specify is that the term 'scaffold' only refers to forms of assistance that can be quantified in some way, and that can be provided and faded according to a perception of what the learner needs. The perception of what the learner needs may be maintained by the technology, by a combination of technology and people, or by people alone.

Let us look at the Homework project as an example. The relationship between the content on the Tablet PC and the learner is important, as it is linked to both the classroom and the out-of-school environment. The teacher 'filters' the manner in which the learner has access to the Tablet PC and the resources it contains in the classroom. S/he also has a role as a MAP for the learner and it was this relationship that the design team aimed to support. The system maintained a model of the learner that was designed to be used to select appropriate activities and assistance for each learner and their family. This involved suggestions being made by the system to the teacher when they were lesson planning and the system and the teacher working together to decide what should be allocated to an individual learner's Tablet PC.

The term 'adjust' is used to refer to the ways in which the relationships between and within the elements identified in the Ecology of Resources model in Phase 2 might be adjusted in support of the learner. For example, in the Homework situation the relationship between school staff and family members, in particular parents, was viewed as a relationship that was in need of strengthening, being currently filtered by the school day, timetabling and accepted practices about how and when teachers and parents talked about a learner's progress. One of the ways in which this need was addressed was through the introduction of a messaging tool on the Tablet. This facility strengthened the relationship between teacher and parent, messages could be linked to the activities on the Tablet PC and past messages could be stored as part of the history of a learner's interactions. It did not however offer support that could be quantified and faded, and was not therefore categorized as scaffolding.

When we consider scaffolds and adjustment, it is useful to examine the manner in which the tabulated representations of the Ecology of Resources as illustrated in Tables 7.2 and 7.3 can be combined with the Learner resources. An illustration of an extract from such a representation is contained in Table 7.4. This encourages the design team to consider the filters from both the perspective of the resource elements and from the perspective of the learner's resources. It also highlights that all adjustments and scaffolding need to be made with reference to the needs of the learner and their resources as identified in Phase 2.

The goal of the design process in this step is to identify the possible ways in which adjustments and scaffolds might be developed. It will, however, be only when the learner is interacting with the different resource elements of their context that the scaffolding will actually be invoked. A useful comparison can be drawn at this point with the early Ecolab software. The system was built so that the environment could be adjusted in a variety of ways, through different phases of complexity for example, and through the provision of different levels of help. It was, however, only when a learner was interacting with the software that the precise selection from amongst these potential scaffolds and adjustments was made, on the basis of that learner's needs at that time.

At the end of design Phase 3 each of the interactions within the Ecology of Resources model developed over Phases 1 and 2 will have been explored to evaluate the extent to which it needs any adjustment or scaffolding. Decisions will also need to be made about the quantification of these adjustments and scaffolding.

There are seven types of interaction that might be the subject of adjustment or scaffolding. The design team should consider each of these.

Type 1 – Scaffolding and adjustment of learner: resource element interaction

Type 1 scaffolding and adjustment are concerned with the filter elements that have been identified through Phase 1. These require attention to assess the extent to which these filters appropriately constrain the access that both learner and MAP will have to the rest of their Ecology of Resources. In the Homework project example, a great deal of early design attention was paid to the environment filter element with respect to the home context. The Homework team worked with families to explore the manner in which the activities that could be provided through the Tablet PC might best fit into existing family and home structures. The team also considered the way in which the design of the activities and technology might enable the extension of the existing structures. For example, families reported that the majority of homework and home learning activities were conducted at a table away from the TV and in shared family space. The manner in which the activities for use at home were provided on the Homework Tablet offered the opportunity for activities to be conducted in different locations both in and out of the home, as and when required.

Table 7.4 Resource elements, filters and learner resources

Resource Element	Filter Element	Learner Resource
Knowledge Numeracy: Counting Addition Subtraction	*influences*	Filter: Curriculum Understand the relationship between addition and subtraction, using number bonds to ten	*influences*	Maths current attainment level
Influences	*Influences*	*Influences*
Resources Mum and Siblings	*influences*	Filter: Administration Family and social norms and relationships	*influences*	Confidence level
Influences	*Influences*	*Influences*
Environment Lounge The types of Object include: Table (lounge) Dartboard	*influences*	Filter: Organization The 'rules' of the household, such as bedtimes and where work can be done	*influences*	Reasoning skills

Type 2 – Scaffolding and adjustment of learner: MAP

Type 2 scaffolding and adjustment concerns the relationships between learner and MAPs. The grounding of the Ecology of Resources model in the ZPD means that it embodies a particular view about the relationship between the learner and those performing the role of the MAP. As has already been identified (page 22), the desired relationship between learners and MAP is described nicely by the Russian term '*obuchenie*', a single word that characterizes interactions in the ZPD. I have talked above in terms of the learner and their MAP in order to offer an open definition of the extent to which the MAP is leading the interaction at any one time. At the start of the relationship between learner and MAP it is likely that the MAP will take the lead, but as the relationship develops the learner may take a greater lead, depending of course on age and capability. In some situations, the MAP will be guiding the learner throughout; in others guidance will be more bi-directional. The learner and their MAP may take the lead in interactions with respect to different elements of the learner's context. It may be, for example, that the learner knows more about how to use a particular technology resource than the MAP, whereas the MAP knows more about the subject matter knowledge to be learnt. In this situation, the roles of learner and MAP will change between participants during the development of the relationship. This illustrates the fact that, even in a short interaction, being in the role of a learner or a MAP can change several times. For learning to have taken place it is of course important that the person who was in the role of learner at the start of the episode is receiving less guidance about that episode's task from the person and/or technology in the MAP role.

I have found that the steps described in Table 7.5 are useful in guiding consideration of the learner's interactions with the MAP. These are the interactions for which adjustments and scaffolding may need to be designed and provided.

It should be noted that the representation described in Step 1 in Table 7.5 is an interpretation of the shared situation definition concept of Wertsch (1984), and that clarifying Steps 1 and 2 may require a full iteration from Steps 1–7. If, however, learner and MAP have previously interacted, this process may be relatively brief.

Type 3 – Scaffolding and adjustment of MAP: MAP interaction

Consideration of this type of interaction is aimed at supporting coordination and coherence between the multiple resources that may at any point act in the role of a MAP. The role of the MAP is played by one or more of the Resources with which the Learner interacts within their Ecology. The MAP is responsible for working with the learner to ensure that an optimal subset of resources is pulled together so that the interactions between learner and resources result in a ZPA centred on the needs of the learner. The role of the MAP can be played by technology, as was the case with the Ecolab software, or it can be played by a peer supported by the technology, as was the case with the Riddles Wordcat software, or it may be played by a combination of different people and technology, as was the case with the Homework project. It may also be the case that the learner is at times themselves acting as a MAP for another learner and is a resource in that second learner's Ecology of Resources. The complexity of the potential interactions within and between different Ecologies of Resources, centred on different learners, requires that interactions between these MAP resources are the subject of considerable design effort. Technology can play an important role here. In the Homework project, for example, the Tablet PC acted as a shared representation through which teacher, parent and child could support the learner and could see what the learner had done when working with another MAP. As mentioned earlier, it also offered a communication tool and provided information for parents about how to support the learner in their completion of activities through the 'Grown-ups' button.

Type 4 – Scaffolding and adjustment of inter-element interaction

The relationships between the different types of element that form part of the Ecology of Resources are those between Knowledge and Skills, Tools and People, and Environment elements. As I have discussed earlier, these relationships may need attention in order to support the learner. During the early phases of the design process the existing relationships will have been identified and the need for adjustment may already be clear. For example, the relationships between Knowledge and Skills and the Environment may need attention in some cases so

Table 7.5 The learning and teaching relationship

Step	Actions to be completed by Learner and MAP	Actions to be completed by design team to adjust and scaffold
1	Represent and communicate the way in which they both currently understand the Learner's Ecology of Resources, particularly with respect to the subject or skill being learnt	Provide facilities to enable the learner and MAP to represent and communicate their understanding. Homework example: Parent and Child can discuss child's previously completed activities using the Tablet PC
2	Negotiate a shared representation of the goal or sub-goal of their interactions. Steps 1 and 2 are the way in which the recognition production gap can be identified	Provide facilities to enable the learner and MAP to negotiate. Homework example: Parent and Child can explore a range of activities and select from these as appropriate
3	Explore the resources identified in the learner's Ecology of Resources model. In particular the filter elements and the extent to which these need adjustment	Provide accessible descriptions of the Resources available
4	Select the resources most suitable for the learner and identify at what level of difficulty and in what way these should be introduced	Provide specifications of the range of resources, such as the level of difficulty of different activities or the range of locations for which an activity has been designed
5	Make decisions about who or what will be able to share the representation of the learner's Ecology of Resources	Provide facilities to share/limit access to the evolving Ecology of Resources model of the learner
6	Access and activate the selected resource/s	Provide facilities to enable resources to be accessed
7	Return to Step 1	

that learners can appreciate the relevance of their knowledge to their interactions in the world. In the Homework project example, the careful consideration of activities that might ground the numeracy concepts in the learner's environment is exemplified in the Camera Homework 'Numbers in your Home', which asked learners to work with a grown-up and to 'look around your home to see if you can find different places where numbers are used. Take 3 digital photographs to show the numbers you have found. Talk with a grown-up about what the numbers mean and why the numbers are useful'. This example also considers the relationship between knowledge, environment and the camera resource of the Tablet PC with the grown-up acting as a MAP.

Type 5 – Scaffolding and adjustment of inter-filter interaction

In the same way that the relationships between resource elements require consideration so too do the relationships between the filter elements. For example, the organization of the classroom during the Homework project was influenced by the administration of the physical Tablet PC resources stored in a trolley that needed to be plugged into the mains electricity to ensure that the Tablets were charged. This relationship was the source of some tension in the early evaluation of the prototype system and attention had to be paid, for example, to how adjustment might be made to the organization of the start of the day when the Tablets were being returned from home and needed to be placed back in the trolley until the next mathematics lesson.

Type 6 – Scaffolding and adjustment of within element interaction

Within each of the resource elements there are relationships such as those illustrated in Tables 7.2 and 7.3. On occasions these too can be supported to promote learning. For example, the relationships between different computing resources can be strengthened, such as that between the Homework classroom Interactive Whiteboard and the Tablet PCs that were linked through the program code of the Homework system so that coherent lessons that use both resources could be planned by the teacher.

Type 7 – Scaffolding and adjustment of within filter interaction

Similarly, within each of the filter elements there are relationships that can be supported to promote learning. For example, the rules of the classroom with respect to use of the Tablet PC may or may not be in tune with the school timetable arrangements or the wider school rules.

Phase 3 of the framework is about identifying the possible ways in which adjustments and scaffolding can be provided. There is no expectation that all types of scaffolding and adjustments will be found in all design situations. Each type of scaffolding and adjustment should be explored by the design team in order to evaluate its relevance to their particular situation. It is also the case that the types of scaffolding and adjustments are not mutually exclusive. For example, the Type 3 MAP scaffolding and adjustment example drawn from the Homework project is a special case of Type 6 within element scaffolding and adjustment.

I have explained the Ecology of Resources Design Framework in some detail, using the Homework project as a worked example. I now present a case study that explores a less well-developed design problem to illustrate how the Ecology of Resources Design Framework can be used.

LEARNING CENTRE Case Study

In contrast with the Homework project example, this second case study does not aim to *develop* technologies *per se* but rather to support learners in *deciding what technologies to use* and when, where and how to use them. In this sense, the starting-point and design need in this example are less well-formulated.

Background

The South Downs Learning Centre (SDLC) operates a self-managed learning (SML) process for 11–16-year-old learners in an 'out-of-school' environment. Self-managed learning is about learning to learn within the context of the individual and the wider community. Consequently, learning within the centre is not formalized to the same extent as in more traditional educational contexts. The SML approach to learning provides a structure within which learners can plan, organize and carry out learning activities. It is framed by three key elements: the Learning Agreement, Learning Groups and Learning Group Advisers. Together these comprise the Learning Community. Learner activity at SDLC is supplemented by a range of external activities such as trips and visits. These are identified, planned and organized by the learners themselves. In addition to the external activities generated by the learners at SDLC, learners also participate in other 'external' activities such as hobbies or personal interests, as well as more formalized activities such as National exams, which are taken through a distance education provider. The majority of learners at SDLC are home-educated and additional learning takes place in the home, supported by parents and/or specialist tutors.

A key aim of the design process described in this case study was to explore and model learners' contexts to identify ways in which available resources might best be used to support their learning needs. These issues were addressed through an iterative participatory design approach in collaboration with learners and staff at the learning centre. It took the research team several interview sessions and observations with learners and mentors to identify and clarify the focus of attention used at the start of this case study.

Phase 1 Mapping the Ecology of Resources

Step 1 – Brainstorming potential resources

Initial explorations with learners and staff at the centre revealed that although learners had access to a wide range of technologies for both formal and informal learning, they did not find it easy to make connections between these technologies, their learning activities and the available spaces for learning. A preliminary generic ZAA was generated, based on a loosely framed design need, which focused on learners' selection and use of technologies on trips. This widely framed ZAA fits with the notion that the initial step of Phase 1 of the design framework aims to provide the widest possible ZAA on the basis that this may need to be revisited across several iterations. As with the Homework project described earlier in this chapter, this preliminary ZAA was then refined to generate a particular set of resources. In the SDLC study, this refined ZAA has been ordered according to the category elements of the Ecology of Resources framework to ease presentation and is illustrated in Table 7.6.

The early stages of the use of the design framework involved an iterative approach. Since the resources, filters and learner interactions become more explicit over time, these early stage iterations gradually faded out as the focus of attention became clearer and more easily accessible as recurrent patterns of interaction or social practice were revealed. This is an important point, and highlights the way that the brainstorming stage of the design framework may not only involve many iterations, but also many cycles of iterations. The illustrative example that is based on a single focus of attention needs to be read on the understanding that it represents just one of many possible iterations.

Step 2 – Specifying the focus of attention

The focus of attention explored in this case study is:

> How can we support the learner to make appropriate selection and use of available technologies to learn about the Milky Way whilst on a trip to the London Planetarium?

Step 3 – Categorizing resource elements

As with the Homework example, the identification of a preliminary set of resources enables the generation of a preliminary Ecology of Resources model, as illustrated in Figure 7.3.

This Ecology of Resources model permits a preliminary elaboration of Steps 4, 5 and 6.

The model itself was further refined and reshaped to focus on learning with technologies which in turn made the design process slightly more manageable by focusing on a particular environment or particular person or particular tools. For example, there were no wifi networks available at the Royal Observatory – so these were deleted from the data set. None of the learners or their mentors had Internet connectivity or GPS on their mobile phones, and it was not our intention to buy or design new devices, so these and related elements were also removed. Steps 4–6 are enumerated sequentially, but it may be desirable to develop Steps 3–6 in parallel, because identifying relevant filters and constraints requires a negotiation back and forth between resource elements and learner resources as well as consideration of the role of potential MAPs. It is not a matter, here, of trying to incorporate Steps 4–6 into the Ecology of Resources model generated at Step 3. It is, rather, a matter of identifying relevant resources and asking the following questions in relation to each step.

Table 7.6 Refined ZAA – Trip to Royal Observatory

Refined ZAA (Trip to Royal Observatory to learn about Astronomy): Category Elements

Knowledge	Environment	Resources
Astronomy, information on the sky at night (stars, galaxies, Milky Way, etc.)	Royal Observatory, Planetarium, shop, cafe, GPS networks, wifi connectivity, Internet connectivity, Planetarium Exhibit spaces, Planetarium learning workshops	Learners, staff from learning centre, peers, researcher-designer, museum guides, show narrators, museum attendants, shop assistants, other museum staff), other learners/visitors, interactive exhibits, simulations, models, digital information screens, mobile phones, text messaging, batteries, memory cards, voice recorder, digital still image camera, digital video camera, combined still image/video camera, headphones, Planetarium shows and exhibits with information on the universe, galaxies, stars, black holes, Milky Way, films, video clips, DVDs

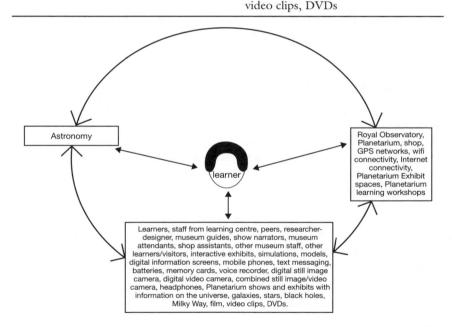

Figure 7.3 Ecology of Resources model – Planetarium visit

Step 4 – What might restrict a learner's access to the forms of assistance identified thus far?

Step 5 – What are the resources brought to the situation by the learner?

Step 6 – Who or what are the MAPs and what role might they play?

Step 4 – Identifying filter elements

At the Royal Observatory, it is possible to attend a Planetarium Show during which learners can learn about the Milky Way as part of a particular scheduled event. The Show as a resource is filtered by event times and by rules: for example, no audio recording or photography is allowed, which means the learner must remember or record in a different way what they are seeing and hearing. The Show as a resource is also filtered by ambiance, with lack of light acting as a constraining filter on the writing of notes. The act of listening to the narrator and the presence of the audience act as a constraining filter on the learner's ability to use available MAPs as *in situ* resources.

Step 5 – Identifying learner resources

The resources reviewed here are those of the learner. These resources include such things as existing competencies, knowledge and skills as well as physical attributes. Some possible resources in the SDLC example were:

> coordination, curiosity, motivation/interest, existing knowledge, problem-solving skills, decision-making skills, planning skills, technical skills, learning models, learning styles, relationships, social skills, collaborative skills, communication skills, self-esteem.

Step 6 – Identifying potential MAPs and defining relationships

As with the Homework example, a range of potential MAPs can be identified in the scenario of the learner at the Planetarium who wishes to learn more about the Milky Way, and these are illustrated in Table 7.7.

The stated purpose of the Ecology of Resources model at Phase 1 is to identify and model a particular design need. Through the various iterations in Steps 1 and 2 and the subsequent review and revision of these resources in Step 3 and Steps 4–6, a subset of resources which were sufficiently scoped and relevant to the stated focus of attention for Phase 1 were produced to enable progress to Phase 2 and the identification of relationships and interactions which might influence the ways in which these resources may or may not be appropriated to act as forms of assistance for learners.

Phase 2 Identifying relationships and filters

As with the Homework example, the resources identified in the SDLC example are organized into groups according to the category elements and the relationships between the elements, in terms of influences, components, typologies and social connections. These are illustrated in Table 7.8.

Figure 7.4 illustrates a sample Ecology of Resources model of a learner's trip to the London Planetarium incorporating resources and filters based on the

Table 7.7 Potential MAPs – Planetarium visit

Name	Explicit/ Implicit MAP	Relationship and Constraints	Resources
Planetarium Show Narrator	Implicit	Infrequent, formal interaction constrained by show timing and constraints of employment	Low familiarity with learner Social skills Astronomy knowledge
Learning Mentor	Explicit	Frequent, formal and informal interactions constrained to time at learning centre/on trip	High familiarity with learner Social skills Some astronomy knowledge
Peer Learner	Implicit	Frequent, formal and informal, constrained by time at centre	Some familiarity with learner Some social skills Some astronomy knowledge
Planetarium Exhibit	Explicit	Constrained by time and space (physical and inhibited by other visitors) at trip setting, linguistic and knowledge constraints (level of learner)	Low familiarity with specific learners Astronomy knowledge (chunked)
Technology	Explicit	Frequent (if personal to the learner), infrequent (if access is shared, local, static); constraints (other people, space, skills, time)	Astronomy knowledge Information storage/ retrieval Simulations, play, interactivity Visualization Communication Evaluation Participatory dialogue

preliminary Table generated at Phase 2 and illustrated in Table 7.8. The model also incorporates arrows that highlight the relationships between these resources and filters. The Ecology of Resources model is still quite broadly framed but can nevertheless be used and reused to consider scenarios and options. For example:

> Jim wants to learn about the *Milky Way*, a type of *Galaxy*. The range of knowledge available to Jim is framed by the knowledge domain of *Astronomy* of which the category '*Galaxie*s' is a component part. Jim is at the *Planetarium* on a trip and therefore has a number of resources available to him to locate information within this knowledge domain. He wanders around his immediate environment and decides to look at the *Exhibit* –'Astronomy Questions'. The Exhibit is part of the Planetarium environment and 'Astronomy Questions' is a type of exhibit.

This exhibit provides both static and interactive resources. Jim is unsure how to use the interactive resources and seeks help from his *learning mentor*. After he has consulted the exhibits, he finds some information he is interested in. He does not have a pen and paper handy but he does have a *digital camera*. The camera's batteries have been charged and there is sufficient storage space on his memory card. The camera *can take photos without the need for flash photography* and a member of the *Museum staff* confirms that *it is permissible to take photos in the Exhibition area*. Jim snaps a photo of the information text about galaxies and then takes a photograph of the interactive animation. When he returns to the learning centre, he uploads these photos to the centre's Flickr site online to share them with his peers and his family and adds comments about his visit. He also uses the photo of the interactive animation as an illustration in the centre's termly newsletter. Jim knew he could have used his *mobile phone* camera to take pictures and upload them directly to the centre's Flickr account but he wanted a better quality image, particularly to read the text from the exhibit, and he had insufficient credit on his phone to transfer the data whilst he was at the Planetarium.

The Ecology of Resources model can then be used to explore the learner's interactions with resource elements. The relationships and filters framing available resources and potential MAPs are made more explicit. Opportunities for cross-location activities are also generated and made visible, the learner's ability to share and comment on their learning via Flickr, for example. Mapping a learner's interactions in this way can provide a preliminary model for considering ways of

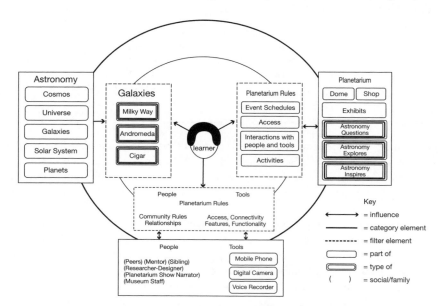

Figure 7.4 Ecology of Resources model for a trip to the London Planetarium

Table 7.8 Identification of resources and filters in the Ecology of Resources

Category Element	Filter Element
Knowledge Astronomy The *component* parts of basic level astronomy knowledge include the following: – Cosmos, Universe, Galaxies, Solar System, Planets, Stars	Filter: Learning goal Scientific classification system and learner's learning goal as part of the *process* curriculum of self-managed learning The *component* parts of the learner's learning goal in this instance are: – Galaxies, The Milky Way
Influences	*Influences*
Tools and People The *types* of resource include: – *People:* Peer learners, learning mentors, researcher-designer, Planetarium show narrator, museum staff, other learners, other visitors – *Artefacts:* Exhibits, books, videos, posters, pens, pencils, paper, batteries – *Technologies:* DVDs, audio and video clips, presentations, interactive exhibits, cinematic exhibits, simulators	Filter: Opportunity and Constraint The *types* of opportunity/constraint are mapped against the *type* of resource – *People:* Time, role, employment demands, location/proximity mode of contact, relationships, learning community rules – *Artefacts:* spatial distribution, opening hours, cost, relevance, ownership, availability – *Technologies:* compatibility, availability, technical skills, spatial distribution, access, relevance, functionality, storage
Influences	*Influences*
Environment The *component* parts of the environment may include: – Royal Observatory *Components:* Planetarium, Shop, Workshops, Exhibits, Activity Room, Cafeteria, outdoor space, Museum, Meridian Line Exhibits – Greenwich World Heritage Site *Components:* National Maritime Museum, park, gardens, The Queen's House, The Old Royal Naval College, The Fan Museum, The Cutty Sark. – SDLC *Components:* Online resources *Types of:* Flickr, blog	Filter: organization As with People and Tools, this filter involves *types* of opportunity/constraint, as follows: *Royal Observatory:* opening hours, rules re copyright, participation, timings of shows, etc., design and layout of interactional spaces (e.g. exhibits or simulations halls), health and safety regulations, time, rules of social engagement in public spaces, learning community rules *Greenwich World Heritage Site:* as above, also proximity, distance, spatial distribution, access. *SDLC:* availability of connectivity, mobile phone credit, technical skills, time

(influences — between Knowledge and Filter: Learning goal)

(influences — between Tools and People and Filter: Opportunity and Constraint)

(influences — between Environment and Filter: organization)

developing effective scaffolds and adjustments in both the learning process and the design process.

Phase 3 Identifying scaffolds and adjustments

The SDLC example was largely exploratory and focused on supporting learners' decision-making processes about appropriate and effective technology use to support their learning. Phase 3 therefore focused more on identifying, for future iterations, potential scaffolds and adjustments.

In contrast to the Homework example, the resource and filter relationships in the SDLC example are much more fluid, and the selection and use of technology is much more 'in the moment' and flexible. Nevertheless, the two examples share common patterns of interaction when it comes to scaffolding and adjustments. For example, in the Homework project, the range of possible interactions between teacher, parents and pupils was adjusted via the addition of a messaging tool, which was added to the tablet PC, thereby transforming participants' access to resources previously filtered by the temporal and distanced nature of the school day and the school environment. In the SDLC Planetarium example, an adjustment to the rules framed by copyright has been made in relation to the Exhibits hall, thus permitting learners to utilize their technology to capture data about their interests in astronomy, which they are later able to share with others via Flickr. A further adjustment to this scenario could, for example, be made by making *in situ* provision within the Planetarium for visitors to share digital data captured in this way online, such as via a shared visitor website. Table 7.9 illustrates the conjoined resources and filters of learners and the Planetarium.

Each of these resources and filters can influence any of the others and it is perhaps only with this understanding that the value of the Ecology of Resource framework really starts to become apparent and the interdependency of the component parts of the learner's context begins to emerge. It helps, here, to consider Table 7.9 as a form of grid, which can be read in every direction, as illustrated in Figure 7.5.

This approach enabled the generation of a grid of learning potentials from which appropriate adjustments and scaffolds might be developed. Once the kinds of relationships and interactions that might occur between the learner and available resources and filters have been explored, along with the ways in which these relate to potential adjustments and scaffolds, it is possible to consider these relationships and interactions in a more fine-grained manner. This process can address the seven types of scaffolding and adjustments outlined in the framework.

There is insufficient space for me to describe how all seven types of scaffolding and adjustment were explored in the SDLC study. I therefore include two examples as an illustration.

Table 7.9 Mapping resources and filters within the Ecology of Resources

Resource Element		Filter Element		Learner Resource
Knowledge Astronomy: Galaxies	*influences*	Filter Learning goal: Learn about the Milky Way and Galaxies	*influences*	Motivation/Interest Prior knowledge about Galaxies or Astronomy
Influences		*Influences*		*Influences*
People and Tools Learning Mentor Planetarium Show Narrator Museum Staff	*influences*	Filter Community rules and relationships Employment demands, time, access Employment role, access Availability, ownership, functionality of tools, e.g. technologies, artefacts	*influences*	Confidence Social skills (formal and informal) Problem-solving skills
Influences		*Influences*		*Influences*
Environment Planetarium *Components:* Dome, Shop, Workshops, Exhibits, Cafe *Types of Exhibit:* Astronomy Questions, Astronomy Explores, Astronomy Inspires	*influences*	Filter Event scheduling Spatial access Design and layout of exhibits Planetarium rules around visitor access, interactions and activities Copyright laws, Health and safety issues	*influences*	Problem-solving skills Social skills (negotiating access, dialogue) Reasoning skills (linking available resources to learning goal)

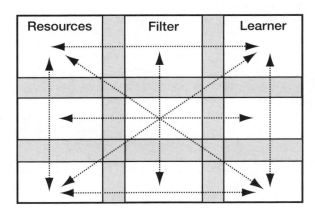

Figure 7.5 Multidirectional grid of resources and filters

Table 7.10 Learner: MAP scaffolding and adjustment

Step	Actions to be completed by learner and MAP	Actions to be completed by design team to adjust and scaffold
1	Represent and communicate their mutual current understanding of the learner's Ecology of Resources, in particular in terms of the knowledge or skill to be learned	Provide facilities to enable the learner and MAP to represent and communicate their understanding *Astronomy example:* Learner and learning adviser can compare and discuss learner's prior engagement with astronomy with available resources in the context of the trip
2	Negotiate a shared representation of the goal or sub-goal of potential interactions (identify the recognition-production gap)	Provide facilities or tools to enable learner and MAP to negotiate the gap *Astronomy example*: Learner and MAP can explore the range of available technologies and discuss their suitability for a particular activity
3	Explore the resources identified in the learner's Ecology of Resources model, in particular the filter elements and the extent to which these need adjustment.	Provide accessible descriptions of available resources *Astronomy example:* Learner consults with museum staff to establish rules of engagement with setting; local signage also contributes to this; researcher-designer and learner discuss functionalities of technologies
4	Select the resources most suitable for the learner and identify at what levels of difficulty and in what way these should be introduced	Provide specifications of the range of resources, e.g. level of difficulty or range of locations *Astronomy example*: learner and researcher-designer discuss opportunities for *in situ* transfer of data using mobile phone and Flickr
5	Make decisions about who or what will be able to share the representation of the learner's Ecology of Resources	Provide facilities to share/limit access to the evolving Ecology of Resources model of the learner *Astronomy example:* learner and learning adviser discuss knowledge-sharing, audience and communicative purpose and transfer of information from Planetarium visit to Flickr or newsletter
6	Access and activate the selected resource/s	Provide facilities to enable resources to be accessed *Astronomy example:* museum staff member gives learner permission to use digital camera to capture data/information about Galaxies
7	Return to Step 1	–

Type 2 – Learner: MAP scaffolding and adjustment

Table 7.10 illustrates the way that the guiding steps can be used to consider the learner who is interested in astronomy and their possible interactions with MAPs.

Type 3 – MAP: MAP scaffolding and adjustment

Table 7.10 indicates that the learner's access to the MAPs identified was continuous and variable. The learner could draw on different MAPs to negotiate different aspects of their Ecology of Resources: knowledge about astronomy from the learning adviser, knowledge about technology from the researcher-designer and information about the environment from museum staff members. In these examples, there are opportunities to explore how the input from these multiple MAPs might be better represented and shared.

Summary

In the definition of context that I proposed in Part 1 of this book I stated that it is the role of the abler participants to scaffold a learner's construction of a narrative that makes sense of the meanings distributed amongst the resources with which they interact. Through this scaffolding the learner at the centre of their context internalizes their interactions and develops increased independent capability and self-awareness. In Chapter 3 I proposed that the concept of scaffolding be refined to emphasize that it involves the evaluation of learner need, the provision of assistance and the withdrawal of that assistance in order to engender learner development. I also suggested that the notion of distributed scaffolding was useful and that it needed to be broadened away from classroom boundaries to consider the learner and their interactions more holistically: we needed to explore and refine how the relationships between the resources that a learner brings to their interactions and the resource elements of their context might be integrated and scaffolded. In this chapter I have presented the Ecology of Resources design framework as a way in which these proposals might be addressed. I have illustrated its application to two different case studies. In Part 3 I consider some of the challenges, limitations and complexities of this approach and the potential that it might offer for the future development of technology-rich learning activities.

Part 3

The future of technology-rich learning

8 New technologies, new interactions?

There are numerous people who make a living from looking into the future, through tracking trends to estimate what might be the next focus of development and what gadget might grab people's attention. In this penultimate chapter of the book I discuss the type of technology that might be available to us and I consider the implications of this for the Ecology of Resources approach. The saturation of our lives with more and different technologies is unlikely to lessen and there are implications of these developments that need to be taken into account when we consider the process of developing technology-rich learning activities. Sometimes we, as learners, choose to select from the increasing range of available technology, and on other occasions the choice is not necessarily ours. For example, I know that if I want to catch a bus into town from the bus stop near my house I can go to the bus company website and look to see when the next bus is due to arrive, or I can use my mobile phone to text the bus stop code to a bus service phone number and receive the information as a text message on my mobile phone. If I do not wish actively to seek such information then the electronic displays at many of the bus stops will also let me know the time till the arrival of the next bus(es). I can of course simply choose to wait and see when the bus arrives. I have a choice about the extent to which I personally engage with these technologies to support my journey planning. Once I arrive in town I can make other choices, but some technologies are not within my control: the surveillance cameras that record activity across large parts of the town, for example, or the photo someone else takes which has me in the background and which they post to their blog.

I stated in Chapter 1 that I was more interested in interactions than in technologies. I therefore consider technology trends in terms of the interactions that they might support rather than the specifics of any individual technologies. I continue to view technologies as digital information and communication technologies, including both hardware and software, although I also consider some of the conditions surrounding the development of these technologies. I see the horizon of this discussion as the next 10 to 15 years.

Technology themes

I do not try to predict the future of technology development but use the trends identified by others[1] to identify seven technology development themes that I consider to have implications for learning and in particular for a context-based model of learning. I discuss each theme in terms of the types of interactions that might be supported as a result. I stress that these themes are not discrete, but interdependent and entwined.

(1) Ubiquity – technology everywhere and anywhere in a learner's Ecology of Resources

Technology will enable more interactions between us and the resource elements inside and outside our bodies. They will be supported by a proliferation in the number of different types of 'smart' device that we carry around with us wherever we go or that are part of the environments with which we interact, including ourselves and the people we meet. These range from familiar technologies, such as personal digital assistants, to less familiar technologies, such as the millions of tiny sensors that can be part of the paint on the walls, sensing when the temperature changes and when more or less insulation may be required, for example. Some devices may be small, but still visible and tangible; others might be embedded and hidden around us and inside us. Body Sensor Networks (Yang, 2006, for example), offer the ability to sense physical and biochemical factors in the human body.

These types of technology developments result in more of the resource elements in a learner's Ecology of Resources being enhanced with computational and interactive capabilities. Learners will therefore be able to interact with more of the resource elements in the Ecology of Resources, should they so choose, and more of the elements in their Ecology will be able to interact with each other. The increased range of interactive resources may of course also result in an increased range of filters for these resources.

A novice gardener, Joe, who wants to grow some vegetables in the soil of a school garden or local allotment, could always use his senses to touch the soil and feel its warmth and moisture. Ubiquitous technology may also mean that he can access the data from a layer of temperature and moisture-sensitive material a few inches under the soil that provides more accurate data collected over a long period of time.

(2) Tagging – more information about more of the elements in a learner's Ecology of Resources, including the learner

In addition to offering us an increased ability to collect data from the world, technology also allows us to add information to the world. This information can then be used by different technology devices and made available to us. For example, we can add digital descriptions, or tags, to physical things, such as buildings; these tags might do the job of describing the building, such as its age and who has lived in it. We can also tag invisible structures such as the cells that make up the mobile phone network so that information can be attached to that cell space. This information might be about the physical location represented by that cell space or it might be some other information, such as a clue in a virtual treasure hunt game (Wyeth *et al.*, 2008).

These types of technology developments result in our being able to add information to the resource elements in a learner's Ecology of Resources. The resource elements we tag could, for example, be different items in a classroom or home that might be examples of arrays, so that when young learners, such as those in the Homework project, are looking for sample arrays these tagged items might be available to the learner and their More Able Partner (MAP). The resource elements we tag might also include MAPs, so that learners are aware of their existence and availability. The information that is added to resource elements could be specifically targeted to a learner's needs. The learner and their MAP might also add their own information to resource elements, both to support a particular learner and to support the learning of others.

These developments might also enhance Joe's gardening activities. It may be, for example, that someone who has previously used this particular piece of land has added information about the poor soil drainage and the likelihood of flooding in this location.

(3) Interfaces – more and different ways to interact with the elements in a learner's Ecology of Resources

For many of us, the keyboard and the mouse are still the tools that we most often use to input information into our computing technology, and the screen, whether on a desktop computer, a mobile phone or some personal computing device, is usually how we see the results of the processing of our inputs. Of course, we may also use touch-sensitive screens to withdraw money from the bank or buy train tickets, and perhaps we use security passes to indicate that we should be allowed to enter a building. This availability of different interfaces is set to continue. Touch, voice, physiological data, environmental data, and movement, for example, all offer ways for us to input information for technology to process. Audio, visual, and tactile feedback can all also be used to indicate the results of the processing that the technology has completed on that input. This increasing range in the variety of ways that we can both input information to technology and receive the results of that input engenders a greater variety of interface possibilities. Additionally, technical advances in particular forms of interface mean that we can expect increased sophistication, for example in the resolution and malleability of visual displays and the quality of our audio experiences. The furniture and fabric of our environments, private and public, small and large, offer potential display technologies. There are also implications for the merging of interfaces, such as sound, vision and touch, and the continuing convergence of virtual and physical reality. We can already enter virtual worlds where, although our input may still be through traditional keyboard technologies, we can see ourselves as avatars within those virtual worlds and we can interact within them in a multitude of ways. Augmented and mixed reality interfaces also allow us to mix our physical and virtual interactions, so that our efforts in the physical world, such as moving a foot, result in some action in the virtual world, such as kicking a ball in a virtual football game. The range and sophistication of interactions that transcend the virtual and physical is set to increase and to support a finer grain and richer set of possibilities.

Learners will be able to interact with the resource elements in their Ecology of Resources in an increasing variety of ways that will more often engage a fuller range of their senses. This offers greater potential for actions in and with the real world, a greater variety of ways in which learners can be engaged and a wider range of ways in which MAPs can offer and shape support for learners.

I can now add even more to my gardening example: Joe unfurls his lightweight computer screen to view a visualization of the data that have been picked up from sensors in the soil of the location where he is standing and the information that other people have added. He can see animations of the plants that have been grown here before and hear commentary about the weather conditions, growing successes and challenges. As he points towards a particular part of his vegetable plot, the view on his screen adapts to that particular location using the information provided by the directional sensors in his sleeve and global positioning information from his mobile phone.

(4) Utilities – more capability to support and sustain interactions with the elements in a learner's Ecology of Resources

Moore's law is often used in discussions to provide evidence that technology will continue to reduce in cost and increase in power and capacity (Foresight Sigma Scan, 2009). At the same time as the costs of computing technology are going down and capability is going up there is a movement away from the need for us to be co-located with this capability. This is the idea behind cloud computing, which promises vast amounts of computing power and resources available from banks of computers as and when we need them, provided through a network, such as the Internet, rather than as part of the devices in our hands, bodies and environment.

These types of developments offer the potential for learners and MAPs to rely on being able to access as much information and media as they want, as much processing power and as wide a range of applications as they need, whenever they need it and wherever they are. Individuals and institutions will no longer need to worry about the capability of the devices they own, since these will merely act as interfaces to the cloud of computing resource distributed around the world. The reducing costs ought also to mean that any learner could have access to technology.

For our gardening novice Joe this means that he can access data about his location and its soil from as many previous years as have been recorded, and he can see high-quality multimedia visualizations on whatever device he can access without having to carry a heavy computer around or wait a long time for data processing. His interactions with the different elements of his Ecology of

Resources can also be stored and accessed by him and his MAPs whenever or wherever they are.

(5) Networks – more connections between all the elements in a learner's Ecology of Resources

The combination of mobile technology devices and robust networks means that the technologies and people with whom we interact are increasingly connected to each other wherever they are and however far apart they might be. These networks of connections enable us to keep in touch with other people, with the work we are doing and with parts of our environment from which we are physically disconnected. These increased connections are not just provided through mobile telephony, but can be provided through the Internet, satellite, cable or broadcast networks.

This theme of technology development offers an increased network of connections to support the learner's interactions with the resources of their Ecology. It can help them keep in touch with their MAPs and can support communication and collaboration between multiple MAPs. It also means that information can be passed between the multiple resource elements that have computing capability.

The variety of information that is available about growing locations all over the world is now potentially available to gardener Joe. Some locations may have embedded sensors and information tags like Joe's plot has, others may have more basic records that have been entered into a computer database. The network of connections means that in principle these different information resources can be linked and accessed by Joe. These resources include other people, such as Anouk, who have indicated a willingness to help novices like Joe.

(6) Webs – richer connections between the elements in a learner's Ecology of Resources, including us

I use the term 'webs' to describe something more than the network of technologies and people. The different ways in which the Internet has enabled information-sharing and communication offer an example. The original World Wide Web (www) enabled us to search, retrieve, browse, shop and learn from an enormous range of multimedia information sources hosted on computer servers all over the world. A few people were also able to write information and make this available to other people. The Social Web or Web 2.0 enabled more people to write to as well as read from the www. Blogs, microblogs, wikis, social networking and media-sharing mean that we can share our thoughts, images, sounds and experiences with just one person, a few people, anyone and everyone. The Web 3.0 or semantic web takes this notion of sharing a step further and sees the www as one big database of open data where individual data elements are linked. The idea is that people and organizations will provide access to their data and will make the detailed meaning of these data explicit.

The development of different webs adds richness to the connections that can support the interactions between the elements in a learner's Ecology of Resources, including those with the learner. By this I mean that elements can be linked in different ways, from individual data elements through to entire multimedia resources and people who share a similar interest or learning need.

This means that Joe can decide to contact Anouk by mobile phone, for example. Anouk answers the call and looks at the information that Joe has made available about his Ecology of Resources. Anouk and Joe decide that French beans look like a suitable crop. Anouk also puts Joe in touch with a community of novice gardeners who share their photos, notes and films via a social networking site. These individuals have also shared their data, as have many seed companies and agricultural specialists. This offers Joe and Anouk the chance to see information about different varieties of French beans from a range of perspectives, including where they have been grown, what conditions have proved optimal, disease profiles associated with different locations and conditions and histories of people who have grown particular varieties in similar conditions, indicating when and how much watering was needed, what pests were experienced, when the seeds were harvested and what their yield was.

(7) Hybridization – more blurring of the boundaries between the learner and the elements in their Ecology of Resources and in between the different elements of their Ecology of Resources

The mixed initiative of man and machine generates advanced outcomes. Robots and cyborgs have been a popular topic for science fiction writers, and although the reality is not perhaps exactly as depicted on screen or in novels, robots are a reality and they do a number of useful jobs, in manufacturing, for example. Increasingly sophisticated technology implants and prosthetics continue to become available and although I would not wish to suggest that people who benefit from smart implants, such as artificial retinas, will be viewed as cyborgs, the boundary between man and machine continues to blur and the creation of computers from biological materials is likely to take this further. This hybridization of man and machine can also take the form of collaborative networks of mixed human and machine elements, in which one may not be sure at any particular point if one is interacting with a human or an artificial collaborator. The power that can be derived from combining human-produced and machine-produced information in what has been called 'blogging the lab', for example (de Roure, 2007). Man and machine are also collaborating in crowd-sourcing initiatives such as Galaxy Zoo (http://www.galaxyzoo.org/) that combine the power of technology to provide images of distant galaxies beyond our own with the power of people to view these images and classify them in their millions.

The implications of this last theme for technology-rich learning and the Ecology of Resources are complex. It suggests, for example, that the distinctions between tools and people may become obsolete and that the proposal of mixed man and machine MAPs is a powerful reality.

This theme may mean that our learner Joe discovers a few weeks after he has planted his French beans that the manner in which the data he found about French beans had been collated and the speed with which appropriate information was available to him were the result of a community of man-machine enterprises that categorized land plots. The technology was good at matching data about conditions such as temperature, moisture, sunlight, altitude, gradient, and depth of water table. People were good at making decisions about disease identification from photographic images and deciding when a crop looked ready to harvest, to complement the data about when it was harvested, again from images. This combined enterprise enabled the most appropriate information to be made available to Joe and Anouk.

I have identified seven themes that can be used to talk about the interactions afforded by trends in computing technology development. I have stressed that these are not mutually exclusive, but interconnected. They also sit within a complex system of other developments that will inevitably impact on their progress. The unprecedented ageing of the global population, the need for environmental sustainability, the increased possibilities for cognitive enhancement provided by pharmaceuticals, gene therapy and personal genomics, and the progress that is likely to be made in understanding more about how the human brain works and its relationships with cognition and emotion are just a few of these. They may impact on the manner in which the technology trends are progressed and for whom the benefits are greatest.

Technology theme implications

In my earlier discussion of the interactions enabled by the technology themes I presented a positive view of the possibilities and the potential for learning. There are, however, enormous implications of technology developments that augment and open up access to more of the world and more of the people who inhabit it. There are naturally concerns about personal privacy, about the security of information, of countries and of individuals, and about what kind of legal framework might effectively protect people. In a similar vein, there are enormous ethical implications in many of these developments and worries about personal autonomy, identity, rights, equality and accountability. These implications need to be considered in any discussion about the future use of technology and any development of technology-rich learning activities. They also offer increased evidence for technology development to be a participatory process, such as that proposed by the Ecology of Resources framework, that engages beneficiaries in discussions of ethics and privacy, for example, to guide the development of technology, policy and law. The participatory approach can also help to increase people's understanding of what technology is and how it might help them to learn. These themes and their implications also illustrate the multiple disciplines that are having an impact upon the nature of the learning interactions that may be possible. If these developments are to be conducted in a manner that is to be of maximum benefit to learners these multiple disciplines need to work with each other and with social scientists to understand how the developments that each of them makes are related to the developments of the others. This is a slow process of understanding that needs to happen on a large scale.

There are also implications that arise because of the combinations of different technology development trends. The combined impact of these technology trends will reshape a whole variety of currently familiar distinctions between what might be considered one thing and what might be considered another. This means, for example, that some distinctions will be less clear:

- The distinction between what is inside a body and what is outside a body, including the human body; the distinctions between human and computer, and the distinction between our interactions with technology that are conscious and voluntary and those that are not.

Other distinctions will become less important:

- The distinctions between where my computing power and my digital 'stuff' reside, and between where my technology interface is and where I am.

There are some tensions and potentially confusing aspects to this. For example, technology allows me to make more connections between myself and the resources of my Ecology; it also allows me to disaggregate myself from my physical environment and to disaggregate and re-aggregate different resources within my Ecology, irrespective of their physical locations. There is therefore the potential for learning to be supported by learners being re-engaged with physical reality, for learning to be enriched by the layers of information that can be built upon that physical reality and revealed through a variety of interfaces, and for all this to be possible when learners are not located near any particular source of computing power.

Future scaffolding

At the end of Chapter 3 I proposed three scaffolding challenges that needed to be explored: the need to refine what we mean by scaffolding; the need to build specifications for distributed scaffolding beyond institutional boundaries; and the need to integrate scaffolding between the resources that a learner brings to their interactions. The technology developments discussed in this chapter offer enormous possibilities for tackling these three challenges and for combining human and computer scaffolding to encompass learning that occurs naturally, as well as learning that is officially orchestrated. It will be possible to provide scaffolding assistance through a range of different people and technologies as part of a distributed scaffolding process. The quantification of assistance will remain a difficult task, one that may benefit from access to a range of information about what resources different learners have used and the extent to which this has proved helpful and enabled their success. This may be a task that could benefit from data mining and crowd-sourcing approaches that uses the combined forces of human and machine intelligence to classify interaction patterns and support fading across an entire Ecology of Resources as well as individual elements within it.

In this chapter I have discussed the changing interactions that may be afforded by the developments in technologies over the next 10 to 15 years. In the final chapter I combine this technology-focused view of the future with a more pedagogically focused view to explore the changing roles of learners, MAPs and institutions, and the way in which the Ecology of Resources might support these changes.

9   New interactions, new opportunities for learning

At the start of this book I used the notion of 'Lines of Desire' to describe learners who are able to take best advantage of the people, buildings, technologies and other artefacts available to them to chart a learning trajectory that meets their needs. I used this metaphor to describe my activity to piece together an understanding of context and to pull together some useful conceptual tools to support my elaboration of a context-based framework for the development of technology-rich learning activities. I suggested that although there is wide recognition that an understanding of how people learn requires consideration of the people and artefacts with which they interact, the current, rather narrow, conceptualizations of context with respect to learning have not served research into educational technology particularly well. I elected therefore to take a broad view, and discussed the common themes of concern with respect to context that straddle multiple disciplines. I proposed a definition of context that I then used to focus my discussion of learning and technology both as it relates to what can be found in the literature and as it has emerged in the findings from my own empirical studies. This discussion grounded my presentation of the Ecology of Resources model and design framework.

In this final chapter I review the definition of context and the Ecology of Resources approach that it has enabled me to generate. I discuss the manner in which the ever-evolving range of interactions enabled by the continuing development of technologies may impact upon the Ecology of Resources model and its elements. I explore the limitations and challenges posed by the Ecology of Resources approach and the opportunities that it offers for the future of technology and learning.

The Ecology of Resources approach

The definition of context that I proposed in Chapter 1 recognizes both the subjective and the objective nature of our experiences with the world, the interconnectedness of all the elements with which we interact and the way in which these interactions shape our understanding of the world. I proposed that context should be considered as something that is defined with respect to an individual person and that it spans their life. A person's context is made up of the billions of interactions that they have with the resources of the world: other people, artefacts and their environment. These resources provide 'partial descriptions of the world' with which the learner can build connections through their interactions. These interactions help the learner to build an understanding of the world that is distributed across both resources and interactions: a distributed understanding that is crystallized with respect to a particular individual through a process of internalization. The intentional nature of the people involved in these interactions results in a degree of unpredictability, because each person brings their own agenda to their interactions and this agenda may not be transparent to others. The spatial and historical contingency of an individual's interactions, however, contribute a certain stability to the manner in which an individual might expect to be hooked into their world through their interactions.

The Ecology of Resources model is offered as an abstraction that represents part of this reality for a learner, an abstraction that can be shared between social and technical researchers and practitioners to support analysis and to generate system design. It is grounded in an interpretation of Vygotsky's Zone of Proximal Development, is concerned with learning and considers the resources with which an individual interacts as potential forms of assistance that can help that individual to learn. These forms of assistance are categorized as being to do with Knowledge and Skills, Tools and People and the Environment. These categories are not fixed, as was made clear in Chapter 7 when the design framework was presented. The categories offer a useful way of thinking about the resources with which a learner may interact and the potential assistance that these resources may offer. This emphasis upon the potential assistance that resources might offer highlights that it is the *role* that a particular element plays that is important, rather than its particularity. It is the role that can help in making decisions about the nature of the category to which an element belongs for the purposes of development and discussion.

Knowledge and Skills

The resource categories are also guides for our thinking about the nature of context. The Knowledge and Skills category focuses the design of technology-rich learning activities upon the nature of what it is that is to be learnt. In Chapter 5 when I introduced the Ecology of Resources model I stressed my intention that this label should encompass the broadest of ways of talking about the 'stuff to be learnt', so that the Ecology of Resources model might be useful for those who wish to develop technology-rich learning activities for topics such as bricklaying, wine-making or farming as well as those who are concerned with formal academic disciplines such as engineering, chemistry, languages or history. This is not because I wish to suggest that all types of Knowledge and Skills are part of one homogeneous group, but because no matter what the nature of the Knowledge and Skills, the 'stuff to be learnt' is a resource in a learner's Ecology of Resources and as such it is related to other resource elements in that Ecology. I locate the differences between the different types of Knowledge and Skills in these relationships between resources. I shall take a moment now to explain this further, because it is important for the future development of the Ecology of Resources.

Initially one can draw a distinction between what is represented by the two words *Knowledge* and *Skills*: the first can be thought of as being about concepts and the second about procedures. The two are related; the understanding of some scientific concepts is connected to the scientific process through which they are understood, for example. However there are aspects of acquiring knowledge that cannot be achieved through the kinds of activities that lend themselves to skill acquisition and therefore there is a distinction between knowledge and skills. This distinction does not preclude the application of the Ecology of Resources approach to both knowledge and skills, because both forms of 'stuff to be learnt' are connected to the circumstances of the task being completed and it is those circumstances that the Ecology of Resources model describes. These circumstances may be very different for knowledge and for skills, but the connections for the learner to those circumstances will still exist and will still need to be taken into account in the design of activities.

The existence of a category with a label that includes the word *Knowledge* suggests that there is some notion of a recognizable body of knowledge within the Ecology of Resources model, a body of knowledge that is the basis for the existence of a filter element that might be described in some instances as a curriculum. The existence of the Knowledge and Skills category is not a call to a neoconservative view of a body of academic knowledge that is not primarily motivated by an interest in epistemology. Nor is the interconnectedness between the Knowledge and Skills category and the other resource elements an indication that knowledge in the Ecology of Resources model is a single type of unit and that all forms of knowledge are essentially the same.

I have made it clear that the Ecology of Resources model is grounded in an interpretation of Vygotsky's Zone of Proximal Development, and it is therefore to Vygotsky's discussions of knowledge that I turn here. Vygotsky made a distinction between scientific and everyday concepts and he recognized the importance of formal school learning. I have discussed these views in Chapter 2; I therefore concentrate here upon the manner in which these views relate to the notion of a body of knowledge and have been further informed by an engaging discussion about Vygotsky's sociocultural approach to knowledge in Young (2008). It is the relationship between the formation of the spontaneous and the scientific concepts that underpins human development and it is the reflexive awareness and systematicity provided through the acquisition of these scientific concepts that highlight their relationship with a body of knowledge. These features of Vygotsky's work provide the capacity for abstraction and generalization and they highlight that the scientific concepts are part of a larger system: a body of knowledge as an objective entity. The objectivity of knowledge arises from humanity's mediated productivity that saw the emergence of higher order psychological processes through the development of language. This human capacity to learn from what are essentially teaching interactions as well as from adaptation grounds the inseparability of learning and instruction in Vygotsky's work. His interest in the acquisition of scientific concepts through formal education in school, as well as out of school, indicates that he saw a role for institutions in learning and in relation to knowledge and curricula. Vygotsky's approach discusses both the distinction between scientific and spontaneous concepts and their interrelatedness. Learning is therefore anchored or, perhaps more accurately, it is weaved into a formal curriculum as well as everyday life. This interweaving in subject matter is not encompassed by situated approaches that ignore formal education and the existence of an objective body of knowledge. Vygotsky's emphasis upon the importance of scientific concepts, formal education and the role of institutions supports the existence of a body of knowledge. This body of knowledge is a product of a community's interactions over time; it is a dynamic entity that continues to develop through human enterprise. Over time it can be distinguished, at least to a degree, from the means of its production and recognized as an evolving entity.

The presence of the filter element for Knowledge and Skills signals the importance of the relationship between the manner in which a particular knowledge or skill is recognized and described by members of the learner's culture, and the body of knowledge itself. It is this relationship that is represented by the connection between the Knowledge and Skills resource element and the Knowledge and Skills filter element in the Ecology of Resources model. And it is this connection that represents the interweaving of learning into the subject matter of a body of knowledge through a curriculum. The word 'curriculum' is a little problematic, because some knowledge is so closely entwined within everyday life that it is hard to differentiate any codification that might be described as a curriculum. The tacit knowledge that is closely bound to institutions, such as that discussed by Gertler and Wolfe (2005) in their study of innovation and knowledge flow in high-tech organizations, is closely embedded in people's Ecologies of Resources through its connections with other resource and filter elements. It is therefore hard to distinguish what might be referred to as a curriculum. Other forms of knowledge are both better defined and more readily distinguished from the other resources to which they are connected and are therefore amenable to being formulated into a curriculum: formal science, for example. The key issue here is that the existence of the Knowledge and Skills filter and its connection to the learner, in combination with the interconnections to all the other resources within a learner's Ecology, signals that learning is weaved into formal subject matter *as well as* everyday life.

Tools and people

The Ecology of Resources model addresses the fact that some of the connections that underpin an individual's interactions with the world are and will increasingly be operationalized through technology. It recognizes that people are needed to help make these connections meaningful for a learner. In particular, the Ecology of Resources approach is concerned with the relationship between learners and their More Able Partners (MAPs) and it is concerned with the manner in which human and machine endeavour might be combined in support of this relationship.

The emphasis that the Ecology of Resources places upon the connections between elements both within and between resource categories also draws attention to the manner in which each element is defined in relation to these connections and interactions. This is true for tools as well as for people. For example, a particular piece of educational media – such as a *Number Crew* video in the Homework project – would be described within the Ecology of Resources model in terms of the way in which it is connected to other resources within the learner's Ecology of Resources. In this example these connections support the learner's interactions with the video, and their associated interactions with other people, other tools and environmental elements. The description of this video resource in terms of these relationships draws attention to the fact that this video represents a different resource when it is used in the school classroom compared with when it is used at home.

The connections between the different resources in a learner's Ecology of Resources, the interactions that these connections enable and the manner in which interactions between resources are coordinated across time and space can be enabled through technology. *The important transformation that needs to take place to support the construction of a learner's ZPA is from the operational network of technology-enabled connections between the different resources of people, places and things to the conceptual network of understanding and knowledge construction between people and within the learner.* The technology alone does not provide this transformational power: such power lies in the way that people use technology to support interactions that enable people to learn through the relationships that they build between the elements in their Ecology of Resources. I refer to the view that this transformational power rests with people and not with technology as the '*The Technology Illusion*' (Luckin 2009).

Environment

In my initial discussions about context in Chapter 1, I considered the manner in which the term is used in conjunction with space and place. This brought to the fore the subjective experience of interacting individuals constrained by temporal and spatial contingencies. Further discussions about the impact of ICT highlighted the manner in which physical space can be 'filled' with digital information (Manovich, 2006) and the changes in the affordances of that physical space that result. The technology themes presented in Chapter 8 suggest even more ways in which a learner's environment might be physical, virtual and hybrid. The Ecology of Resources approach is not prescriptive about the nature of the environmental factors that can be considered. Its role is to highlight the need for us to explore the relationships between different environmental elements and between environmental elements, the learner, the Knowledge and Skills they are learning, and the other Tools and other People who are assisting them. It is about understanding the way that learners' activities are spatially contingent.

are offered to a learner through these resources act as the hooks for interactions in which action and meaning are built'. I also call, however, on Vygotsky's emphasis upon the process of *internalization*, an emphasis that can be found in activity theory more generally, and I add that:

> In this sense, meaning is distributed amongst these resources. However, it is the manner in which the learner at the centre of their context internalizes their interactions that is the core activity of importance.

To my mind there is a tension here that relates to what we mean by *embodied* and what we mean by a *mind that is distributed* across artefacts. This is a tension that caused me some discomfort and prevented me in Chapter 7 from referring to the Learner's Resources as being *internal* and the resource elements of the Ecology of Resources as being *external*. It is to this discomfort that I now return, because it needs to be made explicit in order to clarify what the Ecology of Resources model means and because, as Dourish (2001) makes plain, technology makes new forms of interaction possible. As my discussions in Chapter 8 underline, there are technology-enabled interactions that make the boundary presented by the human body more permeable. My discomfort is caused in part because I acknowledge that the issue of embodiment is complex and that it needs to be handled with great care. I therefore wish to extract some key issues from my understanding of the subject of embodiment that are relevant to the manner in which I have treated it within the Ecology of Resources approach and to clarify what embodiment entails within the definition of context that underpins the Ecology of Resources. For my purposes, the tension with respect to embodiment revolves around what we mean by 'internalization' as the process that transforms the *interpsychological* into the *intrapsychological*. In the Ecology of Resources approach I want to hold onto the integral role played *in cognition* by the elements with which a learner interacts and which might be considered to be external to their body, and I want to hold onto the process of internalization. So the question that crystallizes this tension is concerned with the role played by scientific concepts in providing the systematicity required for everyday concepts to be integrated into our consciousness and the importance of language to the higher psychological processes. This is a factor that sets humans aside from other animals and that enables us to create modifications to the epistemic environment that impact upon future generations (Clark, 2008).

The Ecology of Resources approach recognizes that there are aspects of cognition that do happen outside the boundary of the skin and that cannot necessarily be entirely internalized, for example the use of complex computer modelling software, or some of the sophisticated calculations one can now complete on a mobile phone. This is important because it means that when I talk about the resources that a learner brings to their learning these include the manner in which that learner has previously extended their cognition through their interactions with artefacts, such as sophisticated mobile phones. The experience of these interactions may have been internalized, but it is only when the learner is able once again to interact with this artefact that the benefits of this extension to their mind can be reaped. This prevents me from referring to the learner's resources as being *internal* because although for the most part they are a feature of what happens inside the body, this is not the entire story.

Technology impacts upon this debate in at least two important ways. First, it encourages us towards greater distribution, for example the way in which we can store ever-increasing amounts of information through technology, access new information through networks and access other people to help us. We may feel that we need to do less remembering and organizing for ourselves as a result. Second, it offers increasingly rich possibilities for new ways of interacting with each other and with the world.

Simplifying complexity

My aim for the Ecology of Resources model is to provide a simplified, abstract representation that can be shared by those involved in the design process. One of these forms of simplification can be found in my focus upon the learner at the centre of their Ecology of Resources. The definition of context and the Ecology of Resources model that I have proposed adopt an individual learner as a central unit of analysis. Interactions between resource elements, however, and in particular collaboration between more able and less able people, are also a vital component of the approach. Clearly, there are multiple Ecologies of Resources centred on multiple different learners reflecting their intentions and the intentions of those with whom they interact. These Ecologies interact with each other in complex and important ways to form networks of Ecologies. The exploration of these networks of interacting Ecologies is beyond this book, and is a subject of my future research attention.

Scaffolding and assistance quantification

I have echoed the call for a return to the ZPD roots of scaffolding (see Pea, 2004, for instance). This has motivated me to underline that a useful, but currently rare, focus can be placed upon the quantification of the assistance that a learner uses to succeed, as a means of evaluating their collaborative capability as opposed to their independent achievement. The Ecology of Resources model is therefore grounded in the concept of the Zone of Available Assistance and the idea that we can quantify assistance. My use of the term 'quantification' describes how one evaluates the assistance that a learner has been given and refers to both the *amount or quantity* of assistance and to the *quality* of that assistance. This quantification defines the way in which a task is shared between learner and resource elements, in particular MAPs. Any implementation of scaffolding will require this assistance quantification and the participatory design process should provide an initial quantification as a best first guess that can be improved through later design iterations. Alternatively, the design may specify that the role of the technology is to support MAPs in their ability to quantify the assistance they offer. It is therefore likely that some of the assistance quantification will be performed by technology, some in the heads of the MAPs and some within the design documentation that details any adjustments that have been identified.

Time

One of the extraordinary things about humans is our ability to adapt to changes of circumstances both foreseen and unforeseen and to do so as part of an experience that has a seamless quality. We actively weave some sort of coherence between our interactions so that our experience of the world does not fragment or present interfaces between time and space that grate on our expectations. Our experiences with technology can feel rather less smooth as we move between different digital and physical interfaces and take advantage of the connections afforded by technology. I have already suggested that technology offers the operational connections upon which people must build meaningful interactions to feel the benefits of technology-rich learning. This coherence or narrative that is built upon our interactions with people, things, locations and events may be supported through technology and is conjured up by the Lines of Desire metaphor. There is, however, an aspect of this narrative construction that I have sidestepped until now, and that is the issue of *Time*.

If we accept that context is centred on an individual, then its timescale is that individual's life and its boundaries are those of the totality of that individual's interactions. The Ecology of Resources model and approach are intended, however, to be a useful abstraction for the development of technology-rich learning activities. The emphasis I have put upon participatory methods offers a mechanism for some sustainability, but it is not my suggestion that developments should be for the lifetimes of the learners involved. There will be a time at which the design activity begins, a time at which the activity so designed is initially implemented and a time at which the design process, or perhaps more accurately its most recent iteration, is 'complete' in some sense. We might think of the time between the design activity beginning and the completion of an iteration as an episode, accepting that there may be many episodes for the learner that may be more or less well integrated with each other. I find the concept of landscape particularly useful in the way that it focuses on the fact that landscapes have horizons that draw attention to new possibilities, as well as offering closure on our current view. We can think of the end of a design iteration as closing off what the eye can see, but the knowledge that the learning can continue and that more episodes are to follow are represented through the notion of a horizon of new possibilities.

Benford *et al.* (2009) use the word trajectory to describe a coherent journey through a user experience that involves multiple technologies and interfaces to support interactions over time and space. They suggest that there are 'critical moments' in user experience where continuity and coherence need careful design attention, and examples of these critical moments include the occasions when people change roles and interfaces or move between physical and virtual worlds. Their work is not specifically concerned with learning, and I suspect the learning process would throw up fresh sites for 'critical moments', but their idea of trajectories resonates with the complexities of the Ecology of Resources model and may offer guidelines that could be adapted for technology-rich learning activity development.

New opportunities for learning: learner-generated contexts

The relationship between learners and MAPs supports the negotiation of the learner's ZPA. It is a relationship in which assistance is carefully provided and removed in order to increase the learner's proficiency and capability. Technology can support this negotiation process, by supporting interactions between learners and their MAPs, by taking on the role of a MAP, by supporting collaboration between multiple MAPs and through the storage, analysis, representation and visualization of some of a learner's interactions with their Ecology of Resources. Technology offers increased connectivity between people and between the physical and virtual reality of their world, making the concept of distributed scaffolding a real possibility.

In harmony with my definition of context is the view that communities of people work together to build, shape and reshape those communities and their artefacts using language as a means of organizing their activity and of passing on the results to future generations. This is where technology once again offers new possibilities. Technology brings about collaboration on a massive and global scale, such as that seen through Web 2.0 technology, and collaboration that involves human and machine enterprise, such as the crowd sourcing in Galaxy Zoo. This is significant, because this difference in the scale of information-sharing and collaboration has become a *difference in kind* and because 'anything that changes the way groups get things done will affect society as a whole' (Shirky, 2008: 23). So what might this mean for learning and for learners? Clark (2008) refers to people as 'epistemic engineers' who

> self-engineer ourselves to think and perform better in the world we find ourselves in. We self-engineer worlds in which to build better worlds to think in. We build better tools to think with and use these very tools to discover still better tools to think with. We tune the ways we use these tools to discover still better tools to think with. We tune the way we use these tools by building educational practices to train ourselves to use our best cognitive tools better. We even tune the way we tune the way we use our best cognitive tools by devising environments that help build better environments for educating ourselves in the use of our own cognitive tools (Clark, 2008: 59–60).

If we accept this, then it is worth pondering what cognitive tools are currently being tuned and what kind of tuning is going on. The questions that this pondering accentuates for me concern: the scholarly process of knowledge construction; learner agency and the relationship between learners and their MAPs; and the nature of the cognitive tools that learners (and MAPs) will need in the future if they are to select effectively from the staggering array of potential resources. I tackle each of these questions in turn in the text that follows and stress that they are not discrete entities, but interlinked with each other.

The scholarly process of knowledge construction

Young (2008) discusses the emphasis within the media and amongst policymakers of terms like 'knowledge society' and asks what this usage of knowledge means. He also suggests that we need an account of knowledge as a distinctive category in order to 'account for the distinctive feature of our era – the exponential growth of knowledge and its capacity for transforming the world' (Young, 2008: 62). In my earlier discussions of the Knowledge and Skills resource category I used the grounding of the Ecology of Resources model in Vygotsky's work to confirm that the Ecology of Resources approach acknowledges the existence of an objective body of knowledge produced through a community's interactions over time.

If mass collaboration and the proliferation of new interactions enabled by technology are bringing about *changes in kind,* then perhaps one site where these changes might usefully shape our cognition is with respect to the collaborative and participatory construction of adapted, extended and new bodies of knowledge, changes that may enable more people to engage with the scholarly knowledge cycle. I would suggest that examples of mass collaboration are already displaying elegant examples of distributed intelligence, examples that are beginning to involve novices working with experts and humans working with machines. The classification of new galaxies in Galaxy Zoo may also be contributing to the body of knowledge about astronomy and this contribution will be the result of the efforts of many people who would not previously have considered themselves part of the scholarly knowledge production process. There is a step missing here, however, if these new 'knowledge body constructors' are to signal the step change in cognitive tuning that a *change in kind* ought to yield. This step concerns the need to develop people's understanding of what knowledge is, so that they can both tune and appreciate their own knowledge construction efforts.

My discussion of epistemic cognition in Chapter 2 offers some candidates for consideration with respect to how we might help more people to understand what knowledge is, which involve specifying:

1 What kind of knowledge concepts are the subject of the learning activity and how they are described in terms of their relationships to the other resource elements within the learner's Ecology of Resources. This suggestion is consistent with the Curriculum-Based Ecosystems suggested by Barab and Roth (2006) who recognize that knowledge requires an understanding of the relationship between concepts and the accompanying resources and 'contexts-of-use'. The emphasis is placed upon viewing knowledge with respect to its relationships with other resource elements and upon making these relationships as explicit as is practicable. Relationships such as those

with people draws attention, for example, to the manner in which a teacher's epistemic cognition will influence the learner's interactions with knowledge, as will the medium through which information is presented to learners. For instance, is information presented through video perceived to be more or less authoritative than text?

2   What it means for someone to know something, for example that they can specify the evidence that supports their knowing and justify the validity of this knowledge.

3   What role the learning process plays in helping the learner to know something. This entails identifying the process by which the learner used the resources available to them to specify the evidence and justify its validity.

4   What it would mean for the learner to be aware of the process through which they have come to know something.

Each of these elements contributes to increasing personal agency in the learner's conceptions about the nature of knowledge. This also offers a useful way of talking about the role of teaching. A learner's interactions with those who are helping them to learn will influence the way in which the elements identified above can be developed. Teachers, peers and others can engender a move to a more sophisticated appreciation of each of these elements if their interactions are grounded in such an approach.

My earlier discussion of the Knowledge and Skills category also confirmed that the interconnectedness in the Ecology of Resources model did not signal a belief that all forms of knowledge are essentially the same. Different specialist traditions will offer different methodologies and specifications about how knowledge of that specialism is generated and acquired (Young, 2008). A second step that needs to happen for the desired step change in cognitive tuning is to open up the manner in which these bodies of knowledge are generated and recognized. This step can be extended beyond the well-defined bodies of formal knowledge to encompass new conceptions of vocational practice, for example, such as the multifaceted approach proposed by Guile (2009) in his rethinking of the relationship between vocational practice, qualifications, and learners transitioning into employment. Some specialisms may be more suitable than others, and we need to take care here to ensure that the specialisms are operating as gatekeepers of this knowledge in a manner that is appropriate and not by dint of some embedded 'technology' as in the case of the early scribes who mastered the art of writing (Shirky, 2008). This is important if we are to realize the power inherent in a more democratically distributed growth of knowledge.

Learner agency and the relationship between learners and their MAPs

the general law of cultural development (Vygotsky, 1978) makes plain the responsibility incumbent on society to make available opportunities and tools for shared consciousness and understanding. This responsibility is dynamic and therefore requires that society updates its provision in line with development. To what extent then has the nature of the learning and teaching relationships, at least with respect to formal education, developed in line with the *changes in kind* I discussed above? In particular, has the balance of power between people playing different roles within a learner's Ecology of Resources developed consistently with the new interactions made possible through technology and our changing relationships with it? The Ecology of Resources approach stresses the importance of intentionality and draws attention to the concept of *obuchenie* to describe a learning and teaching process that has a sense of mutual cognitive growth within both the learner and their MAP.

I suggest that we need to consider how we facilitate a learner to take greater agency in the creation of their Ecology of Resources, the negotiation of their ZPA and their learning through a constant series of adjustments to this dynamic. For example, the technological innovations and resultant expansion in the forms of interaction available to a greater number of people mean that MAPs may be faced increasingly with learners who know more about at least certain aspects of the technologies and interactions than they do. The negotiation between learner and MAP in their construction of the learner's ZPA will need to recognize the value of the learner's technology expertise resources and also recognize that this does not diminish the MAPs' knowledge and teaching expertise resources if the mutual growth envisaged in the term *obuchenie* is to ensue. It is also the case that these same technological and interactional innovations offer the opportunity for the generation of contexts for learning by learners. I describe this as a *learner-generated context*: 'a context created by people interacting together with a common, self-defined learning goal' (Luckin *et al.* forthcoming, 2010). The idea behind a learner-generated context is not that learners can necessarily work unaided by MAPs, rather it is that learners can be more active in the construction of their own contexts for learning through appropriate technology and appropriate MAP interaction. Institutions such as schools have a key place within a learner's Ecology of Resources, but this importance is as much about how they enable learners to build links between their experiences outside the school as it is with the way that they support learning experiences within the school. I have referred to this previously as 'The Institutional Illusion' (Luckin, 2009).

The nature of the cognitive tools that learners (and MAPs) will need

I have stated elsewhere (Luckin *et al.*, 2009) that the current exploitation of new technology, such as Web 2.0, is not taking most learners beyond the base level of superficial use that the technology naturally encourages. I have also expressed concern about the extent to which even relatively sophisticated learners are developing an understanding about how knowledge is justified. I build on these concerns here and suggest the kinds of cognitive tools that are needed for a capable population. My discussion of the first two questions has already suggested that learners (and MAPs) will need improved and different *knowledge working* capabilities and improved and different *ZPA negotiation* capabilities. There are other additional capabilities that will be needed if we are to take full advantage of the staggering array of interaction possibilities that has and will continue to come our way. These include:

Perpetual Beta Skills, to be able to see the ongoing process of technology development as a learning opportunity that involves looking beyond the specific instantiation of a technology to the interactions that it permits. This skill needs to take the learner beyond an operational ability to an appreciation of the ways that the new forms of interaction can support their conceptual growth.

Failure Appetite, in order to appreciate the opportunities for experimentation and learning that mass information-sharing and collaboration can offer. Shirky makes this point well when he discusses the Web 2.0 group coordination application *Meetup*, which he suggests succeeded 'not in spite of the failed groups, but *because* of the failed groups' (Shirky, 2008: 236).

Resource Synthesis, so that the connections between resource elements in the learner's Ecology of Resources can be brought together effectively into a ZPA that progresses their learning. These resource synthesis skills extend also to the skills that the learners themselves bring to their learning: their cognitive, affective, metacognitive and epistemic resources need to be brought together in an integrated fashion and in a manner that recognizes the important connections between the learner's resources and those of their Ecology of Resources.

Technological Skills, in order to ensure that particular technologies are not seen as unnecessary filters to the learner's progress and to enable more people to engage with the ongoing development of technologies and the refinement of our relationship to these technologies. As noted by the Foresight Wider Implications of Science and Technology report (WIST) (2007), there is insufficient technological literacy to enable us to recognize and exploit the significant technological advances being made: we need a more technologically literate population, and therefore we need to develop technology-rich learning activities that support this development.

These capabilities are not suggested as an alternative to the media literacy and digital literacy skills proposed by others (Buckingham, 2007, for example) but as a necessary extension that will strengthen these new literacies.

The knowledge illusion

The path that I have sculpted in writing this book is one that has taken me through a wide and varied landscape of partial descriptions of exciting possibilities and complex issues. I have attempted to weave together a meaningful narrative about context, learning and technology from these partial descriptions and am left with a strong impression of the tensions that I have uncovered. These tensions seem particularly tricky when they relate to technology. There is, for example, the tension between the way in which technology enables us to be more connected and hooked into the world and yet it also encourages us towards greater distribution and offers us the possibility to be further separated, in a physical sense, from the resources with which we interact. Technology promises a vision of increased human agency and yet we can feel less in control and can be prone to blaming technology for making us feel this way. The tension that leaves me with the greatest feeling of discomfort is, however, that which can be seen in the rhetoric around the word 'knowledge' and the belief that the proliferation of the information resources and interaction opportunities afforded through technology will, in and of itself, make us a more knowledgeable society. I struggle to find the evidence to support this rhetoric and I conclude that we are doing little more than allowing ourselves to be lured in by an appealing and worrisome illusion. I hope that my re-definition of context through the Ecology of Resources model and framework, and my discussion of the issues that it has enabled me to uncover, may cause people to pause and consider how we might take more of a learner's resources into account when we design technology-rich learning activities and, as a result, how we may do better by our learners.

Notes

5 Modelling a Learner's Context

1 Open Mind Productions and Channel 4 Learning

8 New technologies, new interactions?

1 *Beyond Current Horizons* (2009) Final Report. [Online] Available from: http://www.beyondcurrenthorizons.org.uk/outcomes/reports/final-report-2009/

National Science Foundation Strategic Plan 2006 – 2011. [Online] Available from: http://www.nsf.gov/publications/pub_summ.jsp?ods_key=nsf0648

Engineering and Physical Sciences Research Council ICT funding priority signposting. [Online] Available from: http://www.epsrc.ac.uk/Research Funding/Opportunities/ResponsiveMode/Signpost/ICT.htm

Technology Strategy Board ICT strategy. [Online] Available from: http://www.innovateuk.org/_assets/pdf/corporate-publications/ict%20strategy.pdf

Becta Emerging Technologies for Learning. [Online] Available from: http://emergingtechnologies.becta.org.uk/index.php?section=etr&filter=Art Tec_001

PWC, Technology Forecast Winter 2009. [Online] Available from: http://www.pwc.com/us/en/technology-forecast/winter2009/index.jhtml

Foresight Sigma Scan, UK Government Office for Science (2009). [Online] Available from: http://www.sigmascan.org/Live/

Foresight Wider Implications of Science and Technology (WIST) report, UK Government Office for Science (2007). [Online] Available from: http://www.foresight.gov.uk/Horizon%20Scanning%20Centre/21501%20Foresight%20WIST%20AW%20v6.pdf

References

Aleven, V., McLaren, B. M., Roll, I. & Koedinger, K. R. (2004) Toward Tutoring Help Seeking – Applying Cognitive Modeling to Meta-cognitive Skills. *Lecture Notes in Computer Science* 3220. Berlin, Springer-Verlag, pp. 227–39.

Ames, C. (1992) Classrooms: Goals, structures and student motivation. *Journal of Educational Psychology,* 84 (3), 261–71.

Anderson, J. R. (1976) *Language, Memory and Thought.* Hillsdale, Erlbaum.

Anderson, J. R. (1983) *The Architecture of Cognition.* Cambridge, MA, Harvard University Press.

Anderson, J. R., Farrell, R. G. & Sauers, R. (1984) Learning to Program in LISP. *Cognitive Science,* 8 (2): 87–129.

Aroyo, L., Dolog, P., Houben, G.-J., Kravcik, M., Naeve, A., Nilsson, M. & Wild, F. (2006) Interoperability in Personalized Adaptive Learning. *Educational Technology & Society,* 9 (2): 4–18.

Avramides, K. (2009) *An Investigation into Students' Understanding of Knowledge Justification in Psychology Using a Software Tool: Theory and method in the study of epistemic cognition.* Unpublished PhD thesis. University of Sussex.

Azevedo, R., Moos, D. C., Winters, F. W., Greene, J. A., Cromley, J. G., Olson, E. D. & Godbole-Chaudhuri, P. (2005) Why is Externally-regulated Learning More Effective than Self-regulated Learning with Hypermedia? In Looi, C-K., McCalla, G., Bredeweg, B. & Breuker, J. (eds.), *Artificial Intelligence in Education: Supporting learning through intelligent and socially informed technology* (pp. 41–48). Amsterdam, Netherlands, IOS Press.

Baker, R. S. J. D., de Carvalho, A. M. J. A., Raspat, J., Aleven, V., Corbett, A. T. & Koedinger, K. R. (2009) Educational Software Features that Encourage & Discourage 'Gaming the System'. In Dimitrova, V., Mizoguchi, R., du Boulay, B. & Graesser. A. (eds.). *Proceedings of the 14th International Conference on Artificial Intelligence in Education,* pp. 475–82.

Balaam, M. (2009) Exploring the Emotional Experiences of High School Students with a Subtle Stone Technology. Unpublished PhD thesis. University of Sussex.

Barab, S. A. & Roth, W.-M. (2006). Intentionally-Bound Systems and Curricular-Based Ecosystems: An Ecological Perspective on Knowing. *Educational Researcher,* 35 (5), 3–13.

Baxter-Magolda, M. B. (2004) Evolution of a Constructivist Conceptualization of Epistemological Reflection. *Educational Psychologist,* 39 (1), 31–42.

Beal, C. & Lee, H. (2008) Mathematics Motivation and Achievement as Predictors of High School Students' Guessing and Help-seeking with Instructional Software. *Journal of Computer Assisted Learning,* 24 (6), 507–14.

Beal, C., Qu, L. & Lee, H. (2006) Classifying Learner Engagement Through Integration of Multiple Data Sources. *Proceedings of the 21st National Conference on Artificial Intelligence* (July 16–20), Boston, MA.

Beetham, H. (2004) *Review: Developing e-learning models for the JISC practitioner communities,* e-pedagogy programme report. [Online] available at http://www.jisc.ac.uk/epedagogy [Accessed 2 July, 2009].

Belenky, M., Clichy, B., Goldberger, N. & Tarule, J. (1986) *Women's Ways of Knowing: The development of self, voice, and mind.* New York, Basic Books.

Benford, S. (2005) Pushing the Boundaries of Interaction in Public. *Interactions,* 12 (4) 57–58.

Benford, S., Giannachi, G., Koleva, B. & Rodden, T. (2009) *From Interaction to Trajectories: Designing coherent journeys through user experiences.* CHI 2009 (April 4–9), Boston, MA; New York, ACM, pp. 709–18.

Benyon, D. (2006) Navigating Information Space: Web site design and lessons from the built environment. *PsychNology Journal,* 4 (1), 7–24.

Bergin, D. A., Ford, M. E. & Hess, R. D. (1993) Patterns of Motivation and Social Behaviour Associated with Microcomputer Use of Young Children. *Journal of Educational Psychology,* 85, 437–45.

Bliss, J., Askew, M. & Macrae, S. (1996) Effective Teaching and Learning: Scaffolding revisited. *Oxford Review of Education,* 22 (1), 37–61.

Bloom, B. S., Engelhart, M. D., Furst, E. J., Hill, W. H. & Krathwohl, D. R. (1956) *Taxonomy of Educational Objectives: The cognitive domain.* New York, Longman.

Boehner, K., DePaula, R., Dourish, P. & Sengers, P. (2007) How Emotion is Made and Measured. *International Journal of Human-Computer Studies,* 65 (4), 275–91.

Boekaerts, M. (2003) Towards a Model that Integrates Motivation, Affect and Learning. *BJEP Monograph Series II, Number 2 – Development and Motivation,* 1 (1), 173–89.

Booch, G., Rumbaugh, J., & Jacobson, I. (2005) *Unified Modeling Language User Guide, The* (Addison-Wesley Object Technology Series). Boston, MA, Addison-Wesley Professional.

Bransford, J. D., Brown, A. L. & Cocking, R. (2000) *How People Learn.* Washington, DC, National Academy Press.

Brewster, D. (2009) *Interrupted Conversations: Enhancing Laurillard's conversational framework to take account of disruption.* Unpublished PhD thesis, University of Sussex.

Brown, A. L. (1987) Metacognition, Executive Control, Self-regulation, and Other More Mysterious Mechanisms. In Weinert, F. E. & Kluwe, R. H. (eds.), *Metacognition, Motivation, and Understanding* (pp. 65–116). Hillsdale, NJ, Lawrence Erlbaum.

Brown, J. S. (1990) Toward a New Epistemology for Learning. In Frasson, C. & Gauthier, G. (eds.), *Intelligent Tutoring Systems: At the crossroads of artificial intelligence and education* (pp. 262–86). Norwood, NJ, Ablex.

Brown, J. S., Collins, A. & Duguid, P. (1989) Situated Cognition and the Culture of Learning. *Educational Researcher,* 18, 32–42.

Bruner, J. (1984) Vygotsky's Zone of Proximal Development: The hidden agenda. In Rogoff, B. & Wertsch, J. V. (eds.) *Children's Learning in the 'Zone of Proximal Development'* (pp. 93–97). San Francisco, Jossey-Bass.

Bruner, J. (1996) *The Culture of Education*. Cambridge, MA, Harvard University Press.

Bruner, J. S. & Bornstein, M. H. (1989) On Interaction. In Bornstein, M. H. & Bruner, J. S. (eds.) *Interaction in Human Development* (pp. 1–14). Hillsdale, NJ: Lawrence Erlbaum Associates, Inc.

Brusilovsky, P. & Peylo, C. (2003) Adaptive and Intelligent Web-based Educational Systems. *International Journal of Artificial Intelligence in Education*, 12 (2–4): 159–72.

Brusilovsky, P., Kobsa, A. & Nejdl, W. (eds.) (2007) *The Adaptive Web: Methods and strategies of web personalization*. Berlin & Heidelberg, Springer-Verlag.

Buckingham, D. (2007) *Beyond Technology: Children's learning in the age of digital culture*. Cambridge, UK, Polity.

Bull, S. & Kay, J. (2007) Student Models that Invite the Learner In: The SMILIJ Open Learner Modelling Framework. *International Journal of Artificial Intelligence in Education*, 17 (2), 89–120.

Bull, S. & Kay, J. (2008) Metacognition and Open Learner Models. The 3rd Workshop on Meta-Cognition and Self-Regulated Learning in Educational Technologies. [Online] Available at http://www.andrew.cmu.edu/user/iroll/workshops/its08/papers/Bull.pdf [Accessed 25 July, 2009]

Butler, K. A. & Lumpe, A. (2008) Student Use of Scaffolding Software: Relationships with motivation and conceptual understanding. *Journal of Science Education and Technology*, 17, 427–36.

Carroll, J. M. (ed.) (2002) *Human-Computer Interaction in the New Millennium*. Reading, MA: Addison-Wesley.

Cartwright, K. (2002) Cognitive Development and Reading: The relation of reading-specific multiple classification skill to reading comprehension in elementary school children. *Journal of Educational Psychology*, 94, 56–63.

Casey, E. (2001) Between Geography and Philosophy: What does it mean to be in the Place-World? *Annals of the Association of American Geographers*, 91 (4), 683–93.

Cassell, J. (2004) Towards a Model of Technology and Literacy Development: Story listening systems. *Journal of Applied Developmental Psychology*, 25, 75–105.

Catling, S. (2005) Children's Personal Geographies and the English Primary School Geography Curriculum. *Children's Geographies*, 3 (3), 325–44.

Chalmers, M. (2004) A Historical View of Context. *Computer Supported Cooperative Work*, 13 (3), 223–47.

Chan, T-W. (1996) Learning Companion Systems, Social Learning Systems and the Global Social Learning Club. *International Journal of Artificial Intelligence in Education*, 7, 125–59.

Chan, T. W. & Baskin, A. B. (1990) Learning Companion Systems. In Frasson, C. & Gauthier, G. (eds.), *Intelligent Tutoring Systems: At the crossroads of Artificial Intelligence and education* (pp. 7–33). Norwood, NJ, Ablex.

Chan, T., Chee, Y.S. & Lim, E.L. (1992) COGNITIO: 'An extended computational theory of cognition'. In Frasson, C., Gauthier, G. & McCalla, G. (eds.), Intelligent Tutoring Systems, Second International Conference, ITS '92, Montréal, Canada (June 10–12), Proceedings. *Lecture Notes in Computer Science*, 608 (pp. 244–52). Berlin, Springer-Verlag.

Chan, T. W., Chung, I. L., Ho, R. G., Hou, W. J. & Lin, G. L. (1992) Distributed

Learning Companion System: West revisited. In Gauthier, G. & Frasson, G. M. C. (eds.), *Lecture Notes in Computer Science*, 608 (pp. 643–49). Berlin, Springer-Verlag.

Chen, N., Wei, C-W., Wu, K-T. & Uden, L. (1992) Effects of High Level Prompts and Peer Assessment on Online Learners' Reflection Levels. *Computers & Education*, 52 (2), 283–91.

Chou, C-Y., Chan, T-W. & Lin, C-J. (2003) Redefining the Learning Companion: The past, present, and future of educational agents. *Computers and Education*, 40, 225–69.

Clark, A. (2008) *Supersizing the Mind: Embodiment, action and cognitive extension*. New York, Oxford University Press.

Clarke, D. (2003) Practice, Role and Position: Whole class patterns of participation. Paper presented as part of the symposium 'Patterns of Participation in the Classroom' at the Annual Meeting of the American Educational Research Association (21–25 April), Chicago.

Cole, M. (1996) *Cultural Psychology: A once and future discipline*. Cambridge, MA, Harvard University Press.

Collins, A., Brown, J. S. & Newman, S. E. (1989) Cognitive Apprenticeship: Teaching the crafts of reading, writing, and mathematics. In Resnick, L. B. (ed.), *Knowing, Learning, and Instruction: Essays in honour of Robert Glaser* (pp. 453–94). Hillsdale, NJ, Lawrence Erlbaum Associates.

Conati, C. & Maclaren, H. (2009) *Modelling User Affect from Causes and Effects*. [Online] Available at http://www.cs.ubc.ca/~conati/my-papers/UMUAI-Affect-Conati.pdf [Accessed 2 August, 2009].

Conole, G., Littlejohn, A., Falconer, I. & Jeffery, A. (2005) *The LADIE Lit Review*. [Online] Available at http://www.elframework.org/refmodels/ladie/ouputs/LADIE%20lit%20review%20v15.doc [Accessed 12 August, 2008].

Cosgrove, D. (2004) Landscape and Landshift. Lecture delivered at the 'Spatial Turn in History' Symposium, German Historical Institute, Washington, DC. 19 February.

Crabtree, A. & Rodden, T. (2008) Hybrid Ecologies: Understanding cooperative Interaction in Emerging Physical-digital Environments. *Personal and Ubiquitous Computing*, 12 (7), 481–93.

Craig, S. D., Graesser, A. C., Sullins, J. & Gholson, B. (2004) Affect and Learning: An exploratory look into the role of affect in learning with AutoTutor. *Journal of Educational Media*, 29: 241–50.

Crippen, K. J. & Earl, B. L. (2007) The Impact of Web-based Worked Examples and Self-explanation on Performance, Problem solving, and Self-efficacy. *Computers & Education*, 49 (3), 809–21.

Crook, C. (1994) *Computers and the Collaborative Experience of Learning*. London, Routledge.

Cummins, S., Curtis, S., Diez-Roux, A. & Macintyre, S. (2007) Understanding and Representing 'Place' in Health Research: A relational approach. *Social Science and Medicine*, 65, 1825–38.

Damon, W. & Phelps, E. (1989a) Strategic Uses of Peer Learning in Children's Education. In Berndt, T. J. & Ladd, G.W. (eds.), *Peer Relationships in Child Development* (pp.135–57). New York, Wiley.

Damon, W. & Phelps, E. (1989b) Critical Distinctions Among Three Approaches to Peer Education. *International Journal of Educational Research*, 13, 9–19.

Daniels, H. (2001) *Vygotsky and Pedagogy*. London, RoutledgeFalmer.

Darnon, C., Muller, D., Schrager, S. M. & Pannuzzo, N. (2006) Mastery and Performance Goals Predict Epistemic and Relational Conflict Regulation. *Journal of Educational Psychology*, 98 (4), 766–76.

Davis, E. A. & Miyake, N. (2004) Explorations of Scaffolding in Classroom Systems. *Journal of Learning Sciences*, 13 (3), 265–72.

Davydov, V. & Kerr, S. (1995) The Influence of L.S. Vygotsky on Education Theory, Research and Practice. *Educational Researcher*, 24 (3), 12–21.

Dawes, L., Mercer, N. & Wegerif, R. (2004) *Thinking Together: A programme of activities for developing speaking, listening and thinking skills*. Birmingham, Imaginative Minds Ltd.

Day, P. (2008) Community Networks: Building and sustaining community relationships. In Schuler, D. *Liberating Voices! A pattern language for communication revolution*. London, The MIT Press.

Day, P. & Farenden, C. (2007) Community Network Analysis – Communications, Neighbourhood and Action (CNA²): A community engagement strategy and research methodology. In Williamson, A. & de Souza, R. (eds.), *Researching with Communities*. Auckland, New Zealand, Muddy Creek Press.

De Bra, P., Aerts, A., Berden, B., Lange, B. D., Rousseau, B., Santic, T., Smits, D. & Stash, N. (2003) *AHA! The adaptive hypermedia architecture*. Proceedings of the fourteenth ACM conference on hypertext and hypermedia. Nottingham, UK, ACM Press.

de Roure, C. (2007) *The New e-Science*. [Online] Available from: http://www.semanticgrid.org/presentations/NeweScience.html [Accessed 22 June, 2009].

Denzin, N. (1984) *On Understanding Emotion*. San Francisco, Jossey-Bass.

Dey, A. K. (2001) Understanding and Using Context. *Personal and Ubiquitous Computing Journal*, 5 (1), 2001, 4–7.

Dillenbourg, P. (1999) What Do You Mean by Collaborative Learning? In Dillenbourg, P. (ed.), *Collaborative-learning: Cognitive and computational approaches* (pp.1–19). Oxford, Elsevier.

Dillenbourg, P. (2002) Over-scripting CSCL: The risks of blending collaborative learning with instructional design. In Kirschner, P. A. (ed.), *Three Worlds of CSCL: Can we support CSCL?* (pp. 61–91). Nederland, Heerlen, Open Universiteit.

Dillenbourg, P. & Hong, F. (2008) The Mechanics of CSCL Macro Scripts. *Computer-Supported Collaborative Learning*, 3 (1), 5–23.

Dillenbourg, P., Baker, M., Blaye, A. & O'Malley, C. (1995) The Evolution of Research on Collaborative Learning. In Spada, E. & Reiman, P. (eds.), *Learning in Humans and Machine: Towards an interdisciplinary learning science* (pp. 189–211). Oxford, Elsevier.

D'mello, S. & Graesser, A. (2007) Mind and Body: Dialogue and posture for affect detection in learning environments. In Luckin, R., Koedinger, K., Greer, J. & Johnson, L. (eds.), *Building Technology Rich Learning Contexts that Work* (pp. 161–68). Amsterdam, Netherlands, IOS Press.

Doise, W. (1990) The Development of Individual Competencies Through Social Interaction. In Foot, H. C., Morgan, M. J. & Shute, R. H. (eds.), *Children Helping Children*, (pp. 43–64). Chichester, J. Wiley & Sons.

Doise, W. & Mugny, G. (1984) *The Social Development of the Intellect*. Oxford, Pergamon Press.

Dorst, K. (2003) *Understanding Design*. The Netherlands, BIS.

Dourish, P. (2001) *Where the Action Is: The foundations of embodied interaction*.

Cambridge, MA, MIT Press.

Dourish, P. (2006) Re-space-ing Place: 'Place' and 'Space' ten years on. In *Proceedings of ACM CSCW06 Conference on Computer-Supported Cooperative Work*, pp. 299–308.

Dourish, P. & Bell, G. (2007) The Infrastructure of Experience and the Experience of Infrastructure: Meaning and structure in everyday encounters with space. *Environment and Planning B: Planning and Design*, 34 (3), 414–30.

Dragon, T., Arroyo, I., Woolf, B. P., Burleson, W., Rana, E. & Eydgahi, H. (2008) Viewing Student Affect and Learning through Classroom Observation and Physical Sensors. In Woolf, B. P., Aïmeur, E., Nkambou, R. & Lajoie, S. (eds.), *ITS 2008. Lecture Notes in Computer Science*, 5091 (pp. 29–39). Berlin, Springer.

Druin, A. (2002) The Role of Children in the Design of New Technology. *Behaviour and Information Technology*, 21 (1), 1–25.

du Boulay, B., Avramides, K., Luckin, R., Martínez-Mirón, E., Rebolledo Méndez, G. and Harris, A. (forthcoming) Towards Systems That Care: A conceptual framework based on motivation, metacognition and affect, *International Journal of Artificial Intelligence and Education*.

du Boulay, B. & Luckin R. (2001) Modelling Human Teaching Tactics and Strategies for Tutoring Systems. *International Journal of Artificial Intelligence in Education*, 12, 235–56.

Dweck, C. S. & Leggett, E. L. (1988) A Social-cognitive Approach to Motivation and Personality. *Psychological Review*, 95 (2), 256–73.

Dyke, M., Connole, G., Ravenscroft, A. & de Freitas, S. (2007) Learning Theory and its Application to e-learning. In Connole, G. and Oliver, M. (eds.), *Contemporary Perspectives in e-learning Research: Theme, methods & impact on practice*. London, Routledge.

Engeström, Y. (1987) Learning by Expanding: An activity theoretical approach to developmental research. Cited in Cole, M. (1996) *Cultural Psychology: A once and future discipline*. Cambridge, MA, Harvard University Press.

Engeström, Y. (2009) From Communities of Practice to Wildfire Activities and Mycorrhizae. Webcast of lecture given at the 'Talking Practice' event, Practice-based Professional Learning Centre for Excellence in Teaching and Learning. Available from: http://www.open.ac.uk/pbpl/resources/details/detail.php?itemId=48563c324dc5c [Accessed 22 July, 2009].

Feng, M., Heffernan, N. T. & Beck, J. (2009) Using Learning Decomposition to Analyze Instructional Effectiveness in the ASSISTment system. In Dimitrova, V., Mizoguchi, R., du Boulay, B. & Graesser, A. (eds.), *Proceedings of the 14th International Conference on Artificial Intelligence in Education* (pp. 523–530). Brighton, UK.

Fitzpatrick, G. (2003) *The Locales Framework: Understanding and designing for wicked problems*. Dordrecht, The Netherlands, Kluwer Academic Publishers.

Flavell, J. (1979) Metacognition and Cognitive Monitoring. *American Psychologist*, 34 (10), 906–11.

Flavell, J. H. & Wellman, H. M. (1977) Metamemory. In Kail, R. V. & Hagen, J. W. (eds.), *Perspectives on the Development of Memory and Cognition* (pp. 3–33). Hillsdale, NJ, Erlbaum.

Foresight Sigma Scan (2009) *School's In: Learning for the twenty-first century*. [Online] Available from: http://www.sigmascan.org/Live/Issue/ViewIssue.aspx?IssueId=505&SearchMode=1 [Accessed 22 August, 2009].

Foresight Wider Implications of Science and Technology (WIST) report. (2007) UK Government Office for Science [Online] Available from http://www.foresight. gov.uk/Horizon%20Scanning%20Centre/21501%20Foresight%20WIST%20 AW%20v6.pdf [Accessed 22 August, 2009].

Freedman, S. W. (1995) Crossing the Bridge to Practice. *Written Communication*, 12 (1), 74–92.

Fretz, E. B., Wu, H-K., Zhang, B., Krajcik, J. S. & Soloway, E. (2002) An Investigation of Software Scaffolds Supporting Modeling Practices. *Research in Science Education*, 32, 567–89.

Gagne, R. (1965) *The Conditions of Learning and Theory of Instruction*. New York, CBS College Publishing.

Gagne, R. (1987) *Instructional Technology Foundations*. Hillsdale, NJ, Lawrence Erlbaum.

Gamma, E., Helm, R., Johnson, R. & Vlissides, J. (1995) *Design Patterns: Elements of reusable object-oriented software*. Reading, MA, Addison-Wesley.

Garnett, F. & Cook, J. (2004) The Community Development Model of Learning. Presented at ALT-C September 14 – 16, 2004. University of Exeter, Devon, England.

Ge, X. & Land, S. (2004) A Conceptual Framework for Scaffolding Ill-structured Problem-solving Process Using Question Prompts and Peer Interaction. *Educational Technology Research and Development*, 52 (2), 5–22.

Gertler, M. S. (2003) The Undefinable Tacitness of Being (There): Tacit knowledge and the economic geography of context. *Journal of Economic Geography*, 3, 75–99.

Gertler, M. and Wolfe, D. (2005) Spaces of Knowledge Flows: Clusters in a global context. DRUID Conference: Dynamics of Industry and Innovation: Organizations, Networks and Systems. Copenhagen (June 27–29).

Goldstein, P. (1982) The Genetic Graph: A representation for the evolution of procedural knowledge. In Sleeman, D. & Brown, J. S. (eds.), *Intelligent Tutoring Systems* (pp. 51–78). New York, Academic Press.

Good, J. & Robertson, J. (2006) CARSS: A framework for learner centred design with children. *International Journal of Artificial Intelligence and Education*, 16 (4): 381–413.

Goodwin, C. (2003) The Body in Action. In Coupland, J. & Gwyn, R. (eds.), *Discourse, the Body and Identity* (pp.19–42). New York, Palgrave/Macmillan.

Goodwin, C. (2007) Participation, Stance, and Affect in the Organization of Activities. *Discourse and Society*, 18 (1), 53–73.

Goodwin, C. (2009) Calibrating Bodies and Cognition through Interactive Practice in a Meaningful Environment. Keynote presentation at Computer Supported Collaborative Learning (June). Rhodes, Greece.

Goodyear, P. (2005) Educational Design and Networked Learning: Patterns, pattern languages and design practice. *Australian Journal of Educational Technology*, 21 (1): 82–101, available online at http://www.ascilite.org.au/ajet/ajet21/goodyear.html [Accessed 7 August, 2009].

Goos, M., Galbraith, P. & Renshaw, P. (2002) Socially Mediated Metacognition: Creating collaborative zones of proximal development in small group problem solving. *Educational Studies in Mathematics*, 49, 193–223.

Green, H. & Hannon, C. (2007) TheirSpace: Education for a digital generation. London, Demos.

Griffiths, A. K. &. Grant, A. C. (1985) High School Students' Understanding of Food

Webs. *Journal of Research in Science Teaching,* 22 (5), 421–36.

Guile, D. (2009) Conceptualizing the Transition from Education to Work as Vocational Practice: Lessons from the UK's creative and cultural sector. *British Educational Research Journal,* [online] at http://www.informaworld. com/10.1080/01411920802688713 [Accessed September 13, 2009].

Gulson, K. N. & Symes, C. (2007) Knowing One's Place: Space, theory, education. *Critical Studies in Education,* 48 (1), 97–110.

Guzdial, M., Kolodner, J., Hmelo, C., Narayanan, H., Carlson, D., Rappin, N., Hubscher, R., Turns, J. & Newstetter, W. (1996) Computer Support for Learning Through Complex Problem Solving. *Communications of the ACM,* 39 (4), 43–45.

Hadwin, A., Wozney, L. & Pontin, O. (2005) Scaffolding the Appropriation of Self-regulatory Activity: A sociocultural analysis of changes in teacher-student discourse about a graduate research portfolio. *Instructional Science,* 33, 5–6.

Hammer, D. & Elby, A. (2000) Epistemological Resources. In Fishman, B. & O'Connor-Divelbiss, S. (eds.), *Proceedings of the Fourth International Conference of the Learning Sciences* (pp. 4–5).

Harris, A., Bonnett, V., Luckin, R., Yuill, N. & Avramides, K. (2009) Scaffolding Effective Help-seeking Behaviour in Mastery and Performance Oriented Learners. In Dimitrova, V., Mizogucji, R., du Boulay, B. & Graesser, A. (eds.), *Artificial Intelligence in Education* (pp. 425–32). Amsterdam, Netherlands, IOS Press.

Harris, A., Yuill, N. & Luckin, R. (2008) The Influence of Context-specific and Dispositional Achievement Goals on Children's Paired Collaborative Interaction. *The British Journal of Educational Psychology,* 78 (3), 355–74.

Hedegaard, M. (1998) Situated learning and cognition: Theoretical learning and cognition. *Mind, Culture, and Activity,* 5, 114–26.

Heraz, A. & Frasson, C. (2009) Predicting Learner Answers Correctness through Brainwaves Assessment and Emotional Dimensions. In Dimitrova, V., Mizoguchi, R., du Boulay, B. & Graesser, A. (eds.), *Proceedings of the 14th International Conference on Artificial Intelligence in Education* (pp 49–56). Amsterdam, Netherlands, IOS Press.

Holmes, J. (2005) Designing Agents to Support Learning by Explaining. *Computers and Education,* 48 (4), 523–47.

Howe, C. J. & Tolmie, A. (2003) Group Work in Primary School Science: Discussion, consensus and guidance from experts. *International Journal of Educational Research,* 39, 51–72.

Howe, C., Tolmie, A., Duchak-Tanner, V. & Rattray, C. (2000) Hypothesis Testing in Science: Group consensus and the acquisition of conceptual and procedural knowledge. *Learning and Instruction,* 10, 1–31.

Hughes, R. I. G. (1997) Models and Representation. *Philosophy of Science,* 64, S325–36.

Hutchins, E. (1995) *Cognition in the Wild.* Cambridge, MA, MIT Press.

Irwin, D. (1991) Art Versus Design: The debate 1760–1860. *Journal of Design History,* 4 (4): 219–32.

Jackson, S. L., Stratford, S. J., Krajcik, J. & Solloway, E. (1994) Making Dynamic Modeling Accessible to Precollege Students. *Interactive Learning Environments,* 4 (3), 233–57.

Jackson, S. L., Stratford, S. J., Krajcik, J. & Solloway, E. (1996) A Learner-centred Tool for Students Building Models. *Communications of the ACM,* 39 (4), 48–50.

Jenkins, H., Clinton, K., Purushotma, R., Robison, A. & Weigel, M. (2006)

Confronting the Challenges of Participatory Culture: Media education for the 21st century. Chicago, The MacArthur Foundation.

Johnson-Laird, P. (1983) *Mental Models: Towards a cognitive science of language, inference and consciousness.* Cambridge, MA, Harvard University Press.

Jonassen, D. (1997) Instructional Design Models for Well-Structured and Ill-Structured Problem-Solving Learning Outcomes. *Educational Technology Research and Development,* 45 (1), 65–94.

Jones, P. (2005) Performing the City: A body and a bicycle take on Birmingham, UK. *Social & Cultural Geography,* 6 (6), 813–30.

Kapler, T. & Wright W. (2005) Geotime Information Visualization. *Information Visualization,* 4, 136–46.

Kapoor, A. & Picard, R. (2005) Multimodal Affect Recognition in Learning Environment, *ACM International Conference on Multimedia,* pp. 677–82.

Kapoor, A., Ahn, H. I. & Picard, R.W. (2005) Mixture of Gaussian Processes for Combining Multiple Modalities. In Oza, N. C., Polikar, R., Kittler, J. & Roli, F. (eds.), *Proceedings of Multiple Classifier Systems, 6th International Workshop, MCS 2005, (June), Seaside, CA,* PDF, (pp. 86–96).

Kaptelinin, V., Nardi, B. A. & Macaulay, C. (1999) Methods & Tools: The activity checklist; A tool for representing the 'space' of context. *Interactions,* 6 (4), 27–39.

Kay, J. (2009) Lifelong Learner Modelling for Lifelong Personalized Pervasive Learning. *IEEE Transactions on Learning Technologies,* 1 (4), 215–28.

Keller, J. M. (1987) Development and Use of the ARCS Model of Motivational Design, *Journal of Instructional Development,* 10 (3), 2–10.

Kerawalla, L., Pearce, D., Yuill, N., Luckin, R. & Harris, A. (2005) *The Design and Implementation of Classroom Activities to Teach 7–9 year-old Children Argumentation and Listening Skills.* Cognitive Science Research Paper 580, University of Sussex.

Kerawalla, L., Pearce, D., Yuill, N., Luckin, R. & Harris, A. (2008) 'I'm Keeping Those There, Are You?' The role of a new user interface paradigm – Separate Control of Shared Space (SCOSS) – in the collaborative decision-making process. *Computers and Education,* 50 (1), 193–206.

Kerckhove, D. D. & Tursi, A. (2009) The Life of Space. *Architectural Design,* 79 (1), 48–53.

King, P. M. & Kitchener, K. S. (2004) Reflective Judgement: Theory and research on the development of epistemic assumptions through adulthood. *Educational Psychologist,* 39 (1), 5–18.

Klaebe, H. G., Adkins, B., Marcus, F. & Hearn, G. (2009) Embedding an Ecology Notion in the Social Production of Urban Space. In Foth. M. (ed.), *Handbook of Research on Urban Informatics: The practice and promise of the real-time city* (pp.179–94). Hershey, PA, Information Science Reference, IGI Global.

Kluwe, R. (1982) Cognitive Knowledge and Executive Control: Metacognition. In Griffin, D. R. (ed.), *Animal Mind – Human Mind* (pp. 201–24). New York, Springer-Verlag.

Koedinger, K. R., Anderson, J. R., Hadley, W. H. & Mark, M. A. (1997) Intelligent Tutoring Goes to School in the Big City. *International Journal of Artificial Intelligence in Education,* 8, 30–43.

Kornell, N. (2009) Metacognition in Humans and Animals. *Current Directions in Psychological Science,* 18, 11–15.

Kornell, N. & Bjork, R. A. (2008) Learning Concepts and Categories: Is spacing the 'enemy of induction?' *Psychological Science,* 19, 585–92.

Koskela, H. (2000) Video Surveillance and the Changing Nature of Urban Space. *Progress in Human Geography*, 24 (2), 243–265.

Kraftl, P. & Adey, P. (2008) Architecture/Affect/Inhabitation: Geographies of being-in buildings. *Annals of the Association of American Geographers*, 98 (1), 213–31.

Kuhn, D. (1999) Metacognitive Development. In Balter, L. & Tamis-LeMonda, C. (eds.), *Child psychology: A handbook of contemporary issues* (pp. 259–86). Philadelphia, PA, Psychology Press.

Lajoie, S. (2005) Extending the Scaffolding Metaphor. *Instructional Science*, 33 (5–6), 541–57.

Lambert, D. & Morgan, J. (2009) *Teaching Geography 11–18: A conceptual approach*. Maidenhead, Open University Press.

Laurel, B. (1991) *Computers as Theatre*. Reading, MA, Addison Wesley.

Laurillard, D. (1993, 2002) *Rethinking University Teaching: A conversational framework for the effective use of learning technologies*. London and New York, RoutledgeFalmer.

Laurillard, D. & McAndrew, P. (2002) Virtual Teaching Tools: Bringing academics closer to the design of e-learning. *Network Learning 2002: A Research Based Conference on e-Learning in Higher Education and Lifelong Learning*, Sheffield, University of Sheffield.

Lave, J. (1988) *Cognition in Practice*. Cambridge: Cambridge University Press.

Lave, J. & Wenger, E. (1991) *Situated Learning: Legitimate peripheral participation*. Cambridge, Cambridge University Press.

Lazarus, R. (1991) Cognition and Motivation in Education. *American Psychologist*, 46 (4), 352–67.

LeBlanc, G. & Bearison, D. J. (2004) Teaching and Learning as a Bi-directional Activity: Investigating dyadic interactions between child teachers and child learners. *Cognitive Development*, 19, 499–515.

Leont'ev, A. N. (1979) The Problem of Activity in Psychology. In Wertsch, J. V. (ed.), *The Concept of Activity in Soviet Psychology*. New York, M. E. Sharpe.

Li, D. & Lim, C. (2008) Scaffolding Online Historical Inquiry Tasks: A case study of two secondary school classrooms. *Computers and Education*, 50 (4), 1394–410.

Light, P. & Glachan, M. (1985) Facilitation of Individual Problem Solving Through Peer Interaction. *Educational Psychology*, 1469–5820, 5 (3), 217–25.

Light, A. & Luckin, R. (2008) *Social Justice and User-centred Design*. Bristol, FutureLab.

Luckin, R. (1998) *'ECOLAB': Explorations in the zone of proximal development*. DPhil Thesis, Cognitive Science Research Paper 486. School of Cognitive and Computing Sciences, University of Sussex.

Luckin, R. (2008) The Learner-centric Ecology of Resources: A framework for using technology to scaffold learning. *Computers & Education*, 50, 449–62.

Luckin, R. (2009) *Learning, Context and the Role of Technology*. Institute of Education. London.

Luckin, R. & du Boulay, B. (1999) Designing a Zone of Proximal Adjustment. *International Journal of Artificial Intelligence and Education*, 10 (2), 198–220.

Luckin, R. & du Boulay, B. (2001) Embedding AIED in ie-TV through Broadband User Modelling (BbUM). In Moore, J., Johnson, W. L. & Redfield, C. L. (eds.), *Artificial Intelligence in Education in the Wired and Wireless Future* (pp. 322–33). Amsterdam, Netherlands, IOS Press.

Luckin, R., & Hammerton, L. (2002) Getting to Know Me: Helping learners understand their own learning needs through metacognitive scaffolding. In Cerri, S. A., Gouardères, G. & Paraguaçu, F. (eds.), *Lecture Notes In Computer Science*, 2363 (pp. 759–71). Berlin, Springer Verlag.

Luckin, R., Connolly, D., Plowman, L. & Airey, S. (2003) With a Little Help From My Friends: Children's interactions with interactive toy technology. *Journal of Computer Assisted Learning* (Special issue on Children and Technology), 19 (2), 165–76.

Luckin, R., Clark, W., Logan, K., Graber, R., Oliver, M. & Mee, A. (2009) Do Web 2.0 Tools Really Open the Door to Learning: Practices, perceptions and profiles of 11–16 year old learners? *Learning, Media and Technology*, 34 (2), 87–104.

Luckin, R., du Boulay, B., Underwood, J., Holmberg, J., Kerawalla, L., O'Connor, J., Smith, H. & Tunley, H. (2006) Designing Educational Systems Fit for Use: A case study in the application of human centred design for AIED. *International Journal of Artificial Intelligence in Education*, 16, 353–80.

Luckin, R., Clark, W., Garnett, F., Whitworth, A., Akass, J., Cook, J., Day, P., Ecclesfield, N., Hamilton, T. & Robertson, J. (forthcoming, 2010) Learner Generated Contexts: A framework to support the effective use of technology to support learning. In Lee, M. J. W. & McLoughlin, C. (eds.), *Web 2.0-Based E-Learning: Applying social informatics for tertiary teaching*. Hershey, PA, IGI Global.

Lumpe, A. T. &. Staver, J. R. (1995) Peer Collaboration and Concept Development: Learning about photosynthesis. *Journal of Research in Science Teaching*, 32 (1), 71–98.

Manovich, L. (2006) The Poetics of Augmented Space. *Visual Communication*, 5 (2), 219–40.

Marshall, P. (2007) *Physicality and Learning – searching for the effects of tangibility in scientific domains*. Unpublished DPhil Thesis, University of Sussex.

Marshall, P., Fleck, R., Harris, A. Rick, J., Hornecker, E., Rogers, Y., Yuill, N. & Dalton, N. S. (2009) Fighting for Control: Children's embodied interactions when using physical and digital representations. *Proceedings of the 27th International Conference on Human Factors in Computing Systems, l 4–0*. (April) (pp. 2149–52). Boston, MA, ACM.

Martínez-Mirón, E. (2007) *Goal Orientation in Tutoring Systems*. Unpublished PhD thesis. University of Sussex.

Marzano, R. (1998) *A Theory-Based Meta-Analysis of Research on Instruction. Mid-continent Aurora, Colorado: Regional Educational Laboratory*. Available from http://www.mcrel.org/products/learning/meta.pdf [Accessed 2 May, 2000].

Mayes, T. & De Freitas, S. (2004) *Review of e-learning Theories, Frameworks and Models*. Commissioned review report as part of the JISC-funded e-pedagogy desk study on e-learning models [Online] Available at http://www.jisc.ac.uk/uploaded_documents/Stage%202%20Learning%20Models%20(Version%201).pdf. [Accessed 9 August, 2009].

McQuiggan, S., Mott, B. & Lester, J. (2008) Modelling Self-Efficacy in Intelligent Tutoring Systems: An inductive approach. *User Modeling and User-Adapted Interaction*, 18 (1–2), 81–123.

Meece, J. L. (1991) The Classroom Context and Students' Motivational Goals. In Maehr, M. L. & Pintrich, P. (eds.), *Advances in Motivation and Achievement:* Volume 7 (pp. 261–85). Greenwich, CT, JAI.

Mercer, N. (1992) Culture, Context and the Construction of Knowledge in the

Classroom. In Light, P. & Butterworth, G. (eds.), *Context and Cognition: Ways of learning and knowing* (pp. 28–46). Mahwah, NJ, Lawrence Erlbaum.

Mercer, N. (1995) *The Guided Construction of Knowledge: Talk amongst teachers and learners.* Clevedon, Multilingual Matters.

Mercer, N. & Littleton, K. (2007) *Dialogue and the Development Thinking: A sociocultural approach.* London, Routledge.

Miller, R. B. (1953) *A Method for Man-machine Task Analysis* (Tech. Rep. No. 53–137). Wright-Patterson Air Force Base, Ohio: Wright Air Development Center.

Moher, T., Hussain, S., Halter, T. & Kilb, D. (2005) RoomQuake: Embedding dynamic phenomena within the physical space of an elementary school classroom. Conference on Human Factors in Computing Systems, 2–7 April (pp. 1655–68). Oregon, US, ACM Press.

Moher, T., Uphoff, B., Bhatt, D., López Silva, B. & Malcolm, P. (2008) WallCology: Designing interaction affordances for learner engagement in authentic science inquiry. Conference on Human Factors in Computing Systems (5–10 April) (pp. 163–172). Florence, Italy, ACM Press.

Moll, L. C. &. Whitmore, K. F. (1993) Vygotsky in Classroom Practice: Moving from individual transmission to social transaction. In Forman, E. A., Minick, N. & Stone, C. A. (eds.), *Contexts for Learning* (pp. 19–42). Oxford, Oxford University Press.

Montessori, M. (1959) *Education for a New World.* Madras, Kalakshetra Publications.

Montessori, M. (1969) *The Absorbent Mind.* Madras, Kalakshetra Publications.

Nardi, B. (1996) Studying Context: A comparison of activity theory, situated action models and distributed cognition. In Nardi, B. A. (ed.), *Context and Consciousness: Activity theory and human-computer interaction* (pp. 69–102). Cambridge, MA, MIT Press.

Norman, D. A. & Draper, S. W. (eds.) (1986) *User-Centered System Design: New perspectives on human-computer interaction.* Hillsdale, NJ, Lawrence Erlbaum.

Nussbaum M., Alvarez, C., McFarlane, A., Gomez, F., Claro, S. & Radovic, D. (2009) Technology as Small Group Face-to-face Collaborative Scaffolding. *Computers & Education,* 52, 147–53.

Oh, S. & Jonassen, D. (2007) Scaffolding Online Argumentation During Problem Solving. *Journal of Computer Assisted Learning,* 23 (2), 95–110.

Ohlsson, S. (1987) Some Principles of Intelligent Tutoring. In Lawler, R.W. & Yazdani, M. (eds.), *Artificial Intelligence and Education,* Volume 1 (pp. 203–38). Norwood, NJ, Ablex.

O'Malley, C. (1994) Computer Supported Collaborative Learning. NATO ASI Series, F: *Computer & Systems Sciences,* 128.

O'Malley, C. & Fraser, D. S. (2004) *Literature Review in Learning with Tangible Technologies.* Technical Report 12, NESTA Futurelab.

Ortony, A., Clore, G. L. & Collins, A. (1988) *The Cognitive Structure of Emotions.* Cambridge, MA, Cambridge University Press.

Pain, R. (2004) Social Geography: Participatory research. *Progress in Human Geography,* 28, 652.

Palincsar, A. S., Brown, A. L. & Campione, J. C. (1993) First-Grade Dialogues for Knowledge Acquisition and Use. In Forman, E. A., Minick, N. & Stone, C. A. (eds.), *Contexts for Learning* (pp. 43–57). Oxford.

Papert, S. Oxford University Press. (1980) *Mindstorms: Children, computers, and powerful ideas.* New York, Basic Books.

Pea, R. D. (2002) Learning Science Through Collaborative Visualization Over the Internet. In *Proceedings of the Nobel Symposium NS 120*, pp. 1–13.

Pea, R. D. (2004) The Social and Technological Dimensions of Scaffolding and Related Theoretical Concepts for Learning, Education, and Human Activity. *Journal of the Learning Sciences*, 13, 423–51.

Pearce, D., Kerawalla, L, Luckin, R., Yuill, N. & Harris, A. (2005) The Task-Sharing Framework: A generic approach to scaffolding, collaboration and meta-collaboration in educational software. In Looi, C. K. & Jonassen, D. (eds.), *Towards Sustainable and Scalable Educational Innovations Informed by the Learning Sciences* (pp. 338–45). Amsterdam, Netherlands, IOS Press.

Pekrun, R., Goetz, T., Titz, W. & Perry, R. (2002) Academic Emotions in Students' Self-regulated Learning and Achievement: A program of qualitative and quantitative research. *Educational Psychologist*, 37 (2), 91–105.

Perry, W. G. (1970) *Forms of Intellectual and Ethical Development in the College Years: A scheme*. New York, Holt, Rinehart & Winston.

Piaget, J. (1970) *Six Psychological Studies*. Brighton, Harvester.

Preece, J., Rogers, Y. & Sharp, H. (2002) *Interaction Design: Beyond human-computer interaction*. New York, John Wiley & Sons, Inc.

Price, S., Sheridan, J. G., Pontual-Falcao, T. & Roussos, G. (2008) Towards a Framework for Investigating Tangible Environments for Learning. *International Journal of Arts and Technology*. Special Issue on Tangible and Embedded Interaction, 1, (3/4), 351–68.

Puntambekar, S. & Hübscher, R. (2005) Tools for Scaffolding Students in a Complex Learning Environment: What have we gained and what have we missed? *Educational Psychologist*, 40, (1), 1–12.

Puntambekar, S. & Kolodner, J. L. (2005) Distributed Scaffolding: Helping students learn science by design. *Journal of Research in Science Teaching*, 42 (2), 185–217.

Puntambekar, S. & Styllianou, A. (2005) Designing Navigation Support in Hypertext Systems Based on Navigation Patterns. *Instructional Science*, 33 (5–6), 451–81.

Quintana, C. & Fishman, B. J. (2006) *Supporting Science Learning and Teaching with Software-based Scaffolding*. Paper presented at American Educational Research Association, 7–11 April, San Francisco, CA.

Quintana, C., Reiser, B. J., Davis, E. A., Krajcik, J., Fretz, E., Duncan, R. G., Kyza, E., Edelson, D. & Soloway, E. (2004) A Scaffolding Design Framework for Software to Support Science Inquiry. *Journal of the Learning Sciences*, 13 (3), 337–386.

Ratner, C. (1989) A Social Constructionist Critique of Naturalistic Emotion. *Journal of Mind and Behaviour*, 10, 211–30.

Rebolledo-Mendez, G. (2003) Motivational Modelling in a Vygotskyan ITS. In Hoppe, U., Verdejo, M. F. & Kay, J. (eds.), *Frontiers in Artificial Intelligence and Applications*, vol. 97 (pp. 537–8) Amsterdam, Netherlands, IOS Press.

Rebolledo-Mendez, G. B., du Boulay, B. & Luckin, R. (2005) Be Bold and Take a Challenge: Could motivational strategies improve help-seeking? In Looi, C-K., McCalla, G., Bredeweg, B. & Breuker, J. (eds.), *Frontiers in Artificial Intelligence and Applications*, vol. 125 (pp. 459–63). Amsterdam, Netherlands, IOS Press.

Rebolledo-Mendez, G., du Boulay, B. & Luckin, R. (2006) Motivating the Learner: An empirical evaluation. In Ikeda, M., Ashley, K. & Chan, T.-W. (eds.), *Lecture Notes in Computer Science (LNCS)* 4053 (pp. 545–54). Berlin, Heidelberg, Springer-Verlag.

Reiser, B. J. (2004) Scaffolding Complex Learning: The mechanisms of structuring and problematizing student work. *The Journal of the Learning Sciences*, 13 (3), 273–304.

Reiser, B. J., Tabak, I., Sandoval, W. A., Smith, B. K., Steinmuller, F. & Leone, A. J. (2001) BGuILE: Strategic and conceptual scaffolds for scientific inquiry in biology classrooms. In Carver, S. M. & Klahr, D. (eds.), *Cognition and Instruction: Twenty-five years of progress* (pp. 263–305).

Reymen, I., Whyte, J. K. & Dorst, K. (2005) *Users, Designers and Dilemmas of Expertise*, Include, Royal College of Art, 5–8 April.

Rogers, P. (2006) Young People's Participation in the Renaissance of Public Space: A case study in Newcastle upon Tyne, UK. *Children, Youth and Environments*, 16 (2), 105–26.

Rogers, Y. (2006) Moving on from Weiser's Vision of Calm Computing: Engaging UbiComp experiences. In Dourish, P. & Friday, A. (eds.), *Lecture Notes in Computer Science* 4206 (pp. 404–21). Berlin, Springer-Verlag.

Roozenburg, N. F. M. & Eekels, J. (1995) *Product Design: Fundamentals and methods*. Chichester, Wiley.

Roschelle, J. (1992) Learning by Collaborating: Convergent conceptual change. *Journal of the Learning Sciences*, 2, 235–76.

Roschelle, J. & Teasley, S. (1995) The Construction of Shared Knowledge in Collaborative Problem Solving. In O'Malley, C. E. (ed.), *Computer-supported Collaborative Learning* (pp. 69–97). Heidelberg, Springer-Verlag.

Rosson, M. B. & Carroll, J. M. (1996) Scaffolded Examples for Learning Object-oriented Design. *Communications of the ACM*, 39 (4), 46–47.

Ryan, R. M. & Deci, E. L. (2000) Intrinsic and Extrinsic Motivations: Classic definitions and new directions. *Contemporary Educational Psychology*, 25, 54–67.

Salmon, G. (2004) *E-moderating: The key to teaching and learning online*. London, Taylor and Francis. [Online] Available at http://www.e-moderating.com/. [Accessed 19 June, 2009]

Sami, P. & Kai, H. (2009) From Meaning Making to Joint Construction of Knowledge Practices and Artefacts – A trialogical approach to CSCL. *Proceedings of Conference of Computer Supported Collaborative Learning*. June 8–13, University of the Aegean, Rhodes, Greece. pp. 82–92.

Saxe, G. B., Gearhart, M. & Guberman, S. R. (1984) The Social Organisation of Early Number Development. In Rogoff, B. & Wertsch, J. V. (eds.), *Children's Learning in the 'Zone of Proximal Development'* (pp. 19–30). San Francisco, Jossey-Bass.

Saxe, G. B., Gearhart, M., Note, M. & Paduano, P. (1993) Peer Interaction and the Development of Mathematical Understandings: A new framework for research and educational practice. In Daniels, H. (ed.), *Charting the Agenda: Educational activity after Vygotsky* (pp. 107–44). London, Routledge.

Scaife, M. & Rogers, Y. (1999) Kids as Informants: Telling us what we didn't know or confirming what we knew already. In Druin, A. (ed.), *The Design of Children's Technology* (pp. 27–50). San Francisco, CA, Morgan Kaufmann.

Scardamalia, M. & Bereiter, C. (1994) Computer Support for Knowledge Building Communities. *The Journal of the Learning Sciences*, 3, 265–83.

Scardamalia, M., & Bereiter, C. (2003) Knowledge Building. In *Encyclopedia of Education*, 2nd edition (pp. 1370–73) New York, Macmillan Reference, USA.

Schommer, M. (1990) Effects of Beliefs about the Nature of Knowledge on Comprehension. *Journal of Educational Psychology*, 82, 498–504.

Schwanen, T., Djist, M. & Kwan, M. (2008) ICTs and the Decoupling of everyday Activities, Space and Time. *Tijdschift voor Economische en Sociale Geografie*, 99 (5), 519–27.

Seligman, M. E. P. (1975) *Helplessness*. San Francisco, Freeman.

Sharples, M., Taylor, J. & Vavoula, G. (2007) A Theory of Learning for the Mobile Age. In Andrews, R. & Haythornthwaite, C. (eds.), *The Sage Handbook of E-learning Research* (pp. 221–47). London, Sage.

Shirky, C. (2008) *Here Comes Everybody: The power of organizing without organizations*. London, Penguin Press.

Skinner, B. F. (1938) *The Behavior of Organisms: An experimental analysis*. New York, London, D. Appleton-Century Company incorporated.

Skinner, B. F. (1968) *The Technology of Teaching*. New York, Appleton-Century-Crofts.

Smagorinsky, P. & Fly, P. K. (1993) The Social Environment of the Classroom: A Vygotskian perspective on small group process. *Communication Education*, 42, 159–71.

Soja, E. (1989) *Postmodern Geographies: The reassertion of space in critical social theory*. London, Verso Press.

Soller, A. (2002) *Computational Analysis of Knowledge Sharing in Collaborative Distance Learning*. Doctoral dissertation. University of Pittsburgh, Pittsburgh, PA.

Soller, A. (2007) Adaptive Support for Distributed Collaboration. *The Adaptive Web. Methods and Strategies of Web Personalization*, Berlin, Heidelberg, Springer, pp. 573–95.

Soloway, E., Guzdial, M. & Hay, K. E. (1994) Learner-centred Design: The challenge for HCI in the 21st century, *Interactions*, 1, 36–47.

Soloway, E., Jackson, S., Klein, J., Quintana, C., Reed, J., Spitulnik, J., Stratford, S., Studer, S., Eng, J. & Scala, N. (1996) Learning Theory in Practice: Case studies of learner centred design. *Proceedings of CHI '96 Human Factors in Computer Systems*, April 18–18, Vancouver, Canada, pp. 189–96.

Stahl, G. (2009) Collaborative Learning Through Practices of Group Cognition. *Proceedings of Conference of Computer Supported Collaborative Learning*, June 8–13, University of the Aegean, Rhodes, Greece, pp. 33–42.

Stanton-Fraser, D. (2007) The Technical Art of Learning Science. In Luckin, R., Koedinger, K., Greer, J. & Johnson, L. (eds.), Artificial Intelligence in Education: Building technology rich learning contexts that work, *Frontiers in Artificial Intelligence and Applications*, Volume 158 (pp. 5–6). Netherlands, IOS Press.

Steels, L. & Brooks, R. A. (eds.) (1995) *The Artificial Life Route to Artificial Intelligence: Building embodied situated agents*. Hillsdale, NJ, Lawrence Erlbaum.

Stenglin, M. (2008) Binding: A resource for exploring interpersonal meaning in three-dimensional space. *Social Semiotics*, 18 (4), 425–47.

Stremmel, A. J. & Fu, V. R. (1993) Teaching in the Zone of Proximal Development: Implications for responsive teaching practice. *Child and Youth Care Forum*, 22 (5), 337–50.

Suchman, L. A. (1987) *Plans and Situated Actions: The problem of human-machine communication*. Cambridge, Cambridge University Press.

Suthers, D. (2001) Towards a Systematic Study of Representational Guidance for Collaborative Learning Discourse. *Journal of Universal Computer Science*, 7 (3), 254–77.

Suthers, D. & Jones, D. (1997) An Architecture for Intelligent Collaborative Educational Systems. *Proceedings of 8th World Conference on Artificial Intelligence in Education* 19–22 Aug Kobe, Japan. Amsterdam, Netherlands, IOS Press, pp. 55–62.

Tabak, I. (2004) Synergy: A complement to emerging patterns. *Journal of the Learning Sciences,* 13 (3), 305–35.

Tharp, R. G. &. Gallimore, R. (1988) *Rousing Minds to Life.* New York, Cambridge University Press.

Thimbleby, H. (1990) *User Interface Design.* Wokingham, Addison Wesley.

Thorndike, E. L. (1898) Animal Intelligence: An experimental study of the associative processes in animals. *Psychological Review,* Monograph Supplement 2 (4, Whole No. 8).

Thorpe, M. & Lea, K. (2002) From Independent Learning to Collaborative Learning: New communities of practice in open, distance and distributed learning. In Lea, M. & Nicoll, K. (eds.), *Distributed Learning: Social and Cultural Perspectives on Practice.* London, RoutledgeFalmer.

Tolman, E. C. & Honzik, C. H. (1930) Introduction and Removal of Reward, and Maze Performance in Rats. *University of California Publications in Psychology,* 4, 257–75.

Tolmie, A., Howe, C., Mackenzie, M. & Greer, K. (1993) Task Design as an Influence on Dialogue and Learning: Primary school group work with object flotation. *Social Development,* 2 (3), 183–201.

Tuckman, B. (2007) The Effect of Motivational Scaffolding on Procrastinators' Distance Learning Outcomes. *Computers and Education,* 49 (2), 414–22.

Tudge, J. R. H. (1992) Processes and Consequences of Peer Collaboration: A Vygotskian analysis. *Child Development,* 63, 1364–79.

Underwood, J. & Underwood, G. (1999) Task Effects in Co-operative and Collaborative Learning with Computers. In Littleton, K. & Light, P. (eds.), *Learning with Computers: Analysing productive interaction* (pp.10–23). London, Routledge.

Underwood, J., Smith, H., Luckin, R. & Fitzpatrick, G. (2008) E-science in the Classroom – towards viability. *Computers and Education,* 50, 535–46.

Valsiner, J. (1984) Construction of the Zone of Proximal Development in Adult-child Joint Action: The socialisation of meals. In Rogoff, B. & Wertsch, J. V. (eds.), *Children's Learning in the 'Zone of Proximal Development'* (pp. 65–76). San Francisco, Jossey-Bass.

Van Dijk, J. (2005) *The Deepening Divide: Inequality in the information society.* London, Sage.

Van Lehn, K., Jones, R. M. & Chi, M. T. H. (1992) A Model of the Self-explanation Effect. *The Journal of the Learning Sciences* 2 (1), 1–59.

Van Lehn, K., Lynch, C., Schulze, K., Shapiro, J. A., Shelby, R. H., Taylor, L., Treacy, D. J., Weinstein, A. & Wintersgill, M. C. (2005) The Andes Physics Tutoring System: Five years of evaluations. In G. I. McCalla and C-K. Looi (eds.), *Proceedings of the Artificial Intelligence in Education Conference* (pp. 678–85). Amsterdam, IOS.

Vygotsky, L. S. (1978) *Mind in Society: The development of higher psychological processes.* Trans. Cole, M., John-Steiner, V., Scribner, S. & Souberman, E. Cambridge, MA, Harvard University Press.

Vygotsky, L. S. (1979) The Genesis of Higher Mental Functions. In Wertsch, J. V. (ed.) *The Concept of Activity in Soviet Psychology.* New York, Sharpe.

Vygotsky, L. S. (1986) *Thought and Language.* Cambridge, MA, MIT Press.

Vygotsky, L. S. (1987) *The Collected Works of L.S. Vygotsky,* Vol 1. New York: Plenum.

Watson, J. B. and Rayner, R. (1920) Conditioned Emotional Reactions. *Journal of Experimental Psychology,* 3, 1, 1–14.

Wegerif, R., Littleton, K. and Jones, A. (2003) Stand-alone Computers Supporting Learning Dialogues in Primary Classrooms. *International Journal of Educational Research,* 39, 851–69.

Wegerif, R. & Mercer, N. (1997) A Dialogical Framework for Researching Peer Talk. In Wegerif, R. & Scrimshaw, P. (eds.), *Computers and Talk in the Primary Classroom* (pp. 49–65). Clevedon, Multi-lingual Matters.

Wegerif, R., Mercer, N. & Dawes, L. (1999) From Social Interaction to Individual Reasoning: An empirical investigation of a possible sociocultural model of cognitive development. *Learning and Instruction,* 9, 493–516.

Wentworth, W. (1980) Context and Understanding: An inquiry into socialization theory. Cited by Cole, M. (1996) *Cultural Psychology: A once and future Discipline.* Cambridge, MA, Harvard University Press.

Wertsch, J. V. (ed.) (1979) *The Concept of Activity in Soviet Psychology.* New York, Sharpe.

Wertsch, J. V. (1984) The Zone of Proximal Development: Some conceptual issues. In Rogoff, B. & Wertsch, J. V. (eds.), *Children's Learning in the 'Zone of Proximal Development'* (pp. 7–18). San Francisco, Jossey-Bass.

Wertsch, J. V. (ed.) (1985a) *Culture, Communication and Cognition: Vygotskian perspectives.* Cambridge, Cambridge University Press.

Wertsch, J. V. (1985b) *Vygotsky and the Social Formation of Mind.* Cambridge, MA, Harvard University Press.

Wertsch, J. V. &. Stone, C. A. (1985) The Concept of Internalization in Vygotsky's Account of the Genesis of Higher Mental Functions. In Wertsch, J. V. (ed.) *Culture, Communication and Cognition* (pp.162–81). Cambridge, MA, Cambridge University Press.

Whitworth, A. (2009) *Information Obesity: A skill for life.* Oxford, Chandos Publishing.

Wigfield, A. & Eccles, J. A. (2000) Expectancy-Value Theory of Achievement Motivation. *Contemporary Educational Psychology,* 25, 68–81.

Williams, A. (2002) Changing Geographies of Care. *Social Science and Medicine,* 55, 141–54.

Williams, P. (2006) Developing Methods to Evaluate Web Usability with People with Learning Difficulties. *British Journal of Special Education* 33 (4), 173–79.

Williams, P. & Minnion, A. (2007) Exploring the Challenges of Developing Digital Literacy in the Context of Special Educational Needs. In Andretta, S. (ed.), *Change and Challenge: Information literacy for the 21st century.* Adelaide, Auslib Press.

Winograd, T. & Flores, F. (1985) *Understanding Computers and Cognition.* Norwood, NJ, Ablex.

Wood, D. J. (1980) Teaching the Young Child: Some relationships between social interaction, language and thought. In Olson, D. (ed) *Social Foundations of Language and Cognition: Essays in honor of J. S. Bruner.* New York, Norton.

Wood, D. (1988) *How Children Think and Learn.* London, Basil Blackwell.

Wood, D. (2001) Scaffolding, contingent tutoring, and computer-supported learning. *International Journal of Artificial Intelligence in Education,* 12, 280–91.

Wood, D. J. &. Middleton, D. J. (1975) A Study of Assisted Problem Solving. *British Journal of Psychology,* 66, 181–91.

Wood, D. J., Bruner, J. S. & Ross, G. (1976) The Role of Tutoring in Problem Solving. *Journal of Child Psychology and Psychiatry,* 17 (2), 89–100.

Wood, D., Underwood, J. & Avis, P. (1999) Integrated Learning Systems in the Classroom. *Computers and Education,* 33 (2/3), 91–108.

Wood, D. J., Wood, H. A. & Middleton, D. J. (1978) An Experimental Evaluation of Four Face-to-face Teaching Strategies. *International Journal of Behavioural Development*, 1, 131–47.

Wood, D., Wood, H., Ainsworth, S. & O'Malley, C. (1995) On Becoming a Tutor: Towards an ontogenetic model. *Cognition and Instruction*, 13 (4), 565–81.

Wood, D., Shadbolt, N., Reichgelt, H., Wood, H. & Paskiewitz, T. (1992) EXPLAIN: Experiments in planning and instruction. *Society for the Study of Artificial Intelligence and Simulation of Behaviour Quarterly Newsletter*, 81, 13–16.

Wood, H. A. & Wood, D. (1999) Help Seeking, Learning and Contingent Tutoring. *Computers and Education*, 33, 2–3, 153–69.

Woodgate, D. & Stanton-Fraser, D. (2005) *e-Science and Education 2000, A Review*. Bath, University of Bath Press.

Wyeth, P., Smith, H., Ng, K. H., Fitzpatrick, G., Luckin, R., Walker, K., Good, J., Underwood, J. & Benford, S. (2008) Learning Through Treasure Hunting: The role of mobile devices. In *Proceedings of Mobile Learning 2008*, 11–13 April, Algarve, Portugal, pp. 27–34.

Yang, G-Z. (2006) *Body Sensor Networks*. London, Springer-Verlag.

Young, M. (2008) *Bringing Knowledge Back In: From social constructivism to social realism in the sociology of education*. London, Routledge.

Yuill, N. (1997) A Funny Thing Happened on the Way to the Classroom: Jokes, riddles and metalinguistic awareness in understanding and improving poor comprehension in children. In Cornoldi, C. & Oakhill, J. (eds) *Reading Comprehension Disabilities: Processes and intervention* (pp. 193–220). Mahwah, NJ, Lawrence Erlbaum Associates.

Yuill, N., Pearce, D., Kerawalla, L., Harris, A. & Luckin, R. (2009) How Technology for Comprehension Training Can Support Conversation Towards the Joint Construction of Meaning. *Journal of Research in Reading*, 32 (1), 109–25.

Zimmerman, B. J. (2000) Self-efficacy: An essential motive to learn. *Contemporary Educational Psychology*, 25, 82–91.

Zurita, G. & Nussbaum, M. (2004) Computer Supported Collaborative Learning Using Wirelessly Interconnected Handheld Computers. *Computers & Education*, 42 (3), 289–314.

Index

Note: page numbers in **bold** refer to figures and tables.